Fame Attack

Fame Attack

The Inflation of Celebrity and Its Consequences

Chris Rojek

BLOOMSBURY ACADEMIC

First published in 2012 by

Bloomsbury Academic
an imprint of Bloomsbury Publishing Plc
50 Bedford Square, London WC1B 3DP, UK
and
175 Fifth Avenue, New York, NY 10010, USA

CIP records for this book are available from the British Library and the
Library of Congress

ISBN 978-1-84966-071-6 (paperback)
ISBN 978-1-84966-072-3 (hardback)
ISBN 978-1-84966-805-7 (ebook)

This book is produced using paper that is made from wood grown in managed,
sustainable forests. It is natural, renewable and recyclable. The logging and
manufacturing processes conform to the Environmental regulations
of the country of origin.

Printed and bound in Great Britain by the MPG Books Group, Bodmin, Cornwall

Cover image © Miramiska/Shutterstock

www.bloomsburyacademic.com

Contents

As for fame, consider ... that as one heap of sand
thrown upon another covers the first, so it happens in life,
a new glory soon eclipses an old one
Marcus Aurelius, 'Meditations'

Who are the men, who, without our realizing it, give us ideas,
tell us whom to admire and whom to despise, what to believe
about ... how our houses should be designed, what furniture we
should put into them, what menus we should serve at our table,
what kind of shirts we must wear, what sports we should indulge
in, what plays we should see, what charities we should support,
what pictures we should admire, what slang we should affect,
what jokes we should laugh at?
Edward Bernays

Stars are recorded people
John Castles

The quest for power is, as we have seen, a protection against
helplessness and against insignificance. This latter function it
shares with the quest for prestige. The neurotic that falls in this
group develops a stringent need to impress others, to be admired
and respected. He will have fantasies of impressing others with
beauty or intelligence or with some outstanding accomplishment;
he will spend money lavishly and conspicuously ... He will not be
able to have anyone as a friend, husband, wife, employee, who
does not admire him. His entire self-esteem rests on being admired,
and shrinks to nothingness if he does not receive admiration
Karen Horney

Fame is not a normal state of affairs for the human being.
It takes a lot of strength and a lot of patience and a tremendous
amount of reality checks to live through something like being
The Fonz [his character on *Happy Days*]. But if you get
caught up in it, it will eventually cut you in half
Henry Winkler

Preface: The New Aristocracy of Fame

I n the *ancien régime*, unbowed insistence upon being judged by title in precedence to deeds was the downfall of monarchy. Charles I in England and Louis XIV in France were executed ultimately because public opinion ceased to accept their divine right to rule. Charles and Louis were *ascribed celebrities*. That is their fame and influence derived from bloodline and was supported by Court protocol and precedent. As industrialization and democracy began to take root, the principle of the divine right of kings started to be openly rejected.

The social, economic, cultural and political forces in question are complex. It is an oversimplification to propose that all vestiges of ascribed celebrity have been swept aside by the ascendant power of industry and democracy. The wedding of Prince William and Kate Middleton in 2011 dominated the global media and transfixed the public. But it should be recalled that it was a marriage between the heir to the throne and a commoner. Blue blood does not run in the veins of Kate Middleton. Her father worked as an airline steward, and later as a flight dispatcher, for British Airways, and her mother was an airline stewardess.[1]

The marriage illustrates nicely the reframing of celebrity culture since the time of Charles I and Louis XIV. It is not just that people from ordinary backgrounds now have the chance to marry into royalty; rather it is that, if this occurs, they become media flypaper for stories, features, rumours, op-ed pieces, interviews and photo spreads. Their views may be no more substantial or insightful than any other offspring of airline handling staff. Nonetheless, they command the world's headlines and gradually come to the conclusion that they have an entitlement to do so.

It might be thought that *achieved celebrity* is inherently positive. For it replaces an aristocratic order in which birthright is all, with a more open society in which rank ceases to be the primary metric of fame. Ascribed celebrities are famous for their *reputations*; achieved celebrities are famous for their *deeds*. Oh happy land in which such a distribution of fame comes to pass! In fact, the age of achieved celebrity has produced a new aristocracy of fame. It consists of stars who are elevated on to the public horizon and who stay there not so much by virtue of their deeds, but by the power of the PR-Media hub behind them. Little has been written about the relationship of this power hub with celebrity culture.[2] Yet the PR-Media hub is fundamental.

Long ago, in 'The Defence of Poetry' (1821), Shelley claimed that 'poets are the unacknowledged legislators of the world'. Now that privilege has transferred to features line staff, news producers, current affairs editors and TV presenters. The reality TV show impresarios Simon Fuller and Simon Cowell possess the power to present three-minute attractions that overshadow news about unrest in the Middle East, child poverty, hunger in Africa, irregularities in the banking system and youth drug addiction. They preside over a setting in the media that has become an idolatry funfair, spinning insubstantial idols today, only to cast them aside for similar plastic replacements tomorrow. Celebrities are the kings and queens of satellite and terrestrial 'soft news' shows that give audiences headlines and sound bites instead of analysis (Baum, 2007; Castells, 2009: 328). While this is a source of disquiet in the serious media, it is not really an issue for students of popular culture. For it is how the majority of them get their news. News and stories of bona fide achieved celebrities, who have acquired fame by virtue of their talents and accomplishments, are treated as equivalent to sound bites from contestants on *Pop Idol* and *The X Factor* or the latest reality TV shenanigans. For many of our fellow citizens, celebrity media news is the only news that matters. It is easy to dismiss these developments as insignificant and symptomatic of deeper problems in the culture. It is a mistake to do so.

Celebrity culture is functional. That is it has functions for the people that produce it and for the people that receive it. 'Celebrity images,' writes Chris Hedges 'are reflections of our idealized selves sold back to us' (Hedges, 2009: 48). In the age of ascribed celebrities, kings and queens presented themselves as the patriarchs and matriarchs of the people. One of the cardinal principles of monarchy was that the best that is in us is present a thousandfold in them. The new aristocracy of fame provides round-the-clock escapism and a light blusher of life-coaching that offer the comfort of distinction and the illusion of wisdom.

Yet while the media is often censorious and dismissive about the cultural illiteracy of celebrity culture – so biting the hand that feeds them, one might say – it knocks against an open door. Audiences are addicted to celebrities. They mainline on the aura of celebrity and rummage through the media for truffles of stardom. A product endorsement from a leading golfer or fashion model can add millions to the balance sheet. Celebrity TV confessions and memories of rehab are devoured as unimpeachable oracles of how to cope with stress, manage adversity and get ahead. Achieved superstars like Bono, Angelina Jolie, George Clooney, Ben Affleck and Leonardo DiCaprio now take a prominent role in global humanitarianism. It is not enough any longer merely to entertain. Leading celebrities must now save the world by establishing charity foundations, do fieldwork in the world's hotspots and browbeat presidents and prime ministers to do their bit.

It would be perverse to deny celebrities the right to care, or to label them all as fakes. All the same, the aspiration for one person to save the world suggests a degree of self-importance that borders on megalomania. Who elected these people to speak for 'us'? What accountability do we have over them? The public is perfectly able to spot a dud when it sees one. A celebrity who has used skulduggery and other dirty tricks to enter the aristocracy of fame is not treated kindly in the court of public opinion. Yet modern men and women have boundless susceptibility to show faith in fakes.

This book is about the colonization of celebrity culture in everyday life. It examines how the fads, fashions and preoccupations of celebrities enter the popular lifeblood. It explores what is distinctive about contemporary celebrity and evaluates the psychological, social, economic and physical consequences of fame aristocracy upon both stars and stargazers. It tries to be philosophical about fame. The aristocracy of fame is with us for a reason. Even the best of us need someone to look up to, while the worst are content to get by with a hand mirror and a personal journal. Yet when the culture of fame breaks the balance between emotion and reason, when reality becomes boring, and when millions wear the hairdos, parrot the catchphrases and ape the opinions of stars who are mostly staged illusions, it is impossible for serious people not to conclude that something is amiss. To dismiss celebrity as trivial is to see ourselves and the world through blinkers. *Fame Attack* is not just about 'them', it is about 'us'.

1 Celebrity Supernova

Farah Fawcett-Majors and Michael Jackson died on the same day. As events go in the time and tide of newsworthy celebrity culture, the exit of Fawcett-Majors was as perverse as that of Aldous Huxley on 22 November 1963: the day of John F. Kennedy's assassination. A celebrity supernova refers to the death of an individual whose fame is so immense that their existence frames the character of the age. It is an image of a cultural presence of something that is not only bigger, but also higher than ourselves.

All cultures require institutions dedicated to promoting transcendence. That is cultural escalators that transport ordinary men and women from private cares and the dun horizon of daily monotony, into a bigger, richer mental and social space. In premodern society, religion, magic and totemism supplied men and women with a sense of following the grand plan of Creation. In the words of Eliade, in archaic society 'life is lived on a twofold plane; it takes its course as human existence and, at the same time, shares in a transhuman life, that of the cosmos or the gods' (Eliade, 1957: 167).

Modern men and women have mostly lost the belief in magical and totemic cosmology, and organized religion is generally thought to be in decline in the West.[1] These escalators of premodern transcendence have been replaced by general acquiescence to the testable propositions of science and technology. But the human affiliation with the notion of transcendence survives. In modern society, celebrity culture – in sport, popular music, fashion, film and television – provides the overwhelming majority of ordinary men and women with access to intimations of elevated existence. In this regard, celebrity culture rivals our relationship with Nature and, in Western society, now outperforms organized religion in the sheer numbers that it attracts. It is no accident that celebrities are also known as stars. Celebrity culture provides a desacralized highway to transcendence. Hence, John Castles notes the rituals of immortality that surround superstars. They are widely idolized as supremely gifted, luxuriantly equipped, larger-than-life beings that provide millions of people with a sense of meaning in a universe that is habitually regarded as indifferent to mankind (Castles, 2008: 91).

Celebrity supernovas present a sense of being in touch with cultural immensity. With the death of a Michael Jackson or a John F. Kennedy, the age changes. It translates into something else. The occurrence of a celebrity supernova involves the pain of group loss and the bitter gall of personal mourning. There is no other news. When Jackson and JFK died, the biographies and cultural significance of Fawcett-Majors and Huxley and all other news items were snuffed out. They became as moths to a black hole. Everything was sucked in and swallowed by the all-absorbing stellar cataclysm.

Not one, but several riddles demand to be solved here. Of the millions who grieved for JFK and Jackson only an infinitesimal number had what might be called a *primary relationship* with them. That is direct, personal contact in non-public settings. In ordinary life, primary relationships with parents, children, other blood relations and close friends are the main source of joy, desire, wonder, pain, remorse, grief and other deep emotions. The majority of people knew of JFK and Jackson as they were familiar with long-dead figures from history, like Hadrian, Salome or Napoleon, that is by writings and word of mouth. True, modern men and women have access to technologies of fame that would have been beyond the imagination of predigital generations, technologies such as sound recordings, photographs, television clips and film footage. Without doubt, these provide more detailed impressions of famous people. But this scarcely amounts to a primary relationship. Through these technologies celebrities have become vastly more accessible to the general public. Strangers and stargazers know more about the private lives of celebrities than ever before. Yet, curiously, celebrities remain consummately out of reach. It is a peculiar quality of modern culture that, via the media, ordinary men and women possess the means to be familiar with much in the private lives of celebrities without ever having shaken their hands or even set eyes upon them face-to-face. Upon what grounds do the millions who never broke bread or supped with the celebrities grieve a supernova as both an immense cultural event and a matter of *personal* loss?

If fame is truly vanity, as Kolakowski (1999) tells us, the adulation of celebrity is surely a base, shallow emotion. For it is not founded in direct personal contact, but imaginary relationships. Yet why should a celebrity supernova make us sensible of a deep, profound, irrevocable transformation in our lives and the social and cultural composition of things, just as the rise of some celebrities makes us conscious of entering a new epoch?

The contagion effect of celebrity is not limited to the case of the celebrity supernova. Commodities that are authenticated as once owned, or even touched, by celebrities command a high price in the auction market. When Sotheby's auctioned 1,300 items from the estate of the late Jacqueline Kennedy, the optimistic pre-sale prediction was $4.6 million. In the event, the sale netted $34.5 million. Some items possessed iconic significance. For example, President Kennedy's rocking chair was sold for $453,000; his set of golf clubs for $772,500; and the desk upon which he signed the 1963 Nuclear Test Ban Treaty, $1.43 million. Other items that had no iconic significance still fetched remarkably high prices. For example, a tape measure ($48,785) and a set of books on Cape Cod ($21,850) (Newman *et al.,* 2011).

The contagion effect is not limited to figures of historical importance. Notorious celebrities generate the same price inflation. For example, the US government auctioned several possessions of the infamous fraudster Bernie Madoff, including a footstool listed at $360, which was sold for $3,300, and a standard bar set, originally listed for $680, which fetched $2,200 (*New York Times* 15.11.2010). Similarly, Stone (2007) reports staggering prices achieved at auctions for locks of Charles Manson's hair, paintings by the serial killer John Wayne Gacy and personal effects of Saddam Hussein.

In *Auguries of Innocence*, William Blake wrote that we can see a world in a grain of sand. The worlds shown to us when a celebrity supernova occurs stretch much further than the life of the individual who has passed. They embody and reflect the spirit of the times. In their import about the glories, setbacks and achievements of human life, they stand square in the searchlight of eternity. In this generation, and for generations to come, they offer parables for the lives of others. The most prestigious celebrities have replaced the gods of ancient society as the immortals.[2] To some this may seem an excessive proposition. However, is it really fanciful to propose that figures like Michael Jackson, Marilyn Monroe, Elvis Presley, James Dean, John Lennon, Frank Sinatra, Kurt Cobain and JFK have achieved immortality? Probably not. As recorded people, their films, radio broadcasts and TV interviews have a timeless quality. Monroe and Dean are still vivid, instantly recognized presences in our culture, despite being dead for nigh on fifty years.

In October 2010 the entire remastered John Lennon catalogue was rereleased on the seventieth anniversary of his birth and the thirtieth anniversary of his assassination. Reviewers and fans treated the event as a new album release by a living star. They referred to fresh power in the singing and the clarity of arrangements that made the music sound brand new. In doing so they unintentionally revealed an important link between celebrity, technology and immortality.

Technological improvement can perpetually recycle celebrity recordings to renew the fame of dead stars. The effect is to create the illusion of an ever more closer union between the audience and the dead celebrity. According to *Forbes* business magazine's 'Top-Earning Dead Celebrities' list (2010), the Lennon estate earned $17 million in 2009, nearly three times as much as the estates of other dead pop stars such as Jimi Hendrix ($6 million), but well behind Michael Jackson ($275 million) and Elvis Presley ($60 million).

Recorded celebrities die physically, but culture provides them with an afterlife. Their deeds are remembered and talked about just as Apollo, Athena, Aphrodite, Zeus and the other Greek gods are recalled today. Might there be a meaningful parallel here? Why should some of us lean upon a celebrity, as others look to gods for comfort and guidance? Why should others abhor the world of celebrity as some despise the work of the Devil? Is the media and public reaction to celebrity culture more in the nature of an overreaction? Or is the media unintentionally conveying the significant truth that, today, celebrities perform some of the functions once performed by the gods?

Fame attack: Defined

Not infrequently, the media is sweepingly condescending about celebrity culture.

If, for most modern people unschooled in the Classics, Angelina Jolie has replaced Aphrodite, and Russell Brand, until his marriage to Katy Perry (2010), was presented in the tabloids as a modern-day Dionysus, the media is also full of choleric disapproval of reality-show wannabe celebrities and mediocre talents eager to hog the limelight. There is the strong sentiment that celeb culture, especially in the guise of reality TV, has gone too far. Among other things, it is deplored for corrupting personal values so that many vainly strive for fame at any cost, inflating the desire for public acclaim over real achievement and encouraging the development of an engorged, irresponsible entertainment sector in which the values of the lowest common denominator are pampered and cosseted.

When Cheryl Cole's judging process on *The X Factor* or Paris Hilton's drug bust receive headline inches that are as big as those assigned to reports on the peace process between Israel and Palestine or the campaign against child poverty, something is amiss with the fourth estate. But the media reflects public demand as well as shapes it. Today, the unpalatable fact is that the public has a keen, apparently inexhaustible, and in the view of many social commentators, seriously unbalanced interest, in the toings and froings of celebrity culture.

Evidently, the inflation of celebrity culture is connected, by association, with personal traumas and toxic social problems. Yet, to date, among the regular bromides of disapproval issued by the media and the struggle to understand what is really going on, a precise definition of the nature of the personal ills and social malaise caused by celebrity culture is oddly wanting. This book is an attempt to partly redress the situation.

Fame attack refers to the neurotic, obsessional disorders that derive from celebrity culture. Three subdivisions of the condition should be distinguished:

1   Celebrity Worship Syndrome, which means the tendency to formulate an over-close identification with a celebrity, leading to dysfunctional behaviour.

2   Star Paranoia, which refers to the emotional conviction that celebrities behave in unreasonable ways, which, for example, infringe human rights,

ignore human nobility, avoid fiscal responsibilities and ride roughshod over legality. The nub of the matter is that celebrities are seen as getting away with it, while the rest of us suffer. This promotes bitterness, resentment and anger about celebrity culture in general. In some cases this may metastasize into vigilantism against specific celebrities.

3 Narcissistic Personality Disorder, which refers to the onslaught of an innate sense of superiority and entitlement that is indifferent to personal and social consequences.

At the level of psychology, fame attack applies to both stars and stargazers. However, the first two types of disorder clearly apply mostly to audiences rather than stars. Narcissistic celebrity disorder is common in stars who have grown too big for their boots; while celebrity worship syndrome and star paranoia is distributed most widely among vulnerable, isolated fans who develop harmful crushes, injurious dependencies or irrational hostilities around illusory relationships with stars.

There may be a therapeutic gain in this. Celebrity worship syndrome may help some individuals get through life. Attaching oneself to celebrities enables individuals to act out ambitions and desires that have been thwarted in ordinary life. In some cases identification may take the form of copying the physical appearance, cultural values and political beliefs of the celebrity. In extreme cases, people suffering from celebrity worship syndrome may use plastic surgery to physically resemble the features of the celebrity. Playing out a sense of fraternity with stars who are out of reach may be a rational coping device to manage the privations of daily life.

Similarly, star paranoia, which is most widespread among people who develop intense sentiments of resentment towards celebrities for getting ahead in some way that is commonly deemed to be unreasonable, may help to manage anger about other areas of personal life that are experienced as painful and intractable. Mostly, fame is lambasted when it is applied to ignore proper social conventions or skip legal hurdles. In recent years the main examples of star paranoia have occurred in allegations of celebrity verbal abuse, tax dodging, drug use and controversial Third World child adoptions. Accordingly, legislation against star harassment and stalking has expanded. In 1990, following the fan-related attempted murder of the actress Theresa Saldana (1982), and the fan-related stalking and murder of the actress Rebecca Schaeffer (1989), the state of California passed anti-stalking laws. Congress passed the Violent Crime and Law Enforcement Act (1994) and in 1996 extended anti-stalking legislation to encompass interstate stalking and stalking within federal jurisdiction. The UK sought to legally tackle stalking with the Protection from Harassment Act (1994).

The condition of fame attack is not limited to the young; it affects all age groups and both sexes. Usually, the neurotic and obsessional behaviour that it produces is not, strictly speaking, dysfunctional. People with celebrity worship syndrome, star paranoia or narcissistic personality disorder may seem a bit peculiar to the rest of us, and they may experience severe difficulties in forming and developing relationships. However, these conditions do not generally warrant clinical intervention. This is not to say that the effects of fame attack are superficial.

In extreme cases, celebrity worship syndrome, star paranoia and narcissistic personality disorder lead to types of behaviour that pose a threat to the individual and those around them. Celebrity worship syndrome, star paranoia and narcissistic personality disorder are often cited in legal cases of trespass, fraud, attempted suicide, suicide, harassment, physical violence and homicide.

It is more difficult to pin down the social effects of fame attack. To speak of malaise, especially when hard research facts are not available, is open to the objection that we are straying into the territory of mere conjecture. Notwithstanding this, the recurrence and frequency of certain allegations in the media is such that they must be aired here. They have to do with the oft-expressed view that people are becoming ruder in public, more concerned with acclaim than integrity, more preoccupied with self-esteem, and fixated upon narrow, selfish, emotional and material wants than the realization of the public good. Specifically, celebrity culture is seen as creating narcissistic personalities who are addicted to attention-seeking and are quick to represent themselves as victims when they don't get it. Self-promotion has been elevated above social responsibility, with the result that the social bonds that hold society together have grown frayed and decayed. Celebrity expressions of entitlement over property, rights of access, scientific and medical privilege, and even adoption, have produced resentment and paranoia among people who accuse celebrities of economic exploitation and personal oppression.

Fame attack is the result of ordinary social and economic practices that have, so to speak, got out of hand. Among these are the pressures on the media to win ratings wars, the narcissistic tendencies produced by huge acclaim and financial reward, the growth of therapy culture which leads greater numbers of people to seek guidance and role models by looking up to strangers, and the apparent volatility of media and public judgements that can make a star out of someone one day and a has-been or demon the next.

The role of the media is particularly noteworthy here. Take the case of Michael Jackson. For more than a decade prior to his death Michael Jackson was regularly portrayed as an unstable individual, a crank, a spendthrift and, most grievously for his public image, a child molester. In 2005, his five-month court trial on seven counts of child abuse ended in acquittal. However, many were left with a rank taste in their mouths. The media played its part in fuelling this by suggesting that there is no smoke without fire. Over and above this, the cost of the trial created numerous, well-publicized financial problems for Jackson. At the time of his death he was a mired, debt-ridden figure, commonly referred to as a musical has-been, of insalubrious character and shot judgement.

The process of rehabilitation started on the day of his death, 25 June 2009. One by one the bricks of bad publicity were gradually wrested away, and with the mortar surrounding them, swallowed by the celebrity supernova. Inch by inch the media reconstructed an overwhelmingly positive image of Jackson as an irreplaceable superstar, a loving father, an admirable humanitarian and, in jaw-dropping irony, one of the greatest victims of media muckraking and character assassination the world has ever known. Denigration gave way to semi-deification. So much so, that when his memorial service was held on 7 July 2009, at the Staples Center, Los Angeles, where his casket was displayed prominently at the front of the stage, was I alone in half expecting Michael to rise in righteous glory from the dead?

Understandably, when people are told one thing by the media on one day and the opposite on the next, a doubt about what to believe grows and eventually takes hold. Celebrity culture revolves around rumour and hearsay as much as facts and professional reporting. This may fit with the distorted, overblown values that characterize the world of the stars, but it makes it devilishly tricky for ordinary people and social commentators to separate the wheat from the chaff.

'He who sings or dances the best...'

We live in a culture dominated by celebrities. Arguably, there is nothing new in this. All societies have figureheads whom most people recognize as possessing cultural priority and economic power.[3] Paganism recognized other-worldly forces and magical figures. Totems were erected to the ineffable, the binding, the solidifying links between natives. In traditional societies, kings and queens ruled and took their licence from divine authority.[4]

The age of monarchy is now passed. Modern societies are based upon formal principles of individual freedom, equality and justice. Yet we still recognize certain individuals as possessing higher status, and society rewards them with privileges that are not given to the majority. We call these figures celebrities. We like to think that they have risen by merit from the ranks of ordinary mortals. But it is not so. Celebrities are constructed. Even in the age of post-monarchy, the type of figures singled out for recognition and reward has changed.

In the century before 1920, people looked up to political leaders, scientists, writers and engineers. Individuals who succeed in a *career* hogged the limelight as respected celebrities. With the coming of mass communications, the importance of career in the construction of celebrity underwent a profound change (Lowenthal, 1961). Celebrity became based, first and foremost, on visual impact, incident and *frontierism*. The latter term is fundamental in understanding the culture of celebrity, yet oddly it has been under-theorized and under-researched. By frontierism, I mean living on the edge of social mores, sexual conventions, psychological orthodoxy and economic prudence. Superstars often flaunt these commonly observed courtesies of life as if they belong to the world of little, unknown people. The media reinforces with this by flagging stories of superstar tantrums, marriage bust-ups, drug problems, alcohol dependencies, devotion to cranky religions, economic profligacy and so on. Before the 1920s, celebrities were generally presented as possessing to the highest degree the qualities of prudence, orderly balance and modesty of the man in the street. After the 1920s, lives of risk, emergency and incident suddenly became attractive and newsworthy.

There is some disagreement about why this happened. The rise of mass communications, the growth of the importance of people skills in the labour market, the decline of the family and community, the erosion of religion, the development of new public spaces in which seeing and being seen were central have been cited as key instrumental factors (Roach, 2007; Gundle, 2008). What emerges most powerfully from the literature is the proposition that, from the 1920s, visual impact, emergency and incident became essential features of celebrity. The famous occupied the frontier existence that was denied to ordinary odds and sods. As such they inhabited a transcendent space into which millions peered, and through gossip columnists, biographers and TV documentary makers, monitored and savoured.

The frontier was a place beyond the boundary of economic privation, sexual restraint and political insignificance. Symbolically, the individuals who resided on the frontier lived a charmed existence. They were beyond Mammon and morality. In having apparent, media-endorsed, access to everything and everyone, celebrities became magnets of aspiration and models of emulation. Their influence permeated national local politics, where they left their imprint upon the bearing and performance of political candidates in elections; the sphere of global diplomacy, where they provided scripts for fundraising, negotiation and power brokerage; public advocacy, where they promoted issues of health, childcare, adult welfare and the environment; and the economy, where they were used to maximize commodity sales and add a dash of glamour to the dull business machinations of corporations.

The star system has now permeated through every level of society. Thus, charities have their star givers; schools and universities have their star academics; professional musicians and sports teams have players and superstars; and businesses have star managers. Even the criminal world has its bad asses and its *real* bad asses: the Kray Twins, Carlos the Jackal, Peter Sutcliffe, Ted Bundy, Bernie Madoff, O. J. Simpson, Colonel Russell Williams, Fred and Rosemary West, Paul Bernardo and Karla Homolka are not just criminals, they are legends of crime. Their notoriety casts a long shadow in private life and popular culture (Penfold-Mounce, 2009). Stardom is not just a matter of renown; it is a question of cultural clout.

One of the most noteworthy developments in contemporary celebrity culture is *celanthropy* (Bishop and Green, 2008). That is the migration of celebrities from the sphere of entertainment into charity investment and humanitarian work. It's one thing to speak out against ignorance, want and injustice, but if you do so as a George Clooney, Angelina Jolie, Annie Lennox, Michael Stipe or a Bono, it possesses note. The words and deeds of ordinary men and women leave ripples. Celebrities make waves. Some celebrities, like Bono, Angelina Jolie, Brad Pitt, Annie Lennox, Bob Geldof, Youssou N'Dour, Sting, George Clooney, Oprah Winfrey, Michael Stipe and Nicole Kidman, are formidable goodwill ambassadors and campaigners for a variety of human rights causes (Cooper, 2008). They use their fame to act as the unelected tribunes of the people. They purport to speak the plain truths from which politicians and business leaders shrink. Like it or not, fame is the name of the game. Our voices are second or third strings in the orchestra. *They* are the maestros, or at least they are acclaimed as such. How does this happen? Why did it arise? What are its consequences?

Once we dreamt of a better world where all would be equal and judged by the quality of their character. Only those who set their faces against the course of history do so now. In attempting to build societies founded upon incorruptible principles of equality and liberty the great social and political revolutions produced their Robespierres, Stalins, Maos and Pol Pots, to say nothing of their less renowned accomplices, adept in torture, repression and execution; I am thinking of the St Justs, the Berias, the Zhu Des and the Ta Moks. Sadly, the writ of liberty and equality does not run free. It often goes hand in hand with blithe disrespect for the sanctity of life. The boldest builders of brotherhood have seen fit to don the butcher's apron and wield the meat cleaver when historical 'necessity' demands.

Notwithstanding this, decency, respect and generosity for our fellow man are not taken lightly. Brotherhood is alive and well. One sees it in the countless, unrecorded acts of consideration, kindness and selflessness that human beings practise daily among one another. But creating a society of universal brotherhood, in which all are recognized as being made of the same stuff and deserving of equal respect, appears to lie within our imagination, but beyond our competence to attain. A face always rises out of the crowd, one flame always leaps higher than the rest.

Is this simply in the nature of the human condition? Common sense indicates that men and women may be born equal, but their charms and talents are not the same.

Should we not regard celebrity as a question of natural gifts? If you are a superior actor than me, if you are physically more alluring and intellectually more able, do you not have a right to fame? If you can hit a ball on a tennis court with infallible accuracy or captivate the people with the beauty and power of your speech, is it not just that your reward should be great and your acclaim merited? After all, Rousseau, in the *Discourse on the Origin of Inequality*, remarked: 'He who sings or dances the best, he who is most handsome, the strongest, and most adroit or the most eloquent becomes the most highly regarded.' Tellingly, he goes on to observe: 'this is the first step to inequality, and at the same time towards vice' (Rousseau, 1984: 114).

Rousseau meant that the rewards of fame divide celebrities from the crowd and provide licence for improper behaviour and fantastic rewards. At least he was working with the assumption that there is a direct, universal correlation between natural gifts, accomplishment and fame.

In our own day no such iron law exists. Fame can be achieved despite the absence of natural gifts or accomplishments. Anyone who watches *Big Brother, American Idol, The X Factor,* or who buys *Heat, Closer, The National Inquirer, OK!* or *Hello!* knows this. Those of mediocre talents, the clamorous, the attention-seeking, the gaudy, common blusterers, tricksters, jades, clowns, tramps, intriguers and simple misfits are perfectly able to claim the attention of ordinary men and women. They rise without trace and amass fortunes by playing a one-string fiddle. For every Michael Jackson, there is a William Hung; for every Oprah Winfrey a Jade Goody.[5] Nowadays, the high and the low mix easily in the washing machine of celebrity culture.

Domestic and factory systems of fame

There is a reason for this mix. Celebrities are not necessarily the most gifted, or virtuous, of men and women. True, it may happen that a figure with the authority, grace and nobility of a Gandhi or Nelson Mandela arises from our midst and achieves righteous acclaim for their precious, enviable humanity. But this is rare. Even when it does happen it would be an error to mistake an industrial relation for a natural one. An industrial relation involves a team of workers, often located in a factory setting, to turn the resources of nature into commodities that possess market value. Training and expertise in public relations and how to use the media are pivotal. Celebrities are cultural skyscrapers. They hog public space. They are built and maintained for public consumption by public relations and media specialists.

This is not the only way in which celebrity value is produced. In recent years what might be called the *domestic system of fame*, based on utilizing the immense power of the Web, has emerged. How might we categorize this system? It is a means of generating public regard that is self-directed and doesn't involve significant teamwork. It is a do-it-yourself approach to fame acquisition.

Historically speaking, the term is associated with craftwork, in other words pre-industrial forms of manufacturing. This is appropriate, as there is indeed a craft element in the domestic system of fame. Celebrity is custom-built and self-administered. This suggests primitive, unapprenticed qualities. But it's a big mistake to associate the domestic system of fame with low-tech operations. The Internet makes automatic, weightless communication available at the flick of a switch. Do-it-yourself strategies for acquiring fame are compatible with the mobile phone, the laptop and the Web. The proliferation of blogging sites and social network platforms supports the accumulation of fame in ways that the publicity seekers of yore could scarcely imagine. Community exchange sites like MySpace, Facebook and Twitter offer switchboards of communication that have been intensively exploited by individuals and groups intent in acquiring fame. They also permit fans to outflank the celebrity spin produced by the public relations industry and middlebrow features editors, to get the inside story. From the earliest days of the Hollywood studio system fans were keenly aware that the public face of the star constructed by studio moguls and their support personnel was stylized and manicured. There was always strong public interest in ferreting the truth behind the appearances of Tinseltown. Practically speaking, this centred on fan club networks that generated and exchanged data on the private lives and secrets of the stars (Barbas, 2001).

It goes without saying that this was not a relationship between equals. Stars have the full power of the PR-Media hub at their disposal. They are supported by life coaches and communicate through heavily controlled mechanisms such as press releases and staged interviews. Fans organize meetings and conventions but they mostly depend upon a do-it-yourself network of exchange.

Nonetheless, it is a mistake to think of this in terms of a zero-sum game in which all of the power resides with stars and their back-up teams, while fans are powerless. From the beginning, there was a degree of what might be called co-operative labour between fans and stars. Thus, by sifting through press releases and engaging in detective work, fans could dig out some of the secrets of the stars and get a grasp on the truth.

Over the last two decades, the spread of the Internet has vastly increased the opportunities for co-operative labour. The volume of unauthorized data about celebrities has increased exponentially. The proliferation of dedicated websites and blogging sites has inevitably created a demand for rankings and impact factors.

The *Forbes* 'Web Celeb 25' list of top bloggers (2010) places the celebrity gossip hound Perez Hilton as the top blogger. His site attracts 7.2 million people a month and is one of the 500 most visited sites on the Internet.

1   Perez Hilton (Perezhilton.com)

2   Michael Arrington (Techcrunch.com)

3   Peter Cashmore (Mashable.com)

4   Evan Williams and Biz Stone (Twitter.com)

5   Kevin Rose (Digg.com)

6   Guy Kawasaki (Guykawasaki.com)

7   Heather Armstrong (Dooce.com)

8   Tila Nguyen (Tilahotspot.buzznet.com)

9   Gary Vaynerchuk (Garyvaynerchuck.com)

10   Cory Doctrow (Craphound.com)

Figure 1 Forbes Web Celeb 10 (2010)
Source: http://www.forbes.com/2010/02/02

The traditional PR-Media system has learned from the new technology. The Internet offers a new global highway for the exchange of news and personal details about celebrities. Blogging sites provide stargazers with the gossip and the low-down on a star. They also provide stars with the opportunity to give messages and interviews, through the creation of dedicated blogging sites. The Internet constitutes a new basis for the commercial exploitation of stardom by providing novel subscription-based models for acquiring celebrity data and merchandise. It gives stargazers unprecedented opportunities to participate, in conjunction with stars, in building celebrity brands and, through the laptop, the iPad and the mobile phone, increases the saturation of celebrity culture to round-the-clock status. Vicariously, you can always be in the company of your star, even though you never stand by his or her side or exchange the merest pleasantry. The Internet is a body and a dynamic resource for raising awareness of stardom and integrating it into everyday life.

The appeal of notoriety

The domestic system is also associated with less salubrious forms of fame. Because the media is ubiquitous, it has been used by individuals and groups as a shortcut to acquiring fame. Typically, this takes the negative form of public notoriety in which a criminal act, or acts, is used to garner shock attention and column inches. A spree killer, a mass murderer, an assassin who kills a high-profile figure, or a suicide bomber can acquire notoriety and gain celebrity overnight. On 10 September 2001 Mohammed Atta was a nobody. The following day he was the most famous person in the world after being identified as the ringleader of the 9/11 bombing team. Who knows if the desire to acquire fame was a motivation behind Atta's terrorism? Without doubt, it was a consequence of his leading role in the annihilation of the World Trade Center. There is reason to believe that this type of domestic system of generating fame is becoming more significant as individuals and groups exploit the publicity access afforded by the media.

The opportunities to acquire fame without resorting to publicity agents or celebrity managers have never been greater. The Internet makes a do-it-yourself approach valid, accessible and relevant. But it carries a bucket-load of risks. In order to be durable, celebrity must be carefully honed and skilfully promoted. It requires a well-judged target audience, accurate information about group motivations and well-considered supplements to enhance fame. Group and solo performer websites have limited resources to generate innovation and initiative in order to build and expand audiences. A cultural skyscraper needs constant maintenance and polishing. Typically, this is beyond the resources of a do-it-yourself approach.

The problem is compounded in what might be termed *domestic system single-issue* bids for fame. For example, McCutcheon *et al.* submit that the two killers in the Columbine massacre deliberately sought celebrity to highlight their experience of school victimization (McCutcheon *et al.*, 2004: 18–20). They left behind communications, which showed a keen concern for their posthumous public image. They speculated on how the massacre would be presented in the media, what stars would play them in the film of the event and even who would direct the movie. The two killers, assert McCutcheon *et al.*, wanted to be celebrity legends with lasting fame of the kind achieved by Billy the Kid, Jesse James and Al Capone (McCutcheon *et al.*, 2004: 19). But how many people remember the names Eric Harris and Dylan Klebold? Although the event is remembered, their names are more or less forgotten.

Seeking fame through the Internet or an infamous act involves an unstable ratio between energy and achievement. You may spend a good deal of time making your poetry or photography available on the Web and still be ignored. You may develop a personal philosophy of Armageddon and crucifixion and, like the Virginia Tech mass killer, Seung-Hui Cho (2007), kill many in a shooting rampage; you may study serial killing, enrol for a criminology PhD in the history of murder, and kill three female prostitutes, like the Bradford serial murderer, Stephen Griffiths (2010) who, when first asked for his name in court, called himself the 'Crossbow Cannibal' (and, it emerged, was partly motivated to kill to command 'the media metric') but your name will not necessarily endure. Fame notoriety possesses impact but its legacy is mostly in doubt. The public has become habituated to apparently random mass and serial killings. The outrage is remembered, but the assailant generally achieves no more than fleeting fame.

While the importance of the domestic system of fame is real, it should not be exaggerated. Typically, the ratio of energy and achievement is misdirected unless it is governed by public relations and media personnel who understand how to propagandize celebrity and make fame durable. In other words, it requires a professional, salaried team of dedicated expert labourers in emotional management, publicity and promotion to design fame and take the required publicity steps to prolong its life. Comparatively speaking, the domestic system of celebrity is small beer.

The factory system and cultural intermediaries

Today, celebrity is, above all, an industrial relation created through a factory machine process. The fame of Gandhi and Mandela does not emerge like water from the mouth of a spring. On the contrary, it is planned, measured, set and burnished by the hands of trained strategists in image-making and dedicated media relations experts. This is an industrial relationship because it involves a blueprint of fame to turn a naturally given, amorphous set of resources into a symbol of public approval, desire or, at the very minimum, recognition.

The term *cultural intermediaries* is used to designate these labourers. Examples include publicists, bodyguards, chauffeurs, voice coaches, PR assistants, personal trainers, private doctors, accountants, financial advisers, personal chefs and astrologists. They are described as intermediaries, because they are located between the star and the public and charged with the task of forging the chains that unite the two. Their labour power is devoted to matters of culture rather than the manufacture of things.

In a world where seven out of ten workers in the advanced economies gain their livelihood from the service sector, culture is king.[6] It possesses pivotal economic value. We need to know which catchphrases, buzzwords, attitudes, jokes, hairstyles, skin tones and wardrobe are regarded as cool, because our daily world consists of trading in communication, ideas and knowledge. We use these resources in work and personal life to acquire personal note or enhance the impression that we make on others. Service labour revolves around being adept in symbols, ideas and communication. In retailing, marketing, sales and teaching, the most effective workers are those who communicate most forcefully. It is celebrities who are presented and recognized as the most glamorous purveyors of these ways of going about things, which is why they dominate popular culture. They act as unofficial life coaches feeding the impulses, habits and emotions of the public by providing attractive examples and glamorous role models. They provide symbols to assist us in narrating, negotiating and interpreting shared experience and drawing moral boundaries (Butler Breese, 2010: 352). Still, the public face they present is a product of public relations and media specialists. What precisely do these chiefly invisible workers contribute?

If we know more about the love lives, diet, health, political preferences and childhood traumas of celebrities than at any point in human history, it is because cultural intermediaries make it so. They provide and manage the constant data flow about stars, persuading the public that they 'know' these persons whom they have never met and, chances are, will never meet, in the form of a face-to-face relationship.

A given of this is that celebrities must be positioned in the media in ways that maximize public impact factors. This requires cultural intermediaries to cultivate and activate media networks and angle celebrities in the best light. If celebrities behave in ways that are contrary to public expectations, it is cultural intermediaries who intervene and recast celebrity encounters for us. This is an intriguing fact about all forms of factory-based fame: celebrity comes locked-in with a veiled, adaptive back-up system. Before stars are known to us they are *prepared* for public consumption. Questions of hairstyle, skin tone, scent, dress, political values, social beliefs and anger management are sifted by experts in the people-skills/impression management industry. It is an organized, well-oiled business designed to create selected stimuli to exert a captivating effect upon audiences. A public face is constructed to achieve instantaneous, affirmative social responses. Moreover, this mask is carefully constructed and regularly polished to take account of changes in personal behaviour, audience demands, corporate requirements and cultural factors. It is like running a power plant that deals with common-or-garden desire instead of electricity and runs via discrete social networks instead of grids.

The core of this is people skills. The factory system of celebrity holds that fame does not advance by accretion, but by design. There must be a plan and a system of communication. This is not primarily a question of economics or politics; it is a question of culture. Knowing how to put people at their ease, take them into your confidence and get the best out of them has high economic value and cultural cachet. This knowledge is transmitted through the structures of the family, education system and community. But society has also evolved dedicated, professional networks of commerce and governance that engage perpetually in nothing else but transmitting and honing people skills for a ravenous public. The most highly developed of these is the public relations industry. It is impossible to understand how celebrity works today without grasping the fundamentals of this industry.

Edward Bernays and the public relations mill

Public relations has a long history (Ewen, 1996). The leading historical guru in propaganda and public relations is generally accepted to be Edward Bernays. He developed techniques to use what he called 'associational values and dramatic incidents' to dramatize communication and elevate and position 'opinion-leaders' (Bernays, 1928: 154). The aim is to mould the public consumption of celebrity. Bernays emphasizes the positive, constructive role of public relations in 'producing harmony' between government, business and the people (Bernays, 1928; 1935: 82). But he is realistic enough to acknowledge that public relations may also bring about destructive effects.

In public relations, social impact is all. Engineering high impact factors is the epitome of good public relations. Other sectors may have a sentimental or trusting view of the motivations of trust in social groups. In contrast, the public relations industry is hard-headed and cultivates an ethos of cool professional detachment with respect to the question of influencing the passions and opinions of the public.

For moulding public opinion presupposes three things. Firstly, a *leader* through which 'vast numbers of individuals can be reached'. Secondly, *pressure groups* who actively support leaders, interpret ideas and communicate enthusiasm to the wider public. Thirdly, an *assessment* of what matters to the public. Among the issues he mentions in this regard are self-preservation, ambition, pride, love of family and children, patriotism and love of play (Bernays, 1935: 83).

Having got the three elements in place, Bernays continues, public relations works on a couple of fronts: symbols and the media. *Symbols* are 'shortcuts to understanding and to action'. They operate via emotional potency and familiarity. One of the most important tasks of the public relations specialist is to fashion the right symbols and maintain their potency in constantly changing conditions (Bernays, 1935: 84–85).

The *media* is posited as the essential network 'by which his facts and point of view reach his public' (Bernays 1935: 84). The media allows individuals and groups to be brought into instant, perpetual, fruitful juxtaposition. The correct use of the media makes it impossible to ignore appeals based upon dominant motives and the support of group leaders. Control of media output is therefore a precondition for building celebrity.

Upon this basis, Bernays outlines his famous four key steps in a successful programme of public relations (Bernays, 1935: 85–87):

1. Formulation of an objective

This involves defining a corporate or political objective that articulates the goals of leaders and matches them to public motivations. The optimal condition in public relations is when the aims of business and corporate leaders mesh with the public interest. Significantly, Bernays maintains that a public relations exercise should be abandoned if this condition is not met. Properly used, public relations can create a potent match between group needs and political and economic objectives. Of course, it can also be used to cultivate false appetites and obsessions in the public and build forms of leadership that produce domination. For this reason, public relations must be transparent, accountable and bound by strict ethical codes of practice.

2. Gathering data on public attitudes

This is the use of interviews, focus groups and survey questionnaires to elucidate group motivation and public interests. For Bernays, this is the 'scientific foundation' of the public relations industry because it brings to light data that do not arise from ordinary social encounters that reveal the state of 'the group mind' (Bernays 1935: 86).

3. Study of analysis

The analysis of public attitude supplies the basis for the formulation of objectives and the conduct of public relations campaigns. The ideas of leaders and the symbols that they use must be crafted to appeal to the public. Getting the message across may simply be a matter of fact finding and dramatic presentation, but it also involves technologies of 'educating' the public.

4. Use of media

The press, billboards, advertising, newsletters, television, radio and the other branches of the mass media are used to maximize accessibility. Use of the media requires careful planning, continuous monitoring and discriminate targeting to ensure that the basic ideas of the PR campaign stand out from 'the welter of competing ideas' that 'flow naturally to the public through the accustomed channels' (Bernays, 1935: 87). Practically speaking, this means equipping opinion-makers with people skills and investing symbols with potent payloads of associational meaning so as to ensure that they will be noticed and reported by the media.

Bernays writes chiefly about the relationships between party politics, business and mass opinion formation (Bernays, 1928). But the logic and principles of his public relations model are transferable to today's factory system of celebrity culture. Bernays himself pioneered the use of the silent movie star, Clara Bow, and the famous aviatrix of the 1920s, Mrs Stillman, to endorse commodities of the day. In addition he worked as a press agent for Enrico Caruso, Florenz Ziegfeld, Diaghilev and Nijinsky. He was also employed as the public relations mastermind to transform the grey image of the US President Calvin Coolidge into something more exciting and palatable for voters.

Bernays was fully aware of the associational values and dramatic dividend of celebrity upon the public. He was part of the generation for whom motion pictures was a seismic innovation in popular culture and leisure. He quickly recognized the potential of film and film stars in making a mark on the group mind:

> The American motion picture is the greatest unconscious carrier of propaganda in the world today. It is a great distributor for ideas and opinions. The motion picture can standardize the ideas and habits of a nation. Because pictures are made to meet market demands they reflect, emphasize and even exaggerate broad popular tendencies. (Bernays, 1928: 166)

So it is no surprise that Bernays availed himself of the associational values of Hollywood to give Coolidge's image a boost. He did so by organizing high-profile, public, press-related meetings between the President and Hollywood superstars of the day like Al Jolson, Ed Wynn, and the Dolly Sisters.

Bernays operated at the crossroads between celebrity culture, business and government. Among his business clients he numbered Proctor & Gamble, New Jersey Telephone, Dodge Automobiles, the United Fruit Company and Filene's Department Store. He was also employed by the US government for the President's Emergency Committee on Employment (1931–2) and the war effort.

The new electronic technologies of mass communication, especially radio, film and later television, provided public relations with unprecedented new motorways into the public mind. For well-nigh seventy years, Bernays was at the forefront of proselytizing the effective application of these new media in advancing the science of public relations. Bernays was a nephew of Sigmund Freud. The methods of good practice that he developed for public relations were indebted to the theory of psychoanalysis devised by his uncle. Added to them are contemporary insights from Gustave Le Bon, Wilfred Trotter and others, on the social psychology of the crowd. In particular, Bernays follows Freud in maintaining that human beings are directed by unconscious drives that are evident in subconscious motivations, dependencies and other psychological materials, that influence conduct. Freud regarded psychoanalysis to be a benign science that brings order out of chaos. Despite acknowledging latent destructive potential in the enterprise, Bernays sees the science of public relations in the same vein. For him, the purpose of moulding public opinion is to bring the subconscious motivations of the people fit flush with the progressive goals articulated by enlightened leaders for the benefit of mankind.

However, things are not so simple when one turns to underlying questions relating to how Bernays understands the people and the role of leaders. One does not need to delve very far into Bernays's writings before the conviction that he is an elitist emerges and is corroborated. For example, he contends that democratic society consists of 'the herd and the group (who) follow those whom they recognize as leaders' (Bernays, 1928: 126). He continues:

> ... the group mind does not *think* in the strictest sense of the word. In place of thoughts it has impulses, habits and emotions. In making up its mind, its first impulse is to follow the example of a trusted leader. (Bernays, 1928: 73, emphasis in original)

On this logic, the challenge facing what Bernays called 'the intelligent minority' of people-skills professionals, business interests and government is obvious. In short order it follows that the task of public relations is to construct 'the associational values', 'symbols' and 'dramatic incidents' calculated to harness the 'impulses', 'habits' and 'emotions' of the people (Bernays, 1928: 127).

Bernays wrote before the fully developed emergence of Fascist leaders, the Fascist propaganda machines and the rise of related militia groups in interwar Europe who acknowledged no responsibility to be accountable to the public for their actions. Even so, his invention of the phrases 'intelligent minority' and 'trusted leader', to say nothing of his easy use of terms like 'the herd' and 'regimented' to describe the masses, struck a chill in the hearts of many contemporary observers and commentators.

Bernays was not interested in the questions of how 'the intelligent minority' are recruited, the social means by which they are integrated or why the sinews of power that they exert over the majority are largely 'invisible'. Nor was he an apologist for the universal literacy programmes initiated by democracy as the defence against manipulation by an elite. According to him:

> Universal literacy was supposed to educate the common man to control his environment. Once he could read and write he would have a mind fit to rule. So ran the democratic doctrine. But instead of a mind, universal literacy has given him rubber stamps, rubber stamps inked with advertising slogans, with editorials, with published scientific data, with the trivialities of the tabloids and the platitudes of history, quite innocent of original thought. Each man's rubber stamps are the duplicates of millions of others, so that when these millions are exposed to the same stimuli, all receive identical imprints. (Bernays, 1928: 48)

This is a bleak assessment of freedom and justice in modern life. It holds that the game of democracy is not worth the candle. The realpolitik of modern life amounts to rule by an 'invisible government' (consisting of business leaders, educated professionals and specialized technical staff) who operate through 'trusted leaders' to 'regiment' and 'guide' the masses. Celebrities pour the oil that makes this machine run by humanizing the objectives of government.

Optimally, the interests of invisible government and the masses coincide. But this leaves a raft of unresolved questions.

To begin with, it is a very peculiar vision of democracy. For Bernays, the rule of the people is not derived from the will of the people. The challenge of democracy is to ensure that the triumph of decent, healthy popular values – what the people would ideally want – are articulated on their behalf by responsible leaders and trusted celebrities.

Of course, Bernays acknowledges the possibility of corruption. The main checks that he lists against the misuse of power by the elite are the accountability of leaders to the media and the electorate, and the ethical codes of professional and technical staff intended to prohibit irregular or bad practice. However, given that he sees the electorate as pliable and inscribed with 'rubber-stamped' stimuli that prevent them from thinking for themselves, the only practicable checks he advances against the misuse of elite power are the ethics of professional and technical salaried personnel.

Without wishing to discount the probity and fearlessness of public relations and media personnel, it is questionable whether this guarantee amounts to very much. The reward structure of public relations and media personnel is dictated by the 'invisible government' of business and political leaders who demand high impact factors for their investment. The interests of one are consecutive upon the interests of the other. If public relations organizations expose the practices of business and government as corrupt, they bite the hand that feeds them. This is not to say that it is right to assume that they always collude with the interests of invisible government. However, it is naïve to assume that breaking with these interests when matters of corruption are revealed is either an automatic or fail-safe response.

Bernays's discussion raises larger issues about the engineering of consent and the proper uses of power in modern society that go well beyond the concerns of this book. The simple point that needs to be made here is that the principles he formulates and applies have since been adopted and developed by the factory system of celebrity production to manipulate mass motivation and desire. Bernays anticipates the point when he maintains that freedom of speech together with the free press have expanded the American Bill of Rights to include the right of persuasion. The expansion of the media has opened the gateway to communication, providing the basis for good and powerful arguments to be spread to the widest possible number, for the benefit of mankind (Bernays, 1947: 113). As usual, Bernays does not situate this technical development in relation to history or power. He does not ask the big questions, such as who has the real power to use the media as a communication tool or why the majority of people are marginalized or excluded from the open gateway of mass communications. He treats 'the intelligent minority' and 'the herd' as transhistorical facts of the human species and confines himself to the technical problems of effective communication and opinion formation arising therefrom. His benign account of the open gateway of mass communications is dependent upon a Pandora's box of questions of power, inequality and influence remaining firmly shut.

For Bernays, PR practitioners, publicists and media commentators are in the business of positive people-persuasion. They profile celebrities in public life through the strategic use of associational values, dramatic incidents and calculated symbols of prestige in order to shape public opinion. This process is supported by the use of surveys, questionnaires, focus groups and unstructured interviews. This process of data accumulation is the basis for refining objectives and navigating media interventions. The highest cultural value of this process is achieved through media placement and representation. The celebrity factory system does not innocently seek access to the media. Rather, it engages in a war of manoeuvre to ensure that the celebrity skyscraper is presented to achieve the highest impact rating.

It is important to understand that the cultural standing and presentation of celebrities are not just matters of talent, achievement or position. In addition, they are centrally dependent upon the data yield harvested by public relations and media specialists into the motivations and opinions of the group. Nor is the subject of data yield a straightforward matter of fact-finding. Public relations personnel, and cultural intermediary accessories of many shapes and sizes, engage in a variety of celebrity design issues that aim to integrate the public face of celebrity with the public mind. Underlying the qualitative relationships that the public relations industry strives to form, then, is a mass of quantitative data that supports and informs the production of high impact factors.

Bernays lived a long life. His heyday was between the 1920s and 1970s. During this half-century he had the ear of presidents, business moguls, newspaper tycoons, the heads of film production companies, TV network executives and celebrities from the world of popular entertainment. The principles that he carved out to promote associational value and dramatic premium in the public mind have been widely adapted and perpetually refined.

Public relations is now a multi-billion dollar business with multiple international service centres serving a global market. It coordinates interlinked promotion campaigns in both the Northern and Southern hemispheres, using multiple languages and negotiating with a variety of religious and political systems. A campaign founded in New York has to make allowances for cultural differences in London, Athens, Cape Town, Vancouver, Hong Kong, São Paulo and Sydney. These are often handled by employing national celebrities to headline campaigns in different geographical regions. But the message is the same. While there is obvious and real competition between different public relations and media corporations, it is legitimate to think of them as a unified force moulding global opinion.

The public relations-Media hub

In the advanced industrial societies a public-relations-media complex has emerged and taken root. Global public relations corporations such as Taylor Herring, Weber Shandwick, Fleishman-Hillard, Ketchum, Ogilvy, Rogers & Cowan and Edelman combine with international media giants like National Amusements, News Corporation, Disney, Vivendi, Time Warner, Viacom and Bertelsmann AG to form a power bloc which dominates the market in information, opinion formation and taste. Global public relations corporations determine campaigns for multinational businesses, states and voluntary organizations. They endeavour to shape public opinion and boost product awareness through public opinion research, press releases, press kits, photo ops, publicity stunts, talk shows, advertising and other media outlets.

Although they are not ruled by a class of illuminati, it is correct to refer to them as a power bloc. They are the gatekeepers between corporations, celebrities and the public. The personnel that staff them are generally recruited from the same educational backgrounds, and they express uniform business values. They exhibit a good match in cultural interests, political intelligence and economic management skills. They understand that people-persuasion is a business that is ultimately judged on profit/loss criteria. Despite the measurable and intangible shifts in public behaviour that campaigns achieve, the buck stops with the balance sheet. They use remarkably similar tools to reach their ends. The PR-Media hub now operates with a six-stage model of client service:

1 **Strategy Objectives:** Defining the focus, demographics, message, symbol, scope and budget of campaigns.

2 **Audience Analysis:** Locating the audience, examining their motivations and social networks.

3 **Community Demographics:** Mapping the communities that will be the target for strategy objectives. If an audience is not transparent, the onus is placed upon constructing one through the manufacture of associational values and dramatic incidents.

4 **Content Creation:** The production of narratives and storyboards to convey messages directly and unambiguously. A corollary of this is to itemize and manage a production schedule.

5 **Delivery:** Enlisting a variety of multimedia gateways to transmit campaigns from the client base to communities. These include television, video-sharing sites, social network communities, Internet sites, mobile communication devices, podcasts, email and physical encounters.

6 **Result Calibration:** Measuring the impact factor of campaigns through public opinion research into views, comments, links, MSM mentions and social bookmarks.

While celebrities are regularly used to endorse campaigns, it goes without saying that in their own right they also make consummate use of the PR-Media hub. It is not just a matter of positioning celebrities before the public. The PR-Media hub also positions the public before celebrities. Remember, stage three of the six-stage PR-Media programme makes provision for constructing an audience around a set of objectives and a campaign message if one does not exist.

This is a big step on from Bernays's era. Bernays made great play of the scientific status of public relations resting in the capacity of expert staff to glean valid information about the subconscious motivations and desires of the group mind. But when he used the term 'propaganda' to describe what public relations people do, he understood it to mean a strictly technical relation. That is public relations refines objectives and formulates messages that unite the motivations of the public and popularize the outlook of leaders. Politicians and trusted celebrities are meant to articulate the idealized good, honest and true values of the people. For the latter are judged to be incapable of articulating them by their own efforts.

Today, something different is openly discussed as a legitimate end of public relations. Namely, persuading consumers to develop new wants, aspirations of identity and lifestyle goals determined by business interests to achieve business ends. This involves a good deal more than merely bringing the good and true values of the public into harmony with the objectives of leaders. In a word it involves creating a *new* public.

Every step of the process entailed in mounting a campaign in the viewfinder of public consciousness and presenting the public to clients is quantitatively and qualitatively investigated and planned. Nothing is left to chance. Promotional messages and symbols are injected into the public mind by a variety of instruments. Celebrity prestige is just one of them.

The leading public relations corporations see themselves as people-smart. They do not resort to browbeating the public or hectoring them with indignant messages to consume this or that commodity. Rather, they blend campaign messages with building trust, support and empathy between campaign objectives and audiences. Establishing social network communities, customer relations groups and corporate responsibility programmes is indispensable. They convey the message that corporations and campaigns are about confirming belonging, and addressing real-world issues, as well as making money. They contribute to a variety of global stewardship duties with respect to educational, healthcare and environmental issues that matter to us all. The catch is that this agenda of interests is not chosen by the people but imposed upon them by the combination of business interests and media information hubs.

The PR-Media hub expounds accountability and transparency as core ethical values. Bernays himself set great store on the values of probity and fair dealing. However, studies of public relations practice in the pop music business have exposed a long covert history of bribery and intimidation (Dannan, 1991; Segrave, 1994). Allegations persist that aid money to Africa generated through event management is misappropriated and squandered (Theroux, 2006). Since the public does not control what the public gets, there is always room for murky financial seepage and nefarious appropriation of relief commodities. The networks of power that enlist the PR-Media hub in the service of government, business and voluntary sector humanitarianism, support illicit counter cultures that work outside the law to achieve the same ends.

The PR-Media hub is the most advanced version of the factory system of celebrity production. It operates to boost the public standing of celebrities and uses famous people as the face and mouthpiece of testimonials to bolster business and government campaigns. Making money is presented as having fun. The connection is stronger if the distribution of profits is allied to goals of corporate social responsibility. An oil company that makes billions from petroleum sales gives something back by supporting literacy programmes in the Third World or by purifying polluted lakes and waterways. Because celebrities are closely connected with the world of play, they provide immediate associational links with fun/giving culture. The greater use of them by the PR-Media hub demonstrates a business decision that 'celebrity sells'. However, celebrities are not the foundation of the complex.

The state, multinational corporations and international voluntary special interest organizations are the core client base. It is their financial, cultural and political requirements that drive the show. By common consent, the PR-Media hub uses technologies of pleasure accumulation to achieve the end of capital accumulation. It is in their role as catalysts of pleasure accumulation and trust that celebrities possess economic value for the PR-Media hub.

Doug Holt (2004) maintains that iconic brands are powerful symbols connected to a set of ideas or values that society holds to be important or compelling. Brands spill over into lifestyles and aspirations so that buying the brand becomes the insignia for wider and deeper forms of community membership. Celebrities afford shortcuts to preconceived associations of power, influence, empathy and glamour. Iconic celebrities build iconic brands. Isabella Rossellini, Jerry Hall and Bryan Ferry have been employed to advertise the Mandarin luxury hotel chain (Maginini *et al.*, 2008); L'Oreal has used Jennifer Aniston, Natalie Imbruglia, Milla Jovovich, Beyoncé, Jennifer Lopez, Andie MacDowell and Sarah Jessica Parker to enhance the brand (Pringle, 2004: 22); George Clooney and Nicole Kidman advertise Omega watches; Catherine Zeta-Jones is the face of Arden. These examples are hardly exhaustive.

The phenomenon of celebrity endorsement is so generalized that it has become an institutionalized feature of the PR-Media business. Celebrities have the capacity to get under the skin of audiences and consumers. For this reason they are signally attractive to the PR-Media hub pursuing the brief to build demand around brands and maximize sales.

The celebrity skyscraper casts a long shadow. Fame is in short supply. For this reason it is in high demand by the many for whom fame is perpetually elusive. Among the positive associations made with it are economic wealth, social power, cultural influence, free time and sexual licence. Celebrities are seen as leading a life of excitement, emergency, risk and incident. In consumer culture, these qualities are keenly desired as a break from routine, anxiety and inhibition. The PR-Media hub positions celebrities on the horizon of public life to persuade us to consume products and provide coaching in boutique lifestyle choices bearing upon questions of health, diet, welfare, public responsibility, personal bearing and environmental care.

An immense concentration of power is vested here. It is one that is little examined and poorly understood. In conjunction with government and business interests, the PR-Media hub supplies symbols, messages and celebrity personalities that dominate the public horizon. They manage brand reputation, visibility and preference at local, national and global levels. This is much more than a simple matter of brand-building. The PR-Media hub devises lifestyle boutique data to predispose audiences to consume products, formulate humanitarian aspirations and adopt government directives as lifestyle choices. Celebrities personify the plans of business and government. Putting a face to a product or a policy makes consumers and audiences feel that they are operating in a safe comfort zone.

Celebrity culture is a soft target for ridicule. The whirligig of press releases, tweets, publicity stunts and melodrama seems to be an extension of soap opera. The media, who feed off celebrity stories, is blatantly patronizing about the phenomenon. They link it with superficiality, triviality, deceit and the dumbing down of culture. Celebrities make nothing but sound bites and snapshot opportunities for the paparazzi. They add to the white noise in modern life, which makes it hard to separate matters of substance from the vacant trails of data confetti. This is a mistake.

In reality, the PR-Media hub is engaged in a battle for the mind. Celebrities are foot soldiers to win the public over to predetermined campaign messages and provide coaching tips on boutique lifestyle. Their political significance is that they constitute brands that predispose the *polis* to identify with them and emulate them.

Celebrities are as essential to modern capitalism, as the steam engine was to the start of the industrial revolution. Today, people skills are no less important than petroleum in making the system work. If the modern capitalist mode of production truly profits by exchange in communication, information, image and knowledge, celebrities are indispensable in making the wheels go around. Conversely, the guile, sweat and artifice that goes into constructing a celebrity means that it is often impossible to have what you might call a natural relation with them. We can't live with them and we can't live without them. To understand them accurately is not just a challenge for the media pundit, it is a requirement for ordinary men and women living in a society dominated by sound bites, the power of fame and visual culture.

2 The Fame Formula

A reasonable inference of the emphasis put here upon the connection between celebrity and the PR-Media hub is that today, fame is formulaic. If modern celebrity advances by design rather than accretion, it must be right to see fame as partly a product of the labour of cultural intermediaries, especially in the areas of opinion research, personality layering and impression management. On this logic, celebrities are not born. They are made. The purpose of assembling and polishing a celebrity is to achieve high impact factor ratings with the public. The term 'impact factor' refers to the space given to an individual or a brand on the horizon of public life. It is measured quantitatively in press column inches, print citations and airwave time. The objective behind engineering a high impact factor is to consolidate and advance the interests of business, government or special interest groups.

This circle is hardly virtuous, for it is apparent that, unlike Bernays, the PR-Media hub has ceased to confine itself to moulding public opinion so as to ensure that the objectives of leaders coincide with the subconscious good and true motivations of the group. Manipulation, in the sense of charming-up superficial needs and creating new markets, is now blatantly part of the game. Yet all things being equal, it is entirely plausible for the PR-Media hub to claim the capacity to conjure fame and ensure its endurance, by mixing the required impression management and publicity potions. This is indeed what representatives of the complex say that they accomplish for clients.

Publicist Mark Borkowski even offers a formula that claims to put the relationship on a scientific footing: $F(T) = B + P (1 + 10T + 1/2T2)$. Thus:

- F is quantity of fame

- T is the Time, measured at three-month intervals

- B is the baseline of fame at the commencement of the top-up process

- P is the fame increment boosted by PR-Media activity (Borkowski, 2008: 372)

Upon this basis, Borkowski, in effect, contends that public relations activity can make gold from base metal. He submits that a person of negligible talent can be projected in the public eye by fate or the domestic system of celebrity and, if the right media connections are activated, the result is fame.

Andy Warhol, who knew how to manipulate the media better than most, famously predicted that in the future everyone would be famous for fifteen minutes.[1] Borkowski quotes Warhol approvingly, but he modifies the fame spike. From a public relations standpoint, unsupported fame lasts not for fifteen minutes, but fifteen months. This is the typical lifespan of a 'celetoid' in receipt of professional support from cultural intermediaries (Borkowski, 2008: 371).

For example, in September of 2009, Sultan Kösen from Turkey was momentarily a media sensation. Kösen became famous not for his exceptional learning, extraordinary technical abilities, devastating pulchritude, or what have you. There was only one thing that the PR-Media hub deemed sensational about him: his height. At 8 ft 1 in (2.47 m), the 27 year old, who suffers from the medical condition known as pituitary gigantism, was named by the *Guinness Book of World Records* as the tallest man in the world. Various publicity devices were employed to bolster his impact rating. In interviews Kösen expressed the hope that his new-found fame would help him find a girlfriend (he never had one before, his height being viewed as an impediment by eligible women). The press also carried stories of how his height inconvenienced him by savagely limiting his fashion options and prevented him from driving, since no car was big enough to accommodate him. According to the fame formula, Kösen's celebrity has, on average, a fifteenth-month shelf life. Indeed, at the time of writing, his impact factor is on the wane. From being front-page news, he is seldom mentioned and never photographed. He is moving ineluctably, to the graveyard of public oblivion that is the lot of the overwhelming majority of celetoids.

Borkowski's contention is that, with the intervention of professional cultural intermediaries, the fame spike can be extended indefinitely. The method is to build up a narrative of publicity incidents to retain the famous figure in the public eye. This directly follows Bernays, who constantly advocated the value of engineered 'dramatic incidents' to maximize impact ratings (Bernays, 1928; 1935). For Borkowski, all things being equal, professional intervention reboots the impact factor at a fifteen-month interval. Thereafter, unless achieved celebrity status is attained, which requires talent and accomplishment, 'fame follows an exponential slide to obscurity' (Borkowski, 2008: 371). A celetoid becomes a has-been, yesterday's man. Even if achieved celebrity is attained, such is the attention span of the public that cultural intermediaries need to engineer another fame spike to boost the impact factor. This may centre on a programmed episode like the release of a new film or album or a revelation from the private life of the star. The object is to reboot the impact factor of the star in order to boost fame for at least another fifteen months.[2]

Borkowski claims that his fame formula is based upon case histories of celebrity trajectories, notably, Kevin Spacey, Halle Berry, Paris Hilton, Nicole Kidman, Richard Branson, Mel Gibson, Lindsay Lohan, Tom Cruise, Abi Titmuss, Angelina Jolie,

Brad Pitt, Hugo Chavez, Jeffrey Archer, Jade Goody and George Michael. It also reflects the study of branding campaigns for front-line Red Bull, Stella Artois, Heineken, American Express and Adidas. From a public relations standpoint, Borkowski holds, there is no consequential distinction to be made between star personalities and products. Both are commodities whose impact factor will dip without the intervention of cultural intermediaries. He substantiates his argument with brief case studies of the fame trajectories followed by the celetoid Jade Goody and the celebrity idol Madonna.

Jade Goody

Jade Goody first came to the attention of the British public in 2002 when she participated as a contestant in the reality TV programme *Big Brother.* Brash, vulgar, overweight, physically plain and self-opinionated, Jade featured in media coverage as, not to mince words, a representative of white, working-class trash. She failed to win the contest and extended her moment in the limelight by occasionally appearing in gossip columns and participating in charity events like the London Marathon. Her refusal to train for the latter event was well publicized in the press. It was taken to be further evidence of her ignorance and ill-judged self-importance.

After fifteen months, the professionally inspired reboot came with the publication of her autobiography (2006). This was the pretext for a round of tabloid interviews and the chat-show circus. In this way Goody extended her celetoid status, albeit with the strong suspicion among cultural intermediaries that the law of diminishing returns was kicking in. After fifteen months, an attempted celebrity reboot via the autobiography and related publicity, her halo on the public horizon was plainly slipping.

What first transformed the situation was Goody's participation in *Celebrity Big Brother* (2007). More particularly, a publicity incident in the series rocketed her back into public consciousness. It is not clear whether the incident was spontaneous or was staged, i.e. whether Goody acted spontaneously or followed the advice of public relations cultural intermediaries. What happened was that Goody reacted angrily to what she took to be the superiority of a co-contestant, the Bollywood star Shilpa Shetty. She launched into a racist attack, which immediately became headline news and resulted in Goody's expulsion from the house.

Writing in 2008, Borkowsi confidently predicted that Goody had 'little chance' of relaunching into true fame again (Borkowsi, 2008: 374). Fate had a different hand in store. The following year, in August 2008, while appearing on the Indian version of *Celebrity Big Brother*, she was diagnosed with cervical cancer. Her public image changed. The uncouth racist poacher of fame was suddenly rebranded as the tragic prey of a killer disease. Her highly public death in 2009, at the age of twenty-seven, which she faced with courage and dignity, raised public awareness of cervical cancer and prompted a government review of screening processes for the under-25 age group in England and Wales.

The terminal phase of her illness included an expertly managed media-wide publicity event, in the shape of her marriage to 21-year-old Jack Tweed. The ceremony, which the press reported cost a reputed £300,000, was widely covered by the global media. Jade was portrayed as a dying princess snatching a last grasp at happiness while, of course, her estate benefited richly from exclusive photo shoots and transmission fees.

After the wedding, cultural intermediaries also extended Goody's public profile with regular bulletins focusing on her physical condition, Essex funeral plans and general state of mind. During the last days of her illness, she featured regularly on national news. Her death was front-page news and a lead item in television news broadcasts. Her will, published in 2010, announced that she left £3 million to her two sons. Not bad for a celebrity blessed with, no discernible talents who was widely labelled by the industry as 'finished', after the Shilpa Shetty incident in 2007.

Madonna

In contrast to Jade Goody, Madonna is a bona fide contemporary idol. Her fame has now extended for over quarter of a century. Press and audience responses to her *Sticky and Sweet* tour (2009), humanitarian work in Malawi (where she founded an orphanage for girls and, controversially, adopted two children, a son in 2006 and a daughter in 2009), film work, health regime, pedicure and love life, shows no sign of abating. She remains a top-drawer attraction for celebrity product endorsement from the likes of multinational corporations such as Pepsi-Cola, Max Factor, Microsoft Windows XP, BMW, Gap, Estée Lauder, Motorola, H&M and Sunsilk. In the 1980s and early 1990s her sexuality was iconic for an entire generation. They have remained faithful in the subsequent dramatic shifts in public face that have been the trademark of her career. Madonna's refusal to be hidebound by image or typecast by public personality was widely and enthusiastically adopted as a female role model by millions of young girls and mature women, throughout the world.

For Borkowski, she is a classic example of the fame formula at work. He submits that all of the principles of fame promotion and calculated exposure management mentioned in relation to Goody apply to Madonna. She prolonged her fame by staging dramatic publicity incidents, calculated, typically in fifteen-month cycles. Examples include controversial pop promo video work, the *Blond Ambition* (1990) tour in which she simulated masturbation on stage at the end of 'Like A Virgin', the cinéma vérité movie *Madonna: Truth or Dare* (also known as *In Bed with Madonna*) (1991) in which she simulates fellatio with a wine bottle, the soft core, coffee table book *Sex* (1992) in which she posed naked in a variety of private and public settings, and the infamous on-stage kiss with Britney Spears at the 2003 MTV Video Music Awards. In the words of Borkowski:

> From her early days as a sharp-witted 80s party girl, she has moved onwards and upwards in her quest to stay famous, creating controversy through videos of her kissing a black Jesus, her *Sex* book and her flirtation with lesbianism, changing style for every album, acting parts in movies, adopting children, writing books for children and becoming a member of the English landed gentry by dint of marriage and money and taking to it like a duck to water. (Borkowski, 2008: 375)

Borkowski presents these various shifts in public image as part of an industrial programme of fame management involving cultural intermediaries at every stage. Madonna engaged in carefully planned publicity-grabbing events to reboot her public profile. Although she refuses to be confined by image and is critical of a world that is entirely filled with images, she is massively image-conscious. This reflects a deeply saturated and nuanced knowledge of American popular culture, which she and her advisers raid to boost her image. Thus, her 'Material Girl' image drew on public representations of Marilyn Monroe in *Gentlemen Prefer Blondes*; the *Blond Ambition* (1990) stage show included references to Fritz Lang's *Metropolis*, Tamara de Lempicka and *A Clockwork Orange*; while in the movie *Dick Tracy* (1990), she recreated a Jean Harlow look.

For Borokowski then, Madonna is a case study of the fame formula. She and her advisers have exploited her talents and accomplishments by engineering publicity incidents to boost her impact factor with the public. It is not enough to be Madonna. In order to seize the public mind she had to pose naked in a variety of soft-core images for the *Sex* book and challenge codes of racial segregation in the black Jesus video. The fame spike requires the boundaries of public expectation to be broken in roughly, fifteen-month intervals.

The 'fame formula' is a diverting party piece. The first thing to note about it is that is a self-serving concoction. It identifies cultural intermediaries as pivotal in the production of fame. Borkowski is himself a successful PR practitioner and therefore has a vested interest in insisting on the fundamental importance of cultural intermediaries in celebrity culture. This is also the line taken by the pop publicist and reality TV impresario Simon Cowell: Stars do not exist without management (Cowell, 2004: 260).

But it leaves aside the thorny question of why a Tila Tequila or a Miley Cyrus should be elevated from the rank and file to occupy the celebrity limelight. You might say that it is simply a matter of being selected and packaged by a cultural intermediary like Borkowski or Cowell and subject to the fame-formula regime. But two unfortunate things follow from this.

Firstly, it elevates the cultural intermediary into a puppet master and casts celebrities and audiences as puppets.[3] It is understandable why cultural intermediaries present themselves as indispensable for they have a service to sell. But to discount the cultural literacy of celebrities and audiences is a mistake. Madonna ruffled adoption protocols when, as a white, wealthy superstar, she adopted two Malawi children. But the inference that this is a matter of the fame formula undermines her literacy as a humanitarian and activist. It cheapens the motivation of celebrities to engage in some types of positive public acts and misconstrues why audiences recognize cultural prestige in them.

The second result of 'the cultural intermediary is all' argument is that it misunderstands the expanded opportunities for the production of fame offered by new technology. The Internet has revitalized the domestic system of celebrity.

Take a figure like Chris Cocker. He is a small town, Southern, openly gay adolescent who posted rants and performance pieces on his MySpace page. All of this changed in 2007 when he posted a defensive piece on Britney Spears after her performance at the MTV Video Music Awards. Spears's performance had been pilloried by the media as lacklustre and embarrassing. Crocker presented himself as her *Don Quixote*. Within two days Crocker's posting received over 4 million hits. He has gone on to become an Internet celebrity with a cult following.

It is one thing to propose that Crocker is an isolated example of Internet celebrity. In that case his fame might be easily dismissed as a topic of paltry exceptionalism. But when I submit that the Net has revitalized the domestic system of fame, I am referring to a general, well-documented phenomenon.

For example, the Filipina singer Charice Pempengco, who performed at two presidential pre-inaugural events and two post-Oscar award events in 2009, acquired fame by releasing her songs on YouTube. Carol Zara, a Brazilian-Canadian blogger, achieved global fame through her *digitallyblonde.com* site on Twitter. Rebekka Guðleifsdóttir became a celebrity after releasing her photographs on Flickr. By 2006 her site received 1.6 million visits, making it the most popular Flickr site. Her images led to her creating and appearing in a Toyota advertising campaign (Smith, 2006). Zoe Margolis posted a blog, under the name Amy Lee, of a young woman's sexual adventures, which became a bestselling book. Ben Going, under the username *boh3m3,* became a video blog star after posting videos on YouTube.

The list is hardly exhaustive. What it indicates is that the Internet offers unprecedented new pathways to acquire fame. The cultural literacy of performers and audiences can create a significant fan base without the intervention of the established factory system of celebrity.

It would be a gross exaggeration to maintain that the Internet is producing a new generation of stars that in time will overtake the factory system and make the PR-Media hub irrelevant. On the other hand, it is changing the traditional rules of the game that apply to celebrity promotion. Established pathways of being discovered and packaged that are based on the factory system of fame are not exactly being replaced. But they are now supplemented by a reinvigorated domestic system, which uses private laptops, the mobile phone and the Internet to generate a fan base. As we have already noted, the Arctic Monkeys, Lily Allen and Little Boots have credited MySpace with launching their popular music careers. In each case the Web built a following that eventually triggered the interest of managers, promoters and other cultural intermediaries. You might say that the revitalized domestic system is creating peripheral stars and parallel supply chains for the promotion of celebrity. However, once they reach a measurable impact factor, the commercial tendency is for them to be co-opted by the factory system, and professionally repackaged.

The case of Justin Bieber is typical.

Bieber is a 16-year-old musician from Stratford, Ontario, whose album *My World 2.0* debuted at number 1 in the *Billboard* chart in 2010 and has, at the time of writing, sold 850,000 copies. He did not acquire fame as a child model, and his parents did not audition him for reality TV shows like *Star Search* or the Disney Channel. What happened is that his mother posted videos of him performing on YouTube. Although the audience was mainly intended to be relatives and friends of the family, Bieber's performances generated a wider fan base that came to the attention of an Atlanta-based promoter and music manager, one Scooter Braun. Braun masterminded a programme of Internet promotion that eventually produced 2.2 million Twitter followers, 50 million YouTube subscribers and a contract with Def Jam Recordings. Bieber has appeared on *The Late Show with David Letterman, The Tonight Show, Saturday Night Live* and at the White House (Suddath, 2010). He was one of the most commercially successful 'discoveries' in the music industry in 2010. Does this invalidate the fame formula? Not really, since the evidence suggests that durable stardom does eventually require managerial expertise from publicists, promoters and other cultural intermediaries. The domestic system of fame can flag new talent, but the factory system is required for acts to make a real splash with the public and flourish.

Conversely, the idea that the fame formula is a science needs to be handled with caution. If fame is truly only a matter of promotion and packaging at timely intervals to increase the limelight awarded to stars, how are we to explain the descent into comparative obscurity of Simon Dee, Les McKeown, Kelly LeBrock, Justin Guarini or Adam Ant? In aggregate, the factory system has more fame causalities than celebrity successes.

What the fame formula describes is a strategy for engineering sensation and tinting fame. This is very different from explaining why some celebrities have the capacity to produce a social transformation and compel strangers to repose intense faith and unqualified trust in them.

If we return to Borkowski's case studies, it is true that publication of Jade Goody's autobiography, participation in events like the London Marathon and the racist attack on Shilpa Shetty were effective spikes in rebooting her fame. But what made her an enduring national and international figure was the positive and courageous way that she dealt with her terminal illness and the public sentiment that her life had been appropriated by the promotions and media industry. No PR man could have predicted or concocted this. Throughout her illness there is no doubt that Goody was guided by cultural intermediaries on how to present the most winning public face and generate a substantial financial legacy for her children. Her book *Jade: Fighting to the End* (2009) was published during the terminal phase of her cancer. *Forever in My Heart: The Story of My Battle Against Cancer* (2009) and a photo book, *Jade – Remember Me This Way* (2009), appeared immediately after her death was announced. They were stage-managed to milk public sympathy and garner maximum publicity and sales. Infamously, *OK!* magazine published a tribute edition that carried the phrases 'In Loving Memory' and 'Jade Goody 1981–2009' days *before* her death. This shows how consistently the media was already treating Goody first and foremost as a commodity rather than a vulnerable, suffering person.

Turning now to the case of Madonna, it is true that media reports of bisexuality, a wild temperament, simulating masturbation on stage, the soft-core photos in *Sex* and the video of kissing a black Jesus certainly grabbed airwaves space and filled print columns. Madonna may well have been advised by public relations experts to periodically outrage the public in this calculated way. Nevertheless, it is unrealistic to contend that these overt acts are the sum reason for explaining her durable fame. Madonna's celebrity is more than an exercise in effective exposure management. The attractive and powerful force of her fame is based on the popular belief that she is an exceptional, inspirational individual whose personal history is so vivid in culture that it enables society to take stock of itself and its position. Madonna symbolizes qualities of boldness, direct thought, spontaneity, unpredictability, frontier-lifestyle flexibility and heroic conviction that are either absent, or widely felt to be thwarted and underdeveloped in everyday life. In a mainline way, her celebrity fulfils a craving, or set of demands in society that, so to speak, *anticipated* or *craved* her and which are beyond the power of cultural intermediaries to create or control.

3 Celebrity and Sickness

To speak of celebrity 'craving' implies both a compulsion to be famous on the part of would-be celebrities and an emotional dependence upon fame in the celebrity flock. Psychologists argue that, today, pronounced and seductive types of celebrity craving are unprecedented. The risks that they pose to ordinary men and women are unparalleled. The Internet, satellite television and show-business magazines make public news and private details of celebrity lives ubiquitous and offer round-the-clock access. Exposure to celebrity culture is instant and perpetual. With perpetual exposure, there are, of course, gains, but also appreciable risks and high costs.

For example, Madonna's humanitarian work in Malawi suffered a serious blow when an audit report (2011) revealed that $3.8 m (£2.4 m) had been spent on a prestigious academy for underprivileged girls that had never been built. The report alleged outlandish expenditures on salaries, cars, office space, golf course membership and free housing. The controversy led to the resignation of the charity's executive director, Philippe van den Bossche, the partner of Madonna's personal trainer. In addition, eight charity workers sued the singer for unfair dismissal and non-payment of benefits. Madonna was presented in the media as gullible and out of touch. To make matters worse, it was revealed that she had loaned $11 m (£6.9 m) to the charity. This raised the separate, difficult question in the media of whether it is proper to treat a loan as an act of charity. Despite her publicity statement that she intended to team up with the Global Philanthropy Group to focus on schools across the country rather than concentrate her humanitarian efforts on one school, Madonna was widely criticized in Malawi and elsewhere for breaking her promise.

Celebrities have high social prestige. Many ordinary men and women regard specific stars or celebrity genres as occupying the pinnacle of glamour and social achievement. In addition, society showers lavish economic, social and cultural rewards upon stars. It is therefore not unreasonable for many ordinary men and women to look up to stars as role models or inspirational lifestyle leaders.

The snag is that the same social prestige that provides celebrities with status, affords licence for them to behave in ways that would be unacceptable in everyday life.

Stardom is strongly associated with narcissism.[1] That is a psychological syndrome consisting of attention-seeking, bullying, vanity, arrogance, intimidation and superiority. Some psychologists even speculate that narcissism is a *pre-condition* for stardom

(Pinsky and Young, 2009). That is, only persons with a high sense of personal self-worth and social authority are likely to develop a calling for achieved celebrity or celetoid status. Be that as it may, the latitude that the PR-Media hub extends to addictive, hysterical, manipulative, disassociated and superior forms of celebrity behaviour is an unfortunate precedent. It breeds imitation. Daniel Boorstin, who characterized the modern world as an 'age of contrivance', warned of the personal and social dangers of living 'with a wall of mirrors'. In some cases, this escalates into obsessive infatuation (Boorstin, 1962: 255). The results for individuals and society can be problematic. Not to beat about the bush, researchers propose that a) the social prestige afforded to celebrities results in specific types of self-harm and social risks for some stars; and b) there is a 'contagious' relationship or 'mirror effect' between dysfunctional forms of celebrity behaviour and negative psychological and social traits among the general population (McCutcheon et al., 2004; Pinsky and Young, 2009).[2]

We will come to the details and evidence for these propositions presently. Before doing so, a few more observations about the nature of these propositions are in order. Most strikingly, the case that celebrities exert an effect of emulation over segments of the population implies that for a significant part of the population the secondary relations of celebrity culture have supplanted the primary relations of home and community. That is for some appreciable sections of the population, the make-believe world of stargazing provides stronger emotional support and more meaningful rewards than family, school, nature or community. In particular, it provides a basis for copycat behaviour and various forms of self-harm. Self-mutilation, anorexia, bulimia, burning oneself with cigarettes, attempted suicide, suicide and homicide have been directly attributed to an obsessional or borderline-obsessional relationship with celebrity. Psychologists qualify this line of argument with the proviso that introverted personality types and individuals who have suffered some type of psychological and social dislocation through the divorce of parents or environmental disturbance or catastrophe have a greater propensity to develop dysfunctional symptoms.

Rates of celebrity self-harm and copycat types of dysfunctional behaviour among the celebrity fan clusters are directly related to the inflation of celebrity in popular culture. The media is identified as the primary source of inflation. 'Life, for millions of star-struck persons,' write McCutcheon et al., 'is little more than a steady diet of television shows, interspersed with musical CDs, movies, and an occasional fan magazine' (McCutcheon et al., 2004: 24).

What is not often noticed is that this 'steady diet' is calculated and highly processed by the PR-Media hub. The media provides much more than news about celebrities. It purports to offer a window on what Britney is thinking, who Paris is dating and why Lindsay has a history of alcohol abuse. In building powerful secondary relationships between the star and the public, the PR-Media hub operates to invert the order that is customary in primary relationships.

What does it mean to invert the order that is customary in primary relationships? In primary relationships we are bound to relations by blood and a history of face-to-face contact with others with whom we choose to recognize close personal sympathy. We get to know them better, through extended social encounters in which intimate private details are exchanged and provide the glue for an enriching relationship. The details of private life percolate through to us stage by stage, like coffee through a filter. Strong primary relationships depend upon discretion and taste. If too much is revealed too soon, or if we ask too much, the health of the relationship is imperilled.

In contrast, the private details of celebrity lives are full-on in the media and require no gradual, learning process through social encounters that respect boundaries and the development of intimate bonds based on the exchange of personal information. The PR-Media hub requires us to form powerful, emotional attachments with stars in order to boost impact factor ratings. This is why private details of celebrity family life, sexual relationships, medical conditions, rivalries, likes and phobias dominate celebrity culture. Frankness, incident, emergency and excitement are among the hallmarks of celebrity. By implication, the lives of ordinary men and women are inhibited, frustrated and repressed.

The chain of association reinforces star power since it boosts the attraction of celebrity prestige. This inference is psychologically consolidated by the practice of the PR-Media hub to portray the lives of the stars as packed with incidents and emergencies. Nowadays, celebrities, especially in the fields of light entertainment and sport, are routinely promoted as secular gods. The adoration awarded to them is a major challenge to personal health and self-restraint. Stars are reported to live on the edge, take big risks, dance with the Devil and, in general, ignore the boundaries that ordinary people observe. They occupy a frontier existence in which the financial stakes are portrayed as spectacular, emotional relationships are more vivid and personal risks are higher.[3]

In contrast, the PR-Media hub positions fan clusters as eking out predictable, risk-averse, uneventful lives. It is celebrities who stake everything on a dream and cultivate an all-or-nothing discipline in the conduct of private and public life. Look at Paul Potts or Susan Boyle. Despite lacking glamour or influence, they dared to live the dream.

It is ordinary people who pay their bills on time, never step out of line and make themselves scarce when bold, life-changing challenges come along. This contributes to the extension and corroboration of a more permissive licence to govern the conduct of star behaviour. Stars do what the rest of us are too frigid and timid to try.[4]

The idea that stars suffer for their fame results in more relaxed attitudes to the exhibition of symptoms of arrogance, entitlement, hysteria, disassociation, intimidation and megalomania in celebrity conduct. This relaxation reinforces the image of the lives of stars as packed with incident and emergency because it means that celebrities are more likely to get involved in highly public controversies with corporations, rival celebrities, the police, the judiciary, the press and the public. Because of adulation and financial rewards, celebrities may not think twice about confronting authority with a 'Do you know who I am?' attitude, whereas ordinary people are most likely to be compliant. We toe the line, while celebrities take if for granted that they can overstep the mark.

Of course, being on the frontier often means that one loses track of ordinary rules of reality. Hence, for example, Mike Tyson's six-year prison sentence for rape in 1992; Lil' Kim's (2005) one-year prison sentence for conspiracy and perjury; Wesley Snipes's 2008 prison sentence for tax evasion; Boy George's (2009) fifteen-month prison sentence for imprisoning a male escort; or, in 2010, Lindsay Lohan's high-handed violation of a probation order, which resulted in a prison sentence.

Some celebrities behave as if the ordinary rules of everyday life do not apply to them. The resultant controversies are faithfully reported and analysed by the media. They contribute to the image of celebrities as beyond the law. This reinforces the preconception of the celebrity as living a frontier existence far away from the order and humdrum of ordinary life.

A considerable literature has now grown up, which maintains that the proliferation of second-order relationships are socially harmful and, for some vulnerable people, personally destructive. The term 'fame attack' refers to a set of celebrity relationships that are toxic. It is more than a matter of perpetual grandstanding in relations with others, being neurotically attached to presenting a beguiling facade for manipulation, insistently badgering, bullying or obsessively spinning fantasies of humanitarian world-changing contributions to mankind. Fame attack means a distinct set of clinical and subclinical forms of psychological and social illnesses that afflict both stars and stargazers. Among celebrities and would-be celebrities the symptoms of dysfunctional conduct may take various forms, including a lack of empathy, callous indifference, a sense of automatic superiority, exhibitionism, entitlement, exploitativeness and grandiosity. In extreme cases, these result in syndromes of dysfunctional behaviour that produce events or patterns of self-harm for stars and stargazers.

Celebrity mortality and the mirror effect

Some years ago, Fowles investigated mortality data pertaining to 100 US stars and compared it with the average of the US population. He reported that celebrities have much lower life expectancy than the rest of the US population. In 1992 the average age of death for Americans was 71.9 years. For stars it was 58.7. The differences became starker when gender data is compared. In 1974 the average American male died at age 68.1, and the average American male star died at age 59.8, a difference of 8.3 years. For female stars the difference is even more dramatic. In 1974, the average age of mortality for an American woman was 75.8 years (Fowles, 1992: 236). For an American female star it was 54.3 years, a difference of 21.5 years. According to Fowles, American celebrities have a higher than average incidence of death from cancer, accidents, influenza, cirrhosis, suicide, homicide, kidney disease and ulcers (Fowles, 1992: 233).

More recent work by Mark Bellis and associates (2007) at the Centre for Public Health, Liverpool John Moores University, compared survival rates of famous musicians and matched them to general populations in Europe and North America. They found that pop stars who experienced between three and twenty-five years of fame, had significantly higher levels of mortality (more than 1.7 times) than demographically matched populations in the UK and US. Higher mortality rates are explained as a result of the high-stress environments of pop star culture in which the incidence of alcohol, drugs, violence and high-risk behaviour is higher than in mean populations. The inescapable conclusion is that fame is sometimes a killer.

Pinsky and Young (2009) extend the argument from celebrities to celebrity culture. They argue that celebrity produces a 'mirror effect'. The frontier, risk-taking existence of celebrities is mirrored by negative adaptive behaviour among the public.[5] Outwardly, media coverage rewards the bad behaviour of celebrities. Paris Hilton, Lindsay Lohan, Britney Spears, Pete Doherty, Jude Law, Mel Gibson, Nicole Richie and Kiefer Sutherland engage in highly public displays of rule breaking and irresponsible conduct. While they are subject to vociferous disapproval from gossip columnists and talk-show hosts who deplore their irresponsibility and outlandish disrespect for convention, they are not exactly knocked off the perch of celebrity prestige. On the contrary, there is evident public approval for bloody-minded behaviour that dares to go where ordinary people fear to tread. Celebrities appear to have it all, do it all, and get away with it all. For Pinsky and Young (2009) this sets a malign precedent. Bad behaviour is copied by some sections of the general population who act upon the precept that they will have their cake and eat it, just like their celebrity idols.

Doubtless the propensity for emulation varies with age, gender, income, education and a range of other factors. However, for Pinsky and Young (2009) the cultural prevalence of fame attack often correlates with personal histories of physical abuse, hypersexuality, emotional harassment, aggression, introversion, an irrational sense of entitlement, exhibitionism, heavy drinking, drug dependence, dietary irregularities, egoism, panic attacks, delusions, low self-esteem and various types of self-harm among the population. Although the authors acknowledge that fame can harness positive energy and produce inspiring role models, they conclude that the balance is currently terribly out of kilter. The magnification of fame in popular culture is fraying the fabric of society. It creates morbid dependencies and avoidable illnesses that will only be rooted out with considerable determination and struggle on the part of parents, medical and therapeutic personnel and opinion-makers.

At its worst, celebrity culture infests ordinary people with false values, base aspirations and abusive character traits. It sweeps all participants and components up in a perfect storm of illusory relationships. Fan clusters are basically imaginary communities who devote themselves to celebrities whose public image is itself a combination of fantasy, figments of imagination and public relations sound bites.

Pinsky and Young's remedy is to prevail upon parents and educationists to trim sails and batten down hatches. Narcissistic parents should stop producing narcissistic children. The School and University systems must abjure a culture of overpraise for pupils and students in favour of benign realism. The media must stop presenting celebrities as secular gods and cease portraying celebrity culture as a perpetual soap opera.

I am bound to say that I see a King Canute-like element about these remedies. They imply a sea change in psychology, culture and mass communication that would be truly momentous. The central dynamics of celebrity culture and the PR-Media hub are concerned with maximizing publicity and achieving high social impact factors. Trimming sails, battening down hatches and tightening up standards of education and regulation are very likely to get nowhere because the countervailing vested interests of the PR-Media hub and business are too powerful.

Be that as it may, at least Pinsky and Young are trying to be constructively critical. This is refreshing because a good deal of the literature never rises above a sort of high-handed, holier-than-thou level of criticism without suggesting how the renaissance of celebrity culture might be achieved. But what exactly are Pinsky and Young seeking to cure? It is one thing to say that fame is bad for some celebrities and for wide swathes of society. But what are the precise details of the syndromes in question?

Over the last ten years the pathology of celebrity has grown into a large, multifaceted subject. It encompasses issues of celebrity mortality and illness rates, patterns of dysfunctional behaviour among stars, hate mail from fans, stalking, physical attack, patterns of self-harm among fans and dangerous or debilitating fan fantasies. The psychological literature posits two behavioural disorders that are relevant in explorations of celebrity illness and pathology: Narcissistic Personality Disorder and Celebrity Worship Syndrome. These are useful frameworks to organize thought and explore the harmful and pathological consequences of celebrity culture. Let us examine them in consecutive order.

Narcissistic Personality Disorder (NPD)

Although the symptoms apply to fans who develop this partly through imitating the worst traits of celebrity culture, narcissistic personality disorder is a condition that applies primarily to stars. The term narcissistic derives from the Greek myth of Narcissus, a proud and beautiful hunter who was beguiled by his own image in a reflecting pool and subsequently pined away. Self-love is associated with excessive validation of the individual and extravagant invalidation of others. The American Psychological Association distinguishes three types of narcissistic personality disorder:

Type A consists of eccentric, unpredictable behaviour, including paranoia, schizoid personality and a strong propensity to delusion.

Type B consists of antisocial behaviour, borderline identity, attention-seeking, an unreasonable sense of entitlement, exhibitionism, irresponsibility, superiority and vanity.

Type C consists of anxious or inhibited behaviour, neurasthenia, excessive dependency, anger, aggression, suicidal feelings and obsessional compulsive traits.

The diagnostic criteria for identifying NPD are ninefold:

1   A grandiose sense of self-importance. A person with NPD behaves as if they are the centre of the world. They expect unqualified admiration from others, react aggressively to criticism and have a powerful conviction in their superiority without feeling obliged to demonstrate any evidence to support the claim of preferment.

2   A preoccupation with delusions of spectacular success, exceptional beauty and rare brilliance. In some cases there is a strong correlation between these delusions and genealogy. That is persons who label themselves as wonderfully beautiful, of razor-sharp intelligence, possessing amazing powers of expression or superior judgement, and believe that their children are blessed with the same qualities.

3   A belief that a person is unique, unrivalled or specially talented. This carries over into the conviction that only other 'special' people are capable of understanding or mixing with such a person. The implication is that the majority of us constitute a sub-species that is subordinate and incapable of attaining the level of persons who see themselves as 'special'.

4   A ceaseless craving to be admired, flattered and celebrated. This goes hand in hand with seeing life as a perpetual series of special events or treats. A person with NPD craves incident above continuity, and values generosity above prudence.

5   An acute, unyielding sense of entitlement. This translates into convictions that their interests are paramount and the interests of others are insignificant.

6   A readiness to exploit others by manipulation, trickery and sheer deceit. Because NPDs are in touch only with their own reality, they have no inhibitions against making things up when it suits their purpose to do so.

7   An affable outward public face, which conceals a callous manner, ruthless self-interest and lack of empathy. Because the interests of the person with NPD are automatically viewed as paramount and beyond criticism, the rights and entitlements of others are often neutralized or ignored.

8   A delusion that others are the seat of envy. In some cases this translates into suspicious, paranoid forms of behaviour in which others are labelled as grasping, selfish and unreasonable.

9   A supercilious, arrogant manner. A person with NPD is heedless of the needs and wants of others. This is associated with authoritarian, bullying forms of behaviour that bulldoze opposition and smother resistance.

When an individual's behaviour conforms to at least five of these criteria, then that person is diagnosed as having the condition of NPD.

A common symptom is an acute sense of isolation.[6] In celebrity culture, the star is alone with his genius, his demons or his so-called 'unique' issues and unable to relate to others as equals. As a result, a person with NPD may indulge in perpetual distraction, profligate expenditure, be reliant on alcohol, drugs or other stimulants, in order to numb the scalding sense of being alone in a cruel world.

Underlying this condition is often a deep sense of insecurity and unworthiness. Arrogance, self-importance and vanity are coping mechanisms to manage an inner sense of incompetence or damaged credibility. The roots of this are often preverbal, which perhaps accounts for why many NPDs find it so difficult to articulate or comprehend the symptoms of their behaviour. This militates against building enriching relationships with others. NPDs often have a history of broken relationships, divorce and estrangement from children, relations and friends. The more an individual feels trapped into playing the game of perpetual dazzling brilliance, physical perfection and social superiority, the greater the propensity to seek distraction or oblivion through alcohol, narcotics, psychological abuse or profligacy.

Pinsky and Young cite the highly public dysfunctional behaviour of celebrities like Paris Hilton, Nicole Richie, Lindsay Lohan, Britney Spears and the late Anna Nicole Smith as textbook examples of NPD in celebrity culture. It reveals toxic levels of superiority, entitlement, vanity, irresponsibility, high risk and self-harm (Pinsky and Young, 2009: 26–31).

One also thinks of the ITV1 documentary *Living With Michael Jackson,* in which Martin Bashir interviewed the late Michael Jackson (2003). The programme is widely regarded to have tarnished the already troubled public image of Jackson. It showed him to be a lonely, solitary figure, insulated from the real world by the walls of his Neverland Ranch, surrounded by an on-call-all-hours team of cultural intermediaries and in thrall to a disturbing Peter Pan complex in which he saw himself as a pure, misunderstood artist alone in a heartless world of media sycophants and bloodsuckers. A good deal of footage concentrated upon Jackson's unapologetic profligacy as he squandered hundreds of thousands of dollars on tasteless baubles in a West coast luxury department store and his heartfelt, but unconvincing, denial that he had undergone major cosmetic surgery.

Child stardom and its consequences

Jackson always lamented that stardom had robbed him of his youth and the innocence and wonder of being a child. There is nothing new about this. Childhood stardom is often presented, by the celebrities who experience it, as a curse, since it produces a sense of exaggerated entitlement, vanity and arrogance. The list of child stars who have suffered mental breakdowns, alcohol and drug dependency is a long one, especially if stardom does not continue into adult life. If this happens, child stars are trapped by memories of the days of their youthful bloom when they enjoyed a privileged relationship with the public, wealth and effortless access to a life of incident. Not surprisingly, many find the psychological problems intolerable, and cannot cope. The list of child star casualties is sobering.

Corey Haim, star of *The Lost Boys* (1987), died of an accidental drug overdose at 38; Dana Plato, who played Kimberley Drummond in the US sitcom 'Diff'rent Strokes', committed suicide at 35; the singer Lena Zavaroni also died at 35 following a 22-year battle with anorexia; Andrew Koeing who played 'Boner' in the TV series 'Growing Pains' committed suicide at 41; Gary Coleman, who starred in 'Diff'rent Strokes' from the age of 10 to 18, died of a brain haemorrhage at 42, after an adult life as a washed-up child star peppered with a history of charges of assault, disorderly conduct, reckless driving and domestic violence. Judy Garland, Jackie Coogan, Mickey Rooney, the Olsen Twins, Lindsay Lohan and Britney Spears all had troubled adult histories that were explained as part of the struggle to come to terms with the complicated psychological consequences of childhood fame.

Child stars require expert protection. They need counsellors who can advise them on the pitfalls of fame and guide them away from harmful, dysfunctional behaviour and into building solid, enriching relationships with others. The stress of not being able to live up to one's public image or handle the media correctly can be punitive. Child stars may become trapped in a Neverland of eternal youthful fame, which becomes harder to occupy as ageing takes its toll.

In adult life, sudden fame can be just as bad. Unknowns who become overnight sensations are like children in the world of fame. Susan Boyle, the plain, Scottish spinster who was the sensation of the 2009 run of the TV amateur talent show *Britain's Got Talent,* spent time in a psychiatric clinic after coming second in the final. She was said to be emotionally exhausted and unable to deal with the complexities of fame and failing to win the contest outright. After her release, she compared sudden fame to a 'demolition ball'.

Likewise, the Canadian freestyle skier Alex Bilodeau who won a gold medal in the 2010 Winter Olympics, Shane Lynch of *Boyzone,* Lisa Stansfield, Eminem, the late Amy Winehouse, Lily Allen and the late George Best, all testified to being overwhelmed by sudden fame, which resulted in various forms of self-harm, bullying and other forms of dysfunctional behaviour.

Fame, bipolarity and borderline personality disorder

Clinically speaking, fame is also frequently associated with bipolar disorder and borderline personality disorder. The symptoms include depression, belligerence, hypomania, delusions, fatigue, concentration lapses, irritability, loneliness, self-loathing, panic attacks, feelings of personal worthlessness, poor appetite, overeating and suicidal impulses. People who suffer from bipolar disorder and borderline personality disorder see life as a series of fragments. The rules and disclosures that apply to one fragment are not necessarily consistent with the next one. A person may engage in the delusion of presenting herself as a glamorous promiscuous novelist with three book contracts and a TV tie-in in one fragment, and elsewhere as a dedicated, home-loving mother who sees through the fame game, is a principled and trustworthy confidante and supports family values, *without recognizing any inconsistency, delusion, or acknowledging that they are lying.* People with these conditions treat encounters as akin to standing on a precipice and living for the moment. Since much of what they do and who they say they are is based upon lies, they often have a phobia of being found out. Because presence carries with it the risk of disclosure, people with this condition may become reclusive. Alternatively, they adopt a Devil may take the hindmost attitude to publicity and say anything that comes into their heads since, for them, nothing is true. Echoes of this abound in celebrity culture, even though they might not be related to full-blown syndromes.

In his squib on Arnold Schwarzenegger, Gary Indiana (2006) recounts a jaw-dropping *aperçu* about Ronald Reagan. Reagan, the B-list movie celebrity who gained control of the American presidency for two terms in the 1980s, publicly declared that after the collapse of Nazi Germany he participated in the liberation of the Jews. When it was pointed out that this was impossible since Reagan had never been to the war front, he is reported to have replied, 'facts are stupid things'. This is exactly what the bipolar or borderline personality believes when they spin a yarn.

Inevitably, bipolarity carries a fear of failure. As a result, bipolar and borderline personalities have difficulty in formulating a sense of continuity in their personal relationships and a coherent moral perspective. They may be excessively gregarious in public but people who are close to them do not know who they really are. They live for the moment, and have little concern for the connection between actions and consequences. Each fragmentary encounter elicits a different energy rush or energy slide. They cope with this by ever more grandiose flourishes. The spendthrift use of the credit card and immense, ultimately specious, undertakings to love or reform, or the flamboyant undertaking to lavish care upon others, or to devote themselves to saving mankind, are typical coping techniques. Because of this, bipolar and borderline people have difficulty in building durable relationships of trust and mutual respect. Stimulants, especially alcohol, drugs, sleeping pills and sex are used as standbys to combat the psychological frictions that arise.

NPD, bipolar disorder and borderline personality disorder are closely associated with the arts. This has led many commentators to contend that mania and creativity go hand in hand. Among the celebrities that have gone public about suffering from bipolar disorder are Stephen Fry, Carrie Fisher, Russell Brand, Mel Gibson, Sinead O'Connor, Catherine Zeta-Jones and Brian Wilson. It is likely that there is a much bigger silent majority among the 'celebritariat'.

In the appropriate measure, narcissism is usually regarded to be a healthy component in personalities. It correlates with ambition, drive and the desire to be recognized. It follows that all celebrities need a strong measure of narcissism in order to pitch themselves to the public as would-be or bona fide stars. While most celebrities are able to hold narcissistic tendencies in check so as not to become a risk to themselves or others and require clinical intervention, a significant minority are unable to cope with fame. Narcissism is quixotic and volatile. Stars inhabit a looking-glass world in which the praise and adulation of others inherently distorts interaction and relationships. The star and the audience are entangled in a world of surfaces and mirrors. The actress Uma Thurman puts her finger on some of the problems that this poses for the star in relating to others:

When you meet someone who has a very intensely preconceived notion about you because of what you do, it's a hurdle you have to climb over in order to be really interactive with another person. You're not any of that list of clichés that they think you are. Maybe you're some of them, but maybe not in the order that they think you are. (Uma Thurman, quoted in Berlin, 1996: 261)

For a star suffering from NPD, bipolar disorder or borderline personality disorder, the looking-glass world of stardom can lead to an exaggerated sense of entitlement and self-worth. When stars in this position feel threatened they often regress to the childhood coping strategies of anger, disassociation, lying or rejection. The incredulity and incomprehension that this produces in others contributes to the star's sense of insufferable isolation.

Patently, NPD, bipolarity and borderline personality disorder are conditions in which the energy level of projection in social encounters is inappropriate and harmful. It produces dysfunctional and, in some cases, pathological types of conduct. It is especially prevalent among celebrities because one of the prime functions of the PR-Media hub is to layer an exaggerated sense of self-worth and glamour on stars. Stars are portrayed as possessing the mysterious, sought-after X factor that makes them objects of desire, fantasy and admiration among the rank and file. They are courted and pampered as kings or queens and permanently held aloof from the common ruck, who are treated as lucky to touch the hem of their garments. This requires stars to devote an immense amount of emotional labour in personal grounding and reality checks. As Henry Winkler, while discussing the pleasures and pitfalls of fame, puts it:

It's very heady. You can easily start to believe that you're more than you are. They make you believe that you're very special, that all of a sudden you've grown inches. You're handsomer than you were. Your hair is golden blonde and flowing. It's a very seductive thing. Maybe one of the great lessons of life is how to maintain your equilibrium. (Henry Winkler, quoted in Berlin, 1996: 262)

The gulf between the star and the public is deliberately exaggerated by the PR-Media hub that portrays celebrities as living a frontier existence where each life is packed with incident and emergency.

It may be objected that celebrities are not alone in this. The poorest sections in society also have lives packed with incident and emergency. Their daily existence is a struggle to make ends meet and see the light at the end of the tunnel. But, of course, the frontier existence of celebrity culture is categorically different. Celebrity addictions, breakdowns and crack-ups contribute to the aura of stars as special people who deliberately and voluntarily *suffer* for their art. They accept incident, risk and emergency as part of the pact with fame and the inevitable price of affording social impact. This aura is exploited and developed by the PR-Media hub to boost the star's mystique. At a personal level, the hoopla of being portrayed as permanently located in a world of incident and emergency, compounds narcissistic, bipolar and borderline tendencies. It makes stars conscious of living in a special, vulnerable place and acting under pressures that ordinary people do not face and can never truly understand. Arrogance, vanity, entitlement and superiority are legitimated as responses to the challenges of stardom – heroic challenges that ordinary people cannot really imagine.

Celebrity worship syndrome

Fame is also associated with personality disorders and other morbid symptoms in the behaviour of fans. In this regard, psychologists have coined the term 'celebrity worship syndrome' (McCutcheon, Lange and Houron, 2002). By this is meant a type of obsessive-compulsive behaviour involving general states of dissociation and occasional borderline-pathological events. It is essential to make a distinction between non-pathological and pathological/borderline-pathological types of celebrity worship.

Non-pathological types of celebrity worship are founded upon an intense, insistent preoccupation with fame. It may take the form of an obsession with the lives of the rich and famous or it may address genres of celebrities or specific stars. Typical behaviours involve devoting an excessive amount of non-work time to tracking and assimilating news and gossip about celebrities through newspaper reports, celebrity TV channnels, celebrity magazines and other branches of the commercial media; obsessional monitoring work; imitating the physical appearance or characteristic dress of celebrities; adopting celebrity catchphrases, vernaculars or philosophies of life; having tattoos of celebrities inscribed on the body; writing obsessively to celebrities; visiting the addresses or other physical settings associated with stars, and such like.

In most cases these forms of celebrity worship are manageable. They do not lead to the disruption of primary relationships, the interruption of work patterns or extreme forms of conduct such as stalking or physical attack. As such they are compatible with familiar life and do not pose a risk to the celebrity worshipper or others.

However, even the non-pathological form of celebrity worship has a variety of subclinical social effects. It encourages a culture of dependency as fans become addicted to stars and celebrity genres that uproot or replace primary relationships. It proliferates narcissistic tendencies as audiences imitate the bad behaviour of stars. Typical consequences are the production of cultures of entitlement, exaggerated opinions of self-worth, disassociation, mania, fastening upon life as packed with incident and emergency and rejecting ordinary life as routine and uneventful.

The pathological/borderline-pathological type refers to conduct that produces self-harm and/or a risk to others. The main categories of behaviour are twofold: stalking, and suicide or attempted suicide.

Stalking

Stalking refers to a pattern of intrusive attention, contact or surveillance that causes distress in the victim. It encompasses being followed, being physically attacked, having notes pinned to property, receiving unwanted gifts and getting repeated unwanted telephone calls, letters or emails. The murders of John Lennon and the actresses Rebecca Schaeffer and Kathryn Dettman, were all fan-related. In this respect, the late Mexican Tejano singer Selena bears the dubious accolade of ultimate distinction: she was murdered by the deranged president of her fan club!

In addition, celebrity stalkers have been put on probation, referred to psychiatric hospitals or jailed for harassing stars including Richard Gere, Steven Spielberg, Jodie Foster, Gwyneth Paltrow, Theresa Saldana, Uma Thurman, Keira Knightley, Miley Cyrus, Britney Spears, Kirsten Dunst, James Foxx, Bryan Adams, Conan O'Brien, Halle Berry, Janet Jackson, Catherine Zeta-Jones, Anna Kournikova, Ivanka Trump, David Letterman and George Harrison.

Psychologists argue that stalking begins with a narcissistic fantasy focused upon an external object. Desire for people that we don't know is a perfectly normal part of the human condition. However, in the case of the stalker, the line that divides the public person from the self is either weak or wholly erased. Desire is so strong that the public person ceases to be regarded as a separate entity with meaningful, independent feelings. It becomes part of the desiring person's self and is subject to getting into line by intimidation, brinkmanship and harassment. As such, the desiring person naturally proceeds on the basis of having entitlements and jurisdiction. When this is thwarted by acute or chronic rejection, it promotes a sense of injustice and builds the defence mechanisms of anger and rage. This translates into the devaluation of the desired object and behaviour that is intended to hurt, control, damage or destroy (Reid Melloy, 2001).

Celebrities are particularly at risk of being victims of stalkers because the PR-Media hub is dedicated to present them to the public as super-glamorous, irresistible figures. Delusions of intimacy are reinforced by the constant stream of details from the private life of celebrities. The PR-Media hub affects to imply that audiences are being *taken into confidence* by disclosures concerning the health records, sex lives, work histories, family relationships and friendship networks of the stars. Stargazers are deluded into believing that they are entering into relationships of confidence and intimacy with the celebrity, when in fact the data produced by the PR-Media hub is available on an open-access basis.

The popular conception of celebrities as living a frontier existence in which excitement and risk abound, is reinforced by the PR-Media hub in which the celebrity is situated. The dramatic requirements and compressed form of film, television shows, videos or music recordings enhances the public perception of stars as living lives packed with incident and emergency. As Wykes and Gunter put it:

> Stars very often role-play publicly and fictionally, the embodiment of extremes of human emotion, passion, privacy, pain and pleasure and they do so in intense and contracted episodes. Hence, their iconographic status: they symbolize our lives back to us in fast forward – even soaps don't operate in real time – but they also offer us aspects of human life that we don't personally experience, hence their larger than life quality. (Wykes and Gunter, 2005: 104)

Stalkers have a history of seizing upon the private details of the life of a celebrity and forming a proprietorial, obsessive relationship with them. In some cases, stalkers transfer emotions of anger and rage from the desired object on to a separate object that most of us regard as possessing social honour. Psychiatrists and police surmise that through this means the stalker seeks to be recognized by the object of desire. Arguably, the most famous recent example is John Hinckley. In 1981 he attempted to assassinate Ronald Reagan. The assault was apparently motiveless. However, during the police investigation and subsequent trial it emerged that Hinckley was infatuated with the film star Jodie Foster. The assassination attempt on the President was purported to be a strategy to gain Foster's attention. By killing the leader of the American people, Hinckley hoped to win recognition and approval from Foster.

Do stalkers have common personal and social characteristics? Psychologists and criminologists submit that, typically, celebrity stalkers are isolated, introverted and immature. They are likely to hail from broken families and have a history of difficulties in the labour market. Immersion into the world of secondary relationships, focused around stars, is a coping strategy to manage real-world difficulties.

Stalkers are more likely to be men than women. The most common forms of harassment are silent phone calls, physical intimidation, tailing, trespass and unwanted letters (Budd et al., 2000: 10).

Increasing public awareness about stalking has resulted in anti-harassment legislation. In the United States, the state of California made stalking an offence in 1990. By 1993, most states had passed anti-harassment legislation. The United Kingdom followed suit with the Malicious Communications Act (1988) and the

Protection from Harassment Act (1997). But although society now officially recognizes celebrity stalking as a problem, it has not devised the means to modify or prevent it. This is because legislation focuses upon the stalker, rather than the causes of stalking. By criminalizing or pathologizing the stalker, society absolves the rest of us from recognizing unreasonable, possessive tendencies with respect to stars in our own habitual behaviour.

Suicide and attempted suicide

Celebrity worship may take the form of self-harm. The category of self-harm is amorphous and, in relation to celebrity worship syndrome, demands specification.

Three subsets of self-harm should be distinguished. To begin with, fans may harm themselves because they recognize that the distance between the star and the stargazer is unbridgeable. The stargazer can never enter the orbit occupied by the star. The resultant sense of estrangement and isolation may be handled by the stargazer harming themselves as a form of punishment for being permanently 'outside'.

The second subset refers to forms of self-harm that arise from the stargazer nurturing ambitions of achieved celebrity for themselves and the realization that they are never going to make the celebrity grade. When stars are not born they are cast back into the anonymous, indifferent universe. In such circumstances self-harm is resorted to as self-punishment for not being good enough to achieve celebrity status by virtue of their talents and accomplishments.

The third subset refers to obsessional or borderline-obsessional devotion to stars. In this condition stargazers identify so profoundly with the lives of stars that their own existence becomes a metronome of star life. When a star achieves success, this provides an emotional lift in the lives of stargazers. Similarly, when a star experiences falling and decline, the emotional trajectory is replicated in the lives of the stargazers. Perhaps the most dramatic example of this subset of self-harm behaviour in stargazers, is the phenomenon of copycat suicide that follows a celebrity supernova.

Now, it must be allowed that the motivation behind suicide is a complex question. It has to do with the intersection of family history, genetics and wider psychological, cultural and social factors. Research into this subject therefore requires sensitivity and due respect for the unique facts of biography. Fortunately, students of celebrity can draw upon, refer to and enlist well-founded research. Cheung et al. (2007) investigated 270 individuals who attempted suicide following the suicide of Taiwanese TV star M. J. Nee. They found that, compared to the incidences of attempted suicide in 2003 and 2004, there was no less than a 55 per cent increase in suicides in the weeks following media reports about the death of Nee.

Similarly, Fu and Yip (2007) researched the effect of celebrity suicide on the general suicide rate, following the suicide of the Hong Kong pop star Leslie Cheung. They found that 38 per cent of their respondents were influenced by the suicide of a celebrity. There were significant age and gender specific variations. The study found a 'significant' increase in the suicide rate for men aged between 25 and 39 years who used the same method as Cheung to kill themselves (jumping from a great height).

Other researchers into the relationship between celebrity suicide and general suicide rates found that media publicity produced a risk of copycat suicides that lasted for between two and four weeks (Phillips, 1974; Stack, 1987; Howton et al., 2000). Fu and Yip's findings suggested a much longer copycat risk period, stretching to between eight and fifteen months after the celebrity suicide (Fu and Yip, 2007: 544).

Similarly, other researchers have assumed that the copycat effect is concentrated in people who are vulnerable to self-harm and suicide for independent reasons. Fu and Yip's research concludes that 'celebrity suicide may trigger suicide ideation in anyone within the community, regardless of whether he or she were otherwise vulnerable for suicide (Fu and Yip, 2007: 544).'[7]

The 'sensational' nature of the Hong Kong Chinese media's reporting of suicides is cited as a major factor in copycat suicides. It is not unusual for papers to carry graphics, photos and diagrams of suicides on the front page, with emotional banner headlines. As Fu and Yip point out, this method of media reporting does not comply with World Health Organization (WHO) guidelines (Fu and Yip, 2007: 545).

European research conducted by Etzersdorfer, Voracek and Sonneck (2001) refers to a 'dose response' from the media to describe the emotional trigger behind copycat/contagious suicide. This is based upon an analysis of the motivational factors involved in a 43 per cent rise in attempted suicide or suicide from firearms following newspaper coverage of a suicide by shooting of an Austrian celebrity in Vienna.

Copycat/contagious forms are intimately related to media coverage. This is why Etzersdorfer et al. use the term 'dose effect'. The media administer the information dose that produces a reaction in vulnerable fans. Of course, this is not intentional. But it imposes considerable responsibilities upon the media to report celebrity supernovas in ways that are duly sensitive to the impressionable elements in the fan base. Etzerdofer et al.'s (2001) research into the Vienna case demonstrated that the formulation and application of clear media guidelines in reporting celebrity suicide can contain the copycat effect.

All of these subsets arise because stargazers have allowed the secondary relations of celebrity culture to supplant the primary relations of home and community. Where the balance of close primary relationships is disturbed, the resultant emotions of isolation and loneliness may be handled by formulating intense, emotional secondary relationships with stars. It is not so much that stars are a substitute for defective relationships in family life and friendship networks. Rather, it is a matter of identification with the stars in offering a stairway to heaven.

Common, largely unrecorded examples of self-harm involve self-mutilation using cigarette burns or cuts, starvation regimes and withdrawal from communication. Ultimately, as we have seen above, fans may resort to suicide. The most common form of suicide in celebrity worship culture is the so-called copycat or contagious type that follows a celebrity supernova.

Most people might say that celebrity culture has a neutral effect upon the general population. Against this, celebrity worship syndrome proposes that a) dysfunctional behaviour publicized in relation to stars, carries over and generally multiplies, and b) these forms of generally distributed behaviour would not exist without celebrity culture.

A general culture that has developed a preoccupation with fame produces fractured, divided, grandiose, self-important, disconnected, aggressive and intimidating people. They live in a world of mirrors and have perpetual doubts about their authority and their physical and social presence. As a result they struggle to build and maintain fulfilling primary relationships and turn to the secondary relationships of celebrity culture as a shortcut that enables them, voyeuristically, to experience fame, glamour and empowerment.

The resort to secondary relationships as a way of experiencing fame voyeuristically is reinforced by the plainly bad odds for gaining achieved celebrity. Because the desire for fame is universal, but the opportunities for acquiring or participating in celebrity are elusive, strong general propensities are unleashed to disassociate from the world of work and primary relationships. Cast adrift from the well-publicized stimulants of Beverly Hills and the consumer cornucopia of Rodeo Drive or Bond Street, people feel unfulfilled and thwarted by their distance from the lush life of celebrity, and turn to more readily available stimulants, such as living their meaningful lives through celebrities or alcohol and drugs.

The spiral of dependence is fuelled by the PR-Media hub, which employs cultural intermediaries to titillate and inflame the public with images of celebrity libido. The cultural prestige of stars depends upon the receptivity of the public. Because of this, the PR-Media hub devotes significant resources to positioning the public in relation to alluring symbols of fame and stardom.

Typically, this positioning identifies the audience as receptive to images of beauty, power and authority. Public opinion is primed to react positively to the assembly line of stars paraded by the PR-Media hub. The process obediently follows the sixfold model of moulding public opinion that has emerged in the post-war period, namely strategy analysis, audience analysis, determining community demographics, content creation, delivery and the calibration of results. In this way receptivity is *prepared* and *managed*.

Of course, the PR-Media hub is not omnipotent; it is merely the major force in influencing the public's reception to stars. Yet in this role it has immense power to shape the social horizon of fame and set the agenda of consumer aspirations.

McCutcheon *et al.* estimate that up to a third of the population display traits of celebrity worship behaviour (McCutcheon *et al.*, 2004: 166). This figure is not based on a scientifically convincing sample of the population. As such it may be on the high side. Even so, McCutcheon *et al.* are right to suggest that celebrity worship is much more than a minor subcultural phenomenon. Rather it is a general, deeply rooted characteristic of contemporary culture.

Celebrity worship syndrome appears to be related to the experiences of low self-esteem and social exclusion. According to Schlesinger (2006), the most important social characteristics of celebrity stalking at the time of the crime are unemployment, immigration, not being in a relationship and a history of psychiatric treatment and drug abuse. Maltby *et al.* (2001) found that celebrity worship correlates with low levels of self-worth, anxiety, fantasy-proneness and depression. These symptoms are common among people who feel isolated, rootless, inarticulate and unconfident. Where people feel an absence of close, proximate, primary relations celebrities are appropriated as superior, heaven-based makeshifts. These substitutes may become the basis for obsessive-compulsive identification that replaces the demand for primary relationships. Those who suffer from celebrity worship syndrome may hold down steady jobs and appear to be perfectly respectable members of society. But their meaningful lives are spent in a world of make-believe.

The Absorption-Addiction Model

In the age of achieved celebrity, the majority of those who achieve stardom start out as stargazers. Exposure to celebrity culture begins at birth. Infants absorb cultural symbols of glamour and power developed by the PR-Media hub with their mother's milk. Only a third are likely to develop celebrity worship syndrome but a much larger number are schooled in the culture of fan worship, stargazing and stardom. What are the issues here?

Several attempts to explain the pathway of celebrity worship syndrome have been made. McCutcheon *et al.* have developed what is arguably the most cogent psychological explanation: the Absorption-Addiction Model (McCutcheon *et al.*, 2004: 154–63).

This is a developmental theory of celebrity worship which identifies three distinct stages in the emergence of obsessive or borderline-obsessive conduct: Entertainment-Social; Intense-Personal; and Borderline-Pathological. As with all psychological developmental theories it is not proposed that all individuals are bound to pass through the three stages. Progress into the rarer, subclinical or clinical forms of dysfunctional behaviour depends on the strength of primary relationships and the unsatisfactory resolution of intense secondary relationships. However, in the case of a fully developed instance of celebrity worship syndrome the clinical assumption is that the individual progresses through each of the three stages. What are the behavioural characteristics of these stages?

1. Entertainment-social

The normal phase in the process of adolescent socialization in the West is prolonged interaction with the media. The prominence assigned to celebrity culture in the media means that children and adolescents spend a good deal of formative time in the company of images of glamour and stardom processed by the PR-Media hub. Powerful images of what is attractive and powerful in females is presented in pop promo videos of female singers like Lady Gaga or Christina Aguilera. Male heroes like Sam Worthington in *Avatar* (2009) or Jake Gyllenhaal in *Prince of Persia* (2010) are imprinted as glamorous role models for the under-15 demographic. Children absorb these images and in many cases imitate the attitude and behaviour associated with the role models, before they go through the normal stages of psychosexual development.

Absorbing media images of stardom is an ordinary part of growing up. It plays a positive role in enabling young people to adjust to the insecurities and strains that arise from primary relationships in the home and community by empathizing with and projecting onto star worlds. By identifying with a star on screen the adolescent stargazers may find ways of working through emotional blocks or communication breakdowns in the home. In addition, it may assist with peer group membership and breaking down barriers between strangers. Celebrity news and gossip is a medium that ignores the boundaries of class, gender, nation or race. As such, it operates as a global icebreaker. Referring to Miley Cyrus or Justin Bieber may be a calling card to join local peer group relationships, but it also has the capacity to operate as a passport that connects people from different cultures and nation states.

Exposure and, to some extent, absorption in the entertainment-social phase of celebrity culture is portrayed as an orthodox part of growing up. In most cases, children adjust optimally to the heroic and glamorous images presented to them by the media and real-world relationships. But a crucial part of McCutcheon *et al.*'s (2004) thesis, is that optimal adjustment is not invariable. Indeed, they hold that variation from the mean is sufficiently appreciable to constitute a matter of public concern.

2. Intense-personal

In some cases, especially when individuals are introverted or isolated, media bombardment of celebrity news and gossip becomes addictive. Stargazers formulate the delusion that they possess a special or unique relationship with their favoured star. They comb the press, television, the Internet and fan clubs for news of their idol. They adopt the hairstyle, pedicure, vernacular and public outlook of the star. They may have tattoos of the star printed on their bodies. Identification with the recorded life of the star becomes pivotal in establishing the stargazer's personal sense of authority. This is often reinforced by joining Web and blogging sites devoted to the star. Chris Cocker's plaintive video on YouTube and MySpace begging the media to leave Britney Spears alone after her under-par performance at the MTV Video Music Awards in 2007, has become an industry cause célèbre.

As we have already seen, the video generated millions of hits and hoisted Crocker into the national press, produced a development deal for a reality show (*Chris Cocker's 15 Minutes More*) and a recording contract.

If the stargazer suffers from the want of personal success, the life of the star may provide solace and a measure of compensation. By voyeuristically living through the public life of the star, the stargazer may come to acquire a sense of personal authority and social presence. In the fully developed intense-personal stage, this delusional relationship torches primary and secondary relationships to become all-consuming. The stargazer's life is organized around media coverage of the celebrity. The separation between the stargazer and the star becomes weak. The narcissism of the star carries over into the private life of the stargazer, leading to the development of aggressive, arrogant, superior, disassociated forms of behaviour.

3. Borderline-pathological

In the borderline-pathological stage of absorption, stargazers are unable to extricate themselves emotionally or psychologically from the star. Over-identification connects the stargazer to the star in a mechanical metronomic relationship. When the media portrays the star as triumphant, the mood of the stargazer is upbeat; when the star is presented as insecure, withdrawn and emotionally bottled up, the mood of the stargazer follows suit. Over-identification may culminate in the delusion that the autonomy of the star is inconsequential. Stargazers come to the conclusion that they possess the right to besiege or devour the star. This is the product of a progressively stronger immersion in the life of the star.

The borderline-pathological stage of celebrity worship syndrome is marked by neurotic and psychotic behaviour, the inability to recognize personal and social boundaries, the idealization or demonization of secondary relationships and weakly defined primary relationships. The pathological form may involve stalking, harassment and suicide.

It appears to have been behind the motive behind the intimidating and violent behaviour of Robert Dewey Hoskins, a vagrant loner, against Madonna. In 1995 Hoskins was arrested for stalking and making a terrorist threat against Madonna and her bodyguard, Basil Stephens. He had been intercepted trespassing at her Los Angeles home, leaving unwanted notes on the property. When restrained by Madonna's bodyguard, Hoskins threatened to 'slice' Madonna 'from ear to ear' if she did not marry him that evening.

Similarly, in 1998 Jonathan Norman was jailed for 25 years in California after being found guilty of stalking and threatening the Hollywood film director Stephen Spielberg. Prosecutors alleged that Norman trespassed on to Spielberg's Pacific Palisades mansion and was carrying a 'rape kit' that he intended to use on the director. Norman's behaviour was described as 'obsessive and frightening' by the Superior Court Judge Steven Suzukawa.

Likewise, when news broke of Catherine Zeta-Jones's clinical treatment for bipolar disorder in 2011, fan harassment was cited in the media as a factor in her condition. In 2004, an infatuated fan, Dawnette Knight, was jailed for stalking Zeta-Jones. She was found guilty of sending letters to the actress telling her that she would die like John F. Kennedy or Manson Family victim Sharon Tate. Zeta-Jones was reported as testifying that 'this has affected me and it will affect me for the rest of my life. I felt like a ticking time bomb' (Hattenstone, 2011).

Celebrity worship syndrome is directly related to the high–profile exposure that the PR-Media hub gives to portraying the lives of stars as packed with incident, risk and emergency. The drip-line of intimate details of the private lives of celebrities creates the delusion in the minds of some stargazers that they have a special or unique relationship with the celebrity.

Recorded rates of celebrity stalking and harassment have increased dramatically over the last three decades. This reflects the intense colonization of the private lives of ordinary men and women by the PR-Media hub. The saturation and manipulation of celebrity images is a highly accentuated feature of contemporary public life. It is no longer a matter of being bombarded with celebrity images at home. The same images are carried in the breast pocket or handbag on mobile phones and other communication devices.

Celebrity sickness is not just a condition afflicting specific stars and stargazers. It is a social malaise that has become associated with a variety of dysfunctional and antisocial forms of behaviour. Pinsky and Young refer to the fixation on media images which breeds dependent personalities, unable to develop self-motivating growth; the attempts to construct an alluring 'pseudo self'; the development of a culture of entitlement, and ensuing collision between entitlement and reality that precipitates panic; 'the descent into envy'; and 'the insecurity that is at the core of every narcissistic personality' (Pinsky and Young, 2009: 236). This is a long and woebegone list. Added to the material on the conditions of narcissistic personality disorder, borderline personalities and celebrity worship syndrome, it suggests that celebrity culture has much to answer for in explaining the problems and ills of the day.

Moral pundits in the media often twin celebrities with the various personality disorders and social illnesses discussed in this chapter. But does this give the topic of celebrity a fair shake? It is easy to dwell on the misuses of fame. The narcissism of stars, the guile of star-makers and the credulity of stargazers will always sell newspapers and attract big television audiences. However, dealing with celebrity on a dismissive level begs the question formulated by Rousseau (1984) and already raised here, namely why is celebrity universal in human groups? We might scorn the narcissistic behaviour of Heidi Montag and Spencer Pratt of MTV's *The Hills,* and revile the film director Roman Polanski and the pop star Gary Glitter for using their fame to have sex with underage girls. But is it right to cast all fame in the same dye? If it is plausible to attribute some types of psychological sickness and social malaise to celebrity culture, is it not also right to postulate and explore a positive relationship between celebrity, ambition and emulation?

4 Charisma Gulch

Celebrity newshounds and gossip columnists frequently trail the term 'charisma' to describe star power. The excitement and fervour generated at film premieres and pop concerts is described using terms like 'charismatic glamour' or 'stellar events'. During elections and the post-election honeymoon, political leaders like Barack Obama and David Cameron are described as 'bold', 'charismatic visionaries' by the media bandwagon.

These phrases are applied willy-nilly in the media and fan networks, but seldom closely examined or explained. The purpose of this chapter is to consider if it is really valid to describe modern celebrities as charismatic. As we shall see, the term has quite a precise meaning as a quality of leadership in social transformation.

By definition, celebrities attract attention. Because of their self-evident force in stimulating media activity and drawing crowds, special powers are often attributed to them by fan clusters and the PR-Media hub. As figureheads, they can swing votes and win elections. In terms of sponsorship, they can make an event out of a non-event, hence their increasing prominence in charity fundraising activities. As fundraisers, the best of them have a reputation for being able to turn water into wine.

These qualities have not been lost on political strategists. Since the election of John Kennedy in the USA (1960), election campaigns and party rallies have adopted many of the mannerisms and razzmatazz of the Hollywood Oscar ceremonies. Ronald Reagan, Tony Blair, David Cameron and Barack Obama overtly used film-star devices and scripts to enhance their electoral appeal.

Doug Kellner has compared Barack Obama's world tours to entertainment spectacles that are designed to produce a 'rock star reception' with thousands of people lining the streets to get a glimpse of him and his image dominating the media (Doug Kellner, 2009: 736).

Similarly, Jeff Alexander (2010a) has compared Obama's presidential campaign and victory to a series of celebrity performances, using the same crowd-pleasing tactics and conveying the impression of monumentality.

Working on the principle of glamour by association, political strategists encourage endorsement from celebrities from film, television, popular music and sport to add lustre to electioneering. Stars humanize the fine print of election manifestos and bring the dry abstract principles of electioneering to life. Political parties, who depend upon the media to inform and, if possible, transfix the public, are keenly aware of the importance of associational 'star factors' in fundraising and boosting votes. Political campaigns are organized on the principles of a Hollywood film set to produce a 'wow factor' to enlarge public enthusiasm. Wannabes can be transformed into serious contenders if they enlist the right big names to endorse them. Barack Obama's presidential campaign received support from a large group of film, rock and hip-hop stars, including Black Eyed Peas, John Legend, George Clooney, Jennifer Aniston, Will Smith, Jessica Biel and Jay-Z. His inauguration ball boasted a lineup including Bruce Springsteen, Bono, Beyoncé, Miley Cyrus, Sheryl Crowe, Shakira, James Taylor, will.i.am and Stevie Wonder. The overwhelmingly affirmative intended message was 'the good from the entertainment world help the good in the rest of society'. For Manuel Castells this message was no accident:

> Early on his campaign, he brought a number of people on board with experience in mobilizing the youth vote, such as Hans Reimert, of Rock the Vote, who coordinated Obama's youth voting initiative; and Chris Hughes, co-founder of Facebook with a significant pay cut to work full time for Obama's campaign, and is widely considered to be the main inspiration behind Obama's networking strategies. Obama's new media chief was Joe Rospars, who was writer and strategist for the Dean campaign before going on to found *Blue State Digital* (a multimedia firm that designs Web campaigns for Democratic candidates). (Manuel Castells, 2009: 394)

In short, Castells regards Obama's political campaign as astutely freeloading from resistant, oppositional and African-American youth cultures to increase receptivity to his campaign among the tranches of American popular culture that had seen themselves as disenfranchised under the years of George W. Bush.

In the United States, Alice Cooper, Clint Eastwood, Mel Gibson, M. C. Hammer, Sylvester Stallone, Magic Johnson, Mark McGwire and Sammy Hagar are well-publicized supporters of the Republican party; while Kevin Bacon, John Cusack, Sean Combs, Jackson Browne, Will Smith, Matt Damon, Kanye West and Nas are known Democrat supporters.

In the 2010 UK General Election campaign, all of the main parties ostentatiously paraded celebrity supporters. Labour endorsers included Ross Kemp, Bill Bailey, Prunella Scales, David Tennant, Eddie Izzard and Richard Wilson; Liberal Democrat star supporters included Colin Firth, Daniel Radcliffe, Chris Martin, Brian Eno and Floella Benjamin; and supporters of the Conservatives included Michael Caine, Carol Vorderman, Kirstie Allsopp, Frank Lampard, Darren Gough and William Roache.

For event planners and political-PR specialists the logic is simple: star charisma delivers publicity that may yield a rich harvest of votes. Glamour by association is characteristically recognized as an electoral asset. This carries over into wider politics in the use of celebrities from the world of entertainment to support lobbyists, pressure groups and social movements. Stars from the world of entertainment are increasingly prominent in political event branding. Prima facie, the success of celebrity advocacy and celebrity diplomacy in fundraising and mobilizing political support reflects the inspirational qualities that are classically claimed by charismatic leaders and confirmed by their followers. But is it really legitimate to associate modern celebrity with the classical understanding of charisma?

To answer the question we must examine how the inspirational qualities of modern celebrity operate. This requires an assessment of the issues of celebrity advocacy and celebrity diplomacy. In contemporary society, achieved celebrities like George Clooney, Angelina Jolie, Johnny Depp, Orlando Bloom, Bono, Annie Lennox, Richard Branson, Al Gore, Michael Stipe and Bob Geldof have emerged as major players in expanding humanitarian consciousness and in fundraising. They are spokesmen for single-issue events like Tsunami Relief, Save Darfur and the Haiti Disaster Fund, and figureheads for a variety of voluntary sector human rights, welfare and environmental pressure groups. These modern celebrities act like 'big citizens', articulating and proselytizing issues on behalf of an implicitly grateful public. In doing this, they are often popularly regarded to be more sincere and relevant than officially elected representatives of the people. Before coming to consider this matter at greater length, a preliminary task must be accomplished, namely scrutiny of the meaning of the classical concept of charisma.

The meaning of charisma

Charisma refers to the heroic or extraordinary qualities, real or imagined, that an admired person is believed to possess. The term originated in early Christian thought where it was applied to refer to 'the gift of grace'. Mystical and metaphysical connotations abound. The charismatic individual is portrayed as a presence from another world or, less melodramatically, a different realm of custom and power; he or she has powers of healing and second sight; they can win wars, where others taste defeats; they have custody over inspirational gifts that produce major social changes in thought, emotions and spirit. Echoes of the religious connotation of divinely blessed, superhuman or supernatural power remain in the application of the term to modern celebrities by television presenters, journalists and laypeople.

In classical discussions, the concept of charisma is described as a revolutionary force because it enables the individual to exercise unreserved influence and inspire total devotion (Weber, 1948; Rieff, 2007).[1] Genuinely charismatic leadership is completely spellbinding and mould-breaking. No ethical rules apply. Charisma can mobilize behaviour that is attached to destructive as well as constructive ends. It can be a force for evil as well as good.

Genuine charisma irresistibly demands that believers follow the will of leaders regardless of personal considerations of well-being and safety. The leader is supported through thick and thin and against all odds. This is because the leader is understood to be divinely blessed and exalted with a unique command over powers of leadership. In terms of personality characteristics, charisma is an explosive force that demands ultimate passion, absolute faith and unqualified commitment from believers and total licence in the planning and execution of leadership. It is a magical force in human conduct. It brings delight and awe to some. To others it delivers fear and woe. It has a genuinely revolutionary quality. As such, it transforms the lives of those who fall under its spell.

This type of authority is usually contrasted with two other types of governance. Traditional authority is associated with ascribed celebrities and preliterate societies. It means a form of rule based upon custom and reverence for precedent. We follow the King or the Emperor because respect for dynasty is engrained in society, that is until a Cromwell or a Robespierre comes along to challenge the rule of custom and privilege.

The second form of rule is rational-legal authority. That is rule by democratically endorsed, transparent and accountable ways of going about things and achieving decisions. In rational-legal systems of rule we follow the dictates of a person by virtue of the position that the person occupies rather than the qualities of the individual.

These two types of rule differ from one another in many important respects. However, as systems of governance they share the characteristics of being stable, routine and dependable. Because of this, they are often associated with monotony, predictability and a general absence of passion. Compliance is achieved by the dead hand of custom, or the sheer administrative weight of the system, rather than the force of romantic, heroic power. The literature distinguishes between various types of charisma, of which the dominant forms are military, political, ethical, religious and artistic. In the classic use of the term, the most common examples of charismatic leaders are prophets and hero-warriors. The actions of the charismatic individual are seen as blessed and miraculous, whereas, for the ordinary man and woman, life is a chicken run.

Most discussions on charisma conclude that it is an unstable form of rule. Four reasons are usually adduced to support this proposition. Firstly, because it is volatile and passionate, it is also divisive. In modern democratic society that is organized around pluralism and respect for multiculturalism and multi-ethnicity, charisma produces as many foes as followers.

Secondly, charisma requires the repetition of victories or triumphs to maintain its power. A charismatic warrior must consistently defeat his enemies in battle, or achieve miracles. The predictions of a prophet must be perpetually confirmed.

To say the least, in real life continuous success is elusive. While the causes of charisma are ultimately unfathomable, its credibility depends upon the repeated demonstration of personal fitness to rule. For this reason, the claim of charisma is particularly susceptible to the vagaries of history.

Thirdly, charismatic authority resists transfer to substitutes, nor can it be successfully passed on to others. In Ancient Rome the charisma of Augustus and Caesar proved to be a burden for their successors. Death does not extinguish the fame of a charismatic leader. But it is a hard act to follow. Charismatic rule aims to establish a footprint that changes the direction of human history in all walks of life. It is not restricted to this or that segment of society. The stamp of the charismatic rule is to personally transform the conditions in which we live.

Fourthly, in literate cultures the claim to achieve charismatic authority is often immediately associated with deception and subterfuge. This is reinforced by the media, who are flagrantly two-faced about charisma and celebrity. Although temperamentally sceptical of idolatry, they employ devices of communication that encourage idol-worship. The media collude with the interests of PR organizations to create larger-than-life public figures. But they also engage in celebrity muckraking and dirt-digging.

Celebrity and charisma today

For modern commentators, the attribution of the classical term charisma to modern forms of celebrity is a misnomer. Writing of the so-called 'charisma' attributed to popular entertainers in the arts, Wilson contends:

> The manifestation of individual ecstasy and group frenzy at their performances perhaps outdo those at the reception of messianic leaders of the past. But such figures enjoy neither political significance nor enduring social regard. They make no specific claims for themselves: they are simply the recipients of extraordinary social acclaim, and the stimulators of extraordinary psychological responses. (Wilson, 1975: 124–5)

Modern celebrities may make the lives of some of their fans meaningful. Special powers are certainly attributed to them, and political candidates duly strive to make celebrity glamour rub off on their systems of organization and campaign messages. The talents and accomplishments of celebrities are widely celebrated as noteworthy. Semi-miraculous powers of entertainment and persuasion are claimed on their behalf. Compared with the monotony and routine of familiar life, they are celebrated as exalted. What is the glamour and meaning of your life compared with celebrity skyscrapers like Britney Spears, Beyoncé, Leonardo DiCaprio or Jay-Z?

the paradox that Marshall talked about

Their deeds, for that matter, their entire lives are portrayed as more bold and eventful than the lives of ordinary men and women.

However, there are several reasons why Wilson's scepticism that modern celebrity is truly messianic is justified. Celebrity powers are not unfathomable or revolutionary. The principles for generating fame were laid down by Bernays, and the PR-Media hub are well versed in the choreography of celebrity. However, the powers or special qualities claimed on behalf of celebrities are typically understood to be strictly finite. The claims that modern celebrities possess divine powers and qualities of inspirational leadership do not survive scrutiny. The powers of Leonardo DiCaprio as a screen actor and Beyoncé as a pop star depend upon a team of cultural intermediaries to achieve impact factors and are not genuinely tenable beyond the entertainment sector. The fame of these celebrities may enable them to play the effective proxy role of 'big citizen', but they do not constitute a genuine, revolutionary force.

What the PR-Media hub calls 'charisma' today is really commodified magnetism. That is a formation of public influence based upon rational principles of public-relations image construction and brand management. It packs hustings rooms and is good box office, but it is not the manifestation of a genuinely revolutionary force.

In the arena of politics, recent leaders like Ronald Reagan, Bill Clinton, Tony Blair, Arnold Schwarzenegger, Barack Obama and David Cameron were elected on the ticket of charismatic change-makers who offered a definitive and total break with the past. In each case, they enjoyed a honeymoon period before realpolitik transformed their fortunes and exposed the limitations of their leadership. Classical charisma means a convulsive, torrential force that sweeps through politics, religion, work, leisure, entertainment and all sectors of society. In contrast, celebrity magnetism is typically calculated, limited and compartmentalized.

The prospects that a big citizen may, in time, become a 'big brother' have fascinated writers and film-makers. The Orson Welles classic, *Citizen Kane* (1941), is dedicated to the proposition that celebrity humanitarianism can be turned into a vehicle of obtaining public office. In reality, the prospects are remote. Modern celebrities may support political parties and good causes. The phenomenon of celebrity diplomacy has certainly become more significant over the last half-century. Notwithstanding this, celebrities from the world of popular entertainment – figures who command the approval of the media and enthusiasm from the masses – seldom embrace the costs and responsibilities of political candidacy. As a general rule of modern celebrity culture, screen idols, pop music stars, literary giants and sports achievers do not make sound candidates as presidents or prime ministers.

Of course, there are exceptions. The Hollywood B-movie actor Ronald Reagan was indeed a two-term president; and Arnold Schwarzenegger grabbed one of Reagan's mantles when he was elected governor of California in 2003.

Schwarzenegger's campaign milked the tough guy image portrayed in his major film roles *Conan The Barbarian* (1982), *The Terminator* (1984) and *Total Recall* (1990) to launch a war against waste and crime; and Reagan certainly used his film-star career to convey the glamour and confidence of the silver screen in television broadcasts and the hustings of small-town America. However, in both cases it is stretching a point to maintain that either of these simply transferred prestige from the world of entertainment to the world of politics and achieved durable revolutionary transformations. Of course, the PR-Media hub presented them as beacons of transformative leadership, but actually they are in the shadow of money and power. It was in the interests of the establishment to portray Reagan and Schwarzenegger as figures of electricity, utterly transforming the landscape of politics, culture and psychology. Those who see a conspiracy of equals here between entertainment and political leaders, engage in a confederacy of dunces. Genuinely charismatic leaders remould business, the military and the media to make the world in their own image. In contrast, Reagan and Schwarzenegger are not masters, but slaves of the establishment. In both cases, their personalities and policies were openly and repeatedly described as flawed in the media and severe doubts were raised about their conduct of leadership, political judgement and personal probity.

In contrast, a genuinely charismatic leader who dismantles the opposition by the force of his personality and through his deeds stifles dissent.[2] It was the capacity of these two Republican leaders to dutifully articulate and protect the interests of business and the military that attracted them to the PR-Media hub. Commodified magnetism adopts the hyperbole of the PR-Media hub to create the public impression that figures like Reagan and Schwarzenegger are charismatic individuals. But hyperbole is not synonymous with a charismatic whirlwind. Genuine charismatic leadership overthrows established customs and beliefs in every aspect of life. Ronald Reagan's televisual sincerity in banging out the message that 'government is not the solution, government is the problem' slogan, above and beyond his capacity to draw on a reservoir of references from his movie past, made him a strictly finite electoral asset and leader for the Republican party. During his second term of office, when non-partisan sections of the media openly alleged that Reagan's behaviour betrayed symptoms of dementia, he was quickly rebranded as a liability. At his peak, he doubtless utilized training, and exploited public sympathies, from his film-star past. But it was the anti-government and pro-liberty message that caught the spirit of the times and made some sections of the media and numbers of the public regard him as inspirational. Moreover, these messages were not revolutionary in introducing new qualities into political culture and life politics. They were profoundly conservative and relied on the Bible and the old-time values of idealized small-town communities rather than the visionary inspiration of Christ or Mohammed.

Why is the misuse of the term so commonplace in celebrity culture today? The answer is that the press, public relations staff and laypeople describe charisma primarily as a personal endowment. Thus, Ronald Reagan is remembered by many as speaking the plain truth and Arnold Schwarzenegger is viewed as the epitome of daring and do.

The error here is that charisma does not refer to a quality of the individual, but to the relationship between believers and the *presentation* of a leader. Make no mistake, the presentation skills of the PR-Media hub are formidable. But they are not up to conjuring from thin air the miraculous, prophetic and divine qualities that are the requisites for being publicly anointed as a charismatic leader. The political literacy of the people may exasperate radical critics, but it is much greater than the general credulity of traditional societies. Preliterate societies were open to the claim of charisma because their populations were not educated in rationally accountable principles of argument and did not possess an independent media to scrutinize the words and deeds of idols. Salvation or supernatural intervention in human affairs was more readily trusted because deistic and metaphysical systems of belief were scarcely challenged. In modern Western society, which boasts freedom of the press, independent political parties and educates between 35 and 50 per cent of its population to university level, the incidence of blind faith among lay people is much lower. Today, from the start, the claim of charisma is therefore susceptible to being eroded as grandiose or overblown. It is more vulnerable to the condemnation of being finally seen as the product of excessive self-esteem, combined with the organized hyperbole of PR-Media ringmasters.

While the case that modern celebrity culture is rich in charismatic figures is weak, the media attribution of celebrity charisma is widespread. In contrast to Wilson (1975) this is not confined to the entertainment sphere. One of the striking and interesting facts about contemporary celebrity is that it is extending into non-government-based forms of problem-solving. The role of celebrities as figureheads for national and international charities has never been bigger. Celebrities take on the role of ambassadors for the poor, the starving and the powerless with a force and public presence that has never been rivaled. This represents an important extension of commodified magnetism. Celebrity Advocacy and Diplomacy are prominent features in the modern culture of fame and, as such, they require more detailed consideration.

Advocacy and diplomacy

Although advocacy and diplomacy are closely related, they are not synonymous. Advocacy refers to moulding public opinion and fund-awarding bodies to enhance

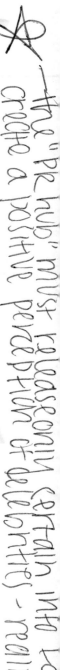

resource distribution for a good cause. Typical methods involving celebrities are celebrity donations, press meetings, field reports, public speaking and media campaigns.

Diplomacy refers to the total arts and practices of non-violent persuasion to achieve ends. Celebrities bring people together, build bridges over parties who are at loggerheads, expedite treaty formation and influence resource allocation.

Advocacy and diplomacy both rely heavily upon people skills, impression management and mass communications. The limitations of commodified magnetism are exposed in organized politics because real world decision-making requires more than media savviness and brand awareness. It demands attention to detail and immense concentrations of time in back-room organization to which most celebrities are not especially partial. These limitations do not apply to relations of advocacy or diplomacy because while the time input may be significant the primary undertaking is public performance. Celebrities provide the acceptable face of care for the cause. As figureheads and fundraisers, they carry over media skills and impression-management accomplishments that they have honed and perfected in the world of entertainment. Working a crowd in an entertainment context draws on the same skill set as persuading people to part with money for a good political or social cause.

There are other reasons why celebrities are well equipped to perform the roles of global advocates and diplomats. Psychologically speaking, narcissistic self-esteem does not simply mean regarding oneself as different from others; it is also associated with being viewed as blessed with the gifts of global empathy and nobility. As a psychological condition it is often manifest in acts of arrogance and entitlement. This superiority complex may go hand in hand with horribly egregious behaviour, but it is also linked to the genuine urge to do good on behalf of mankind.

Celebrity narcissism also goes along with connotations of lives packed with incident and emergency. The extremity of celebrity life parallels the dire situations that charities and relief agencies have to address. Hunger, natural catastrophe, homelessness and poverty are extreme social problems at the opposite end of the scale of the frontier existence in which many celebrities believe themselves to be living. Perhaps this is why so many stars are drawn to humanitarian, philanthropic work of debt relief and feeding the world. Because they see themselves living existences at the frontier of social life, they instinctively relate to those who do not have enough to feed themselves or afford medical care. But there is all the difference in the world between malnutrition in the Third World, watching your children die of malaria or diarrhea, and being stalked by the paparazzi and suffering for your art.

Woody Allen is only too well aware of the vanity of celebrities who complain that they suffer grievously for their art:

> I've always felt that we give artists too much leeway, that we tolerate their cruelties and their narcissism and their temperament because they're artists, when in fact we shouldn't. This started in my life during the McCarthy era. We have a tendency to make allowances for artists because they're in some mystical realm. 'He's a terrible guy, but he can't create unless you give him leeway.' I don't believe we should excuse artists that way. I don't believe you should ever judge an artist's work by his life. I think you can be T. S. Eliot and be an anti-Semite and a great poet at the same time, but I don't think you should excuse artists in their life for being bad people just because they need to create, or claim they do. (Woody Allen in Berlin, 1996: 263–4)

Leaving aside the question of narcissism, celebrities have the time, money and access to influential social networks to activate a humanitarian sense of injustice and a commitment to make the world a better place. Achieved celebrities and celetoids often describe themselves as lucky. Their economic wealth and cultural prestige is the product of upward mobility. So it is no surprise that strong, emotional connections with 'the people' is characteristic of the achieved celebrity outlook. Giving back is a natural aspect of gratitude and a recognition of belonging (Belk, 2010). While there is a close correlation between narcissism and celebrity, it would be an error to suggest or infer that narcissism is at the root of all celebrity advocacy and diplomacy. In many cases it may be a substantial issue, but celebrities are perfectly capable of having and expressing motives of common or garden compassion and decency.

There are a variety of ways in which commodified glamour assists charity work. The simplest act is cash donations. Celebrities who dig into their own pockets to support the charity of their choice make a direct contribution to charity relief efforts. For example, in 2004 Elton John donated $43 million to charities throughout the world; in 2006 Warren Buffett donated $37 million to Bill Gates's charitable foundation; and in 2007 Oprah Winfrey donated $58 million to the Oprah Winfrey Leadership Academy, Oprah's Angel Network and other groups. Bill Gates made the biggest celebrity charity donation to date in 2010, when he pledged $10 billion to the Bill & Melinda Gates Foundation to develop and distribute vaccines for children. Donations of this level make international headlines and raise public awareness.

Celanthropy

Celanthropy refers to the voluntary participation of celebrities in humanitarian fundraising, publicity awareness and charity building.[3] Over the last twenty years

it has emerged as a high-profile adjunct of state, multilateral, corporate and private philanthropic aid programmes. In the case of global single issues such as fundraising to support relief efforts for natural disasters like floods, tsunamis, hurricanes, earthquakes and famines, star power is now regarded to be crucial. In 2010 Haiti Earthquake Disaster Relief Agencies publicized donations of $3 million from Tiger Woods; $1.5 million from Gisele Bündchen; $1 million from Leonardo DiCaprio; $1 million from Oprah Winfrey; $1 million from Brad Pitt and Angelina Jolie and $1 million from George Clooney. These donations are significant, but the real value of celanthropy is the multiplier effect among the public. This takes the form of encouraging the public to make cash donations and participate in event resourcing. The *Haiti Now* (2010) celebrity benefit concert organized by George Clooney and Wyclef Jean, which featured performances from U2, Alicia Keys and Bruce Springsteen, raised $57 million for organizations like Oxfam America, the Red Cross and UNICEF working to help victims of the January 2010 earthquake. Longer-established charities also seek to achieve this effect by enlisting celebrities as figureheads for their activities.

For example, after Christopher Reeve was paralysed in a horse-riding accident in 1995, he became publicly involved with the American Paralysis Association. His participation and endorsement is widely cited to have contributed to doubling the organization's revenue within three years.

The Elton John Aids Foundation (1992) has raised over $55 million in 55 countries for programmes of HIV/AIDS education, the elimination of discrimination and prejudice and care services for people living with the disease. Elton John's annual 'White Tie and Tiara' ball and post-Grammy and Oscar parties are widely publicized vehicles of fundraising for the organization.

Mary Tyler Moore significantly raised the profile of the Juvenile Diabetes Research Foundation in the USA. Jerry Lewis has become a celebrity legend by hosting the annual telephone fundraising event for the Muscular Dystrophy Association.

Greenpeace has received support from Bono, Bryan Adams, Massive Attack, Michael Stipe and Pink. Annie Lennox set up the 'Sing' charity to promote awareness of and raise funds for the prevention of HIV and Aids in South Africa, which has one of the highest rates of HIV in the world. The 'Make Poverty History' campaign was founded by the celebrity screenwriter Richard Curtis, and supported by Alan Rickman, Al Pacino, Bill Nighy, Brad Pitt, Claudia Schiffer, Eddie Izzard, Ewan McGregor, George Clooney, Hugh Grant, Jude Law, Liam Neeson, Mike Myers and Scarlett Johansson. The Look to the Stars celebrity/charity website (www.looktothestars.org) provides an exhaustive list of global links between charities and stars.

In principle, the PR-Media hub supports celanthropy. It builds the celebrity brand by demonstrating that the star has a good heart, a commitment to activism and a social conscience. Celebrity donations and charity work have a halo effect, enhancing the prestige of the star as a responsible, caring citizen.

Forbes business magazine compiles an annual list of the top 100 Power celebrities. The ranking is based upon income, TV/radio impact factors, press ranks, Web ranks and social ranks. The 2010 top ten are listed below:

	Pay ($mil)	Money Rank	TV/Radio Rank	Press Rank	Web Rank	Social Rank
1 Lady Gaga	90	8	3	2	1	1
2 Oprah Winfrey	290	1	1	7	13	13
3 Justin Bieber	53	4	4	8	2	3
4 U2	195	59	59	10	16	17
5 Elton John	100	18	18	19	28	54
6 Tiger Woods	75	6	6	5	40	38
7 Taylor Swift	45	14	14	45	6	6
8 Bon Jovi	125	63	63	49	44	12
9 Simon Cowell	90	22	22	17	62	74
10 LeBron James	48	29	2	6	27	20

Figure 2 Forbes Celebrity Power Top 10 (2011)
Source: http://www.forbes.com/wealth/celebrities [16.05.11]

Celanthropy before Live Aid

Most laypeople would date the rise of celanthropy with the *Live Aid* (1985) event, and Bob Geldof. In fact the history is longer. At this point, celanthropy shifted gear from campaigning to active planning and management. Since Live Aid was invented, organized and managed by stars it was qualitatively different from previous types of celebrity involvement in humanitarian work that generally had taken the form of endorsing or being a patron of non-government charity organizations.

Leaving aside interventions of stars between the 1920s and 1950s, which often went largely unrecorded by the media, the first United Nations Children's Fund (UNICEF) goodwill ambassador was Danny Kaye in 1954. Sir Peter Ustinov was also a prominent international charity worker who, from the 1950s, devoted considerable time and resources to international relief.

However, most authorities maintain that the template for the patron form of celanthropy was Audrey Hepburn in her role as goodwill ambassador for UNICEF (Cooper, 2008). Indeed her field missions in the 1980s and early 1990s in Ethiopia, Sudan, Vietnam and Somalia went beyond passive patronage. In effect, it set the bar for celebrity activism. She directly involved herself in administering care and relief to the distressed, sought out work leaders, forged connections between them, attended appropriate government subcommittee meetings on public-funding questions and the administration of relief, and participated tirelessly in public speaking. Other celebrities fell into the trap of allowing the media to insinuate that they were champagne humanitarians doing good from the trappings of privilege and luxury. Hepburn was careful to avoid this. She eschewed a grandiose attitude in favour of demonstrating empathy for the suffering and a determination to coax the affluent societies to find solutions. By acting as an ordinary citizen, concerned with problems of global powerlessness and compassionate about human suffering, Hepburn used her star status to make connections both with the disadvantaged and powerful elites in government, business and the military. She presented herself as a big citizen in the sense that she adapted her fame and publicity skills to the causes of the poor, the starving, the uneducated and the needy. She portrayed herself as being of the people, rather than above them. For her, fame was the servant of practical problem-solving on behalf of those who would otherwise be invisible or silent.

Live Aid (1985) provided the spur to the growth of campaigning celanthropy. Some of the most prominent celanthropists are explicitly critical of passive forms of celebrity patronage and cultivate humanitarian activism. For example, Bono, Bob Geldof, Richard Gere, George Clooney, Madonna, Johnny Depp, Mia Farrow, Naomi Watts, Shakira and Angelina Jolie are involved in managing and strategy formation rather than mere publicity exercises and fundraising. An important bifurcation in celebrity aid leadership roles has developed between celebrities who adopt an in-your-face approach and a more calculating, brokering role. Authorities cite Bob Geldof as the epitome of the first approach and Bono as the leading representative of the second (Cooper, 2008). However, in both cases the focus is upon using the commodified magnetism of stardom to loosen the brain blindfolds around the government and the public, that limit awareness of the realities of international want, suffering and misery.

The Balance Sheet of Celanthropy

In general, commentators characteristically assert a positive relationship between celanthropy and relief (Cooper, 2008). The PR-Media hub favours philanthropy as a positive characteristic of stardom. Founding a private charity foundation, making well-publicized cash donations, visiting the world's trouble spots and giving aid are good PR. Tiger Woods's donation of $3 million to Haiti disaster relief in 2010 was laudable. That it occurred in the midst of a maelstrom of public disapproval and sponsorship rumbles about his declared marital infidelities must also be noted and weighed.

Celanthropy generates what might be termed philanthropic capital. Philanthropic capital has the virtue of raising funds for the dispossessed. By a happy but not altogether accidental parallel it also builds the celebrity brand. While public association with an established charity can deliver this dividend, the soundest strategy is creating a celebrity foundation. In doing so, celebrities can exercise maximum control over the activities of the charity and regulate the star brand. Celebrity foundations are tax-efficient ways of using income to build fame.

In the United States, as Burke and Barrett (2010) report, donations are tax deductible. A donation of $1 million is eligible for a 100 per cent rate of tax deduction. Legally, foundations are obliged to distribute no more than 5 per cent of their assets to charity work every year. This relatively low percentage means that the accumulation of cash reserves can be significant. They may be used as a handy nest egg if the celebrity needs to burnish his or her public image in the future, when public disquiet about marital infidelities, grandstanding, prima donna behaviour, violence, alcohol dependencies and the like, may rock the celebrity boat.

Although the PR-Media hub sees a booster effect in philanthropic capital, unforeseen events can upset the applecart. There are four sets of negative loop issues that commonly affect celanthropic charities: bureaucratic inefficiency; association with controversial charities; corruption and embezzlement; and accusations of networking being a more important motive in celebrity activism than giving and problem-solving. Each of these issues constitutes serious threats to the reputation of celebrity figureheads or Foundation owners.

1. Bureaucratic inefficiency

Because celebrity foundations and charity relationships are not one-man bands, they carry risks of falling foul of charges of excessive administration costs, second-rate service and bureaucratic inefficiency. In essence, celebrities cede proxy control of the brand to workers, often voluntary staff, who have no background in celebrity culture. As a result, philanthropic capital may be significantly eroded by rumour and bad press reports that celebrity foundations are the charities with which celebrities associate are imprudent or profligate.

Celebrity charity foundations that do not cover administration costs or that reveal a dramatic imbalance between costs and donations can damage the public image of stars. For example, tax returns for 2006 indicated that Tyra Banks's TZONE Foundation paid $35,000 in salaries, while distributing a paltry $32,000 in grants.

Similarly, in the same year the Justin Timberlake Foundation spent $146,000 on operating costs (including $10,000 on travel and loosely defined 'miscellaneous services'). It distributed income of $32,500, of which $30,000 went to the Jane Goodall Institute. An ineffective charity foundation can build the stereotype of dud celebrity in the public mind. Failure in the world of celanthropy may carry over into a waning of star power and economic value.

Research by Burke and Barrett (2010) into the tax returns of 175 non-profit organizations with strong celebrity links revealed a mixed picture. If the foundation is primarily run by the celebrity so that fundraising costs are negligible and if it operates no programmes and simply makes donations to other charities, then overheads can be insignificant. For example, David Letterman's American Foundation for Courtesy and Grooming distributed $1.2 million to a wide range of charities and reported an overhead expense of just $25. Similarly, Alec Baldwin's foundation gave away $555,000 with overheads of only $215; and Steve Martin's foundation disbursed $399,000 with reported overhead costs of $329.

At the other end of the spectrum, foundations associated with Jane Fonda, Hugh Hefner, Larry King, Phil McGraw and Michael Moore reported overhead costs in excess of 20 per cent of grant income received. In 2009 Rosie O'Donnell's For All Kids Foundation distributed $2.9 million in grants, but carried an overhead cost of $1.9 million, i.e. 64 cents in cost for every dollar of grants.

Even long-established and well-known charities sometimes have profit and loss accounts that make little financial sense. For example, Burke and Barrett (2010) refer to the annual Bob Hope Gold Classic tournament in California. On average it generates $1.6 million for charities, but spends nearly five times that sum in expenses. In such circumstances, the media and public may understandably regard celebrities as engaging in grandstanding and glad-handing activity rather than genuine problem-solving. This can taint the public image of the star.

A charity that pays high salaries to executives and is too lax in monitoring overheads plays with fire. Even if celebrities play no role in the day-to-day issues of administration and management, they are guilty by association. The bureaucratic inefficiency of foundations and charities tarnish the public image of the star. It raises sensitive questions about the commitment, prudence and probity of the star, which can undo the positive PR impact factor that charity work brings to celebrity.

One way of tackling the issue is to expand the circle of cultural intermediaries around the celebrity to include advisers and regulators on charity involvement. But this has the effect of introducing another layer of bureaucracy between the celebrity and the public. Ultimately, it runs the hazard of building an image in the public mind of a cosseted celebrity who is out of touch with reality and basks in a reflecting pool of self-approval. This undermines the philanthropic capital of the celebrity and may create a debate among business leaders and the public about whether the celebrity merits the high prestige attributed to him or her.

2. Controversial charities

The identification of celebrities with some charitable voluntary organizations and pressure groups that are perceived by some sections of the media and public as controversial, may garner bad publicity. This is especially true if the organizations are involved in trading or proselytizing activities, services and commodities that are acknowledged to be potentially harmful to the public.

From 1998, until he resigned on grounds of ill health in 2003, Charlton Heston served in the role of President and chief spokesman for the National Rifle Association (NRA) in America. His appeal to the NRA lay in the Hollywood PR-Media portrayal of him and the resultant public perception in film roles like *The Ten Commandments* (1956), *Ben-Hur* (1959) and *El Cid* (1961) as a hero of quasi-biblical proportions. Heston was employed to bring glamour and rectitude to a gun culture that supported hunting and the conviviality of the rifle range as well as unintentionally underwriting American gun crime by making access to weapons so easy. A cinema star of Heston's magnitude was judged by the NRA to make gun ownership acceptable to the general public. He was an accomplished performer in this task, riding the bad publicity of the Columbine massacre and other spree killings with such nonchalant aplomb that he provoked censure from George Clooney. Heston was attacked by Clooney for being out of touch with the anxieties of the majority of ordinary people, being indifferent to polarized opinions about gun ownership and irresponsible in lending his name to the gun lobby.

The tobacco industry has a long history of using movie stars to promote its products. The link between tobacco and premature mortality was conclusively established by the US Surgeon General's Report (1964). However, the risks of tobacco use were widely understood before then. Despite this, research has shown that the tobacco companies invested millions of dollars in Hollywood to achieve testimonials in favour of smoking from stars and product placement in movies. From the late 1930s to the late 1940s, two-thirds of the top box office stars participated in cigarette endorsement campaigns. In the 1950s, John Wayne was a poster boy for Camel cigarettes claiming that the brand offers a product that is milder than the competition and that smoking provides calm and is 'easy on the voice'.

Among others, actors Clark Gable, Spencer Tracy, Joan Crawford, Bette Davis, Betty Grable and Al Jolson endorsed brands like Lucky Strike, Old Gold, Chesterfield and Camel (Lum *et al.*, 2008). For Wayne, who died of cancer in 1979, the close association with Camel cigarettes contributed to the public image of a naïve, irresponsible star who was obtuse about healthy lifestyle issues and gung-ho about personal liberty.

Between the early 1960s and early 1980s greater public knowledge of the health risks, partly achieved by the anti-smoking lobby, resulted in the decline of endorsements and product placement. However, new research implies that after the early 80s, marketing campaigns by Philip Morris, American Tobacco and the University of California digital collection of tobacco industry revived product placement practices to build strong positive images of smoking based around celebrity use of brands in film and television. R. J. Reynolds Tobacco Company hired the public relations firm Rogers & Cowan to develop a 'relationship' of 'positive exposure' between the brand and the motion picture industry. Rogers & Cowan claim that they achieved positive product placement in mainstream movies like *The Jazz Singer* (1980) with Neil Diamond, *Back Roads* (1981) with Sally Field, *Cannonball Run* (1981) with Burt Reynolds, *Pennies from Heaven* (1981) with Steve Martin, and *Blowout* (1981) with John Travolta. They also targeted television shows like *The Tonight Show*, *The Merv Griffin Show* and *The Mike Douglas Show*. The methods they used included providing stars with free supplies of the brand (Maureen O'Sullivan, Rex Reed, Liv Ullman, Shelley Winters and Jerry Lewis are listed as recipients); encouraging stars to light up on talk shows; and placing positive stories of celebrity tobacco use in the press (Mekemson and Glantz, 2002).

For corporations, the value of using stars to endorse high-risk commodities is immense. The right celebrity gives the Midas touch to gun, tobacco and alcohol brands. To have Charlton Heston endorse responsible gun use is tantamount to persuading Moses to speak for your product.

The difficulty is that public knowledge of the risks involved in using potentially harmful products is much greater today. This is a disincentive for stars to participate in direct celebrity product endorsements for risky products. For A-list stars to provide testimonies for alcohol, guns or tobacco would be to enter a career minefield in which short-term gains would almost certainly be wiped out by a contraction in box office appeal.

3. Corruption and embezzlement

A positive public image of the relationship between celebrities and charities depends upon probity in business transactions. Public trust in a charity and a supporting celebrity will be impaired if voluntary donations are subject to charges of financial irregularity or imprudent management. The formation of Band Aid and the 1985 Live Aid global concert marked a new era in celebrity fundraising. Celebrity advocacy on behalf of the excluded became direct and highly publicized. Nothing provided a bigger boost to the twinning of fame with caring in the public mind than star power. Bob Geldof emerged as the leading celebrity conscience and advocate for Africa. In 2005 he organized the Live 8 event, which committed to an ambitious programme of cancelling Third World debt, promoting 'fair trade' and meeting the UN Millennium Development Goals for minimum conditions of life. Geldof fronted Tony Blair's Commission for Africa and, with Bono, participated in the G8 Gleneagles Summit (2005) on world poverty. More than any other celebrity, he symbolized the 'can do' approach in celebrity fundraising and aid programmes. Justifiably, his demands for the affluent world to donate and get involved with the plight of the Third World have been widely applauded and supported.

Yet the era of celebrity fundraising for the Third World has also generated allegations about fraud, the misallocation of funds, and the exclusion of the Third World from decisions about fund distribution. Because of their high profile, the Live Aid and Live 8 events have been given concentrated media scrutiny. In 2010, the BBC reported that 95 per cent of the millions of dollars raised by Band Aid in 1985 were appropriated by Ethiopian rebels to buy arms. The basis of the allegations were interviews with two former senior commanders with the Tigrayan People's Liberation Front (TPLF) who claimed the money was used in the fight to overthrow the Ethiopian government.

The reports provoked a furious reaction from Bob Geldof. While he conceded that some money from Live Aid might have found its way into the hands of rebels, he rejected the figure of 95 per cent, insisted that money laundering had been miniscule, and wrathfully condemned the BBC for gross misreporting.

While the BBC subsequently retracted the allegations, it seems implausible to believe that Live Aid control over funds was watertight. John James, Band Aid's own field director in Ethiopia, is reported to have claimed that between 10 and 20 per cent of the funds were appropriated by rebels and some of the money was used to purchase arms (Gilligan, 2010).

Suzanne Franks (2010) is more scathing. She maintains that relief funds in Ethiopia were monopolized by the Communist government led by the tyrannical Colonel Mengistu Haile Mariam. The government diverted funds to a variety of military purposes designed to bolster the regime rather than finance relief. These included luring conscripts to the army and bankrolling a so-called 'villagization' programme designed to assist enforced population resettlement. According to Franks (2010: 55) the military appropriation of Live Aid funds prolonged the war between Mariam's forces and the counterinsurgents led by the Tigrayan People's

Liberation Front (TPLF). Of course, this was contrary to the intentions of Band Aid and the millions who supported them. Yet it also runs counter to Geldof's attempt to whitewash the organization.

The dispute exposed latent friction between professional aid workers in Africa and Geldof. This reflects wider tensions between the voluntary aid sector and celebrity suitors. Live Aid was criticized by professionals in the sector for misunderstanding relief needs in Africa, by putting supplying food and medical supplies at the top of the agenda. According to many professionals, the real focus should be upon education and transparent government. By implication, corrupt government in Africa is held to misappropriate funds for its own ends.

Professional aid workers are privately critical of celebrity oversimplification of aid issues. They have expressed concerns that celebrity suitors drive relief agendas on the basis of limited and partial knowledge of Third World problems. Celebrity attribution of what is needed in Africa, and other developing countries, is often a response to highly publicized media reports about famine and disease. While these issues are urgent and must be addressed, focusing narrowly and emotionally upon them obscures issues of political culture and economic infrastructure. These issues are, so to speak, beneath the surface of famine and disease yet, in reality, they are the root cause of the problems (Theroux, 2006).

In effect, celebrity suitors are impugned for unwittingly propagating a new type of colonialism. It derives from Western op-ed pieces, sound bites and TV documentaries, rather than prolonged fieldwork and sustained analysis of Third World political economy. Celebrity 'can do' attitudes have a proven track record in creating publicity and generating funds. But aid professionals raise thorny questions about the proper use of celebrity-propelled publicity and the most efficient distribution of star-induced funds.

It would be wrong to imply that all criticism about the era of celebrity fundraising is concentrated in the Live Aid and Live 8 projects. In 2001, War Child UK, which raises money for young victims of war around the world, was accused by the media of financial mismanagement. Specifically, following investigations by the *Guardian* and *Channel 4 News*, the charity was accused of accepting bribes and reckless spending on overheads. The bad publicity resulted in several celebrity patrons, notably Luciano Pavarotti, David Bowie, Tom Stoppard and Juliet Stevenson, withdrawing patronage and support.

We have already referred to the controversy over the mismanagement of Madonna's (2011) project to build an academy for underprivileged girls in Malawi. There are other examples to which one might refer, but in a book of this type there is no need to add to the list because the point has been made. Celebrity involvement in Third World Charity relief is laudable. However, it exposes celebrities to the charges of grandstanding, naivety and viewing African and other Third World problems through a TV screen, rather than dedicated hands-on involvement.

4. Networking overshadows problem-solving

Private charity donations are significant. In 2006 more than 65 per cent of US households with annual incomes of less than $100,000 made charitable donations (Ottinger, 2008). Most of these took the form of 'chequebook philanthropy'. While these donations reflect a genuine humanitarian impulse, they are also about networking and social positioning. Cash-rich celebrities may exploit celanthropy as a way of boosting their own careers. Donating cash and time to high-profile charities boosts star power because it makes celebrity humanitarianism transparently visible (Street, 2002). But chequebook celanthropy can do little to solve problems of inequality and relief unless the accumulation and distribution of funds is independently audited. If celebrities are seen as wearing their hearts on their sleeves and lecturing the public on humanitarian causes without ensuring that fundraising produces genuine relief they are likely to become victims of what we now colloquially call 'tall poppy syndrome'. That is certain sections of the media and the public will seek to cut them down on the grounds of being all mouth and no trousers.

These enumerated risks are not, in themselves, a basis for deterring celebrities from advocacy, diplomacy and celanthropy. Nor do they provide the pretext for dismissing celanthropy as intrinsically hypocritical or ineffectual. Prudent exposure management arrangements can pre-empt many of the problems, albeit at the cost of adding more rungs to the ladder between the celebrity, the public and the targets of relief. Even so, the discussion will have served its purpose if it alerts readers to the point that there is a trade-off between the good publicity attached to celebrity advocacy and diplomacy and public literacy about the limitations of the commodified magnetism of celebrity.

It goes without saying that this trade-off would not be an issue in cases where genuine charisma is manifest. The charismatic leader is beyond criticism. But today's celebrities are not genuinely charismatic. Although superstar celanthropists appear to have the power to move from the entertainment sector to wider forms of activism, they do not possess the revolutionary power to transform social, economic and cultural conditions. Hobnobbing with world political leaders and engaging in fieldwork in zones of distress is not the same as changing the world. The glamour and star power of superstar celanthropists is limited by competing career commitments and is subject to media scrutiny and public evaluation. Therefore, the application of charisma to the activities of modern celebrities is indeed a misnomer. Ours is an age of commodified magnetism, not charismatic rule.

5 Exposure Management

Fame only attacks civic culture when that fame is unmerited and produced by orchestrated hyperbole. Present-day unease with what is sometimes called the 'froth of celebrity culture', derives from the proposition that it is in the interests of the PR-Media hub to subject society to a perpetual fame blitz. The result is that individuals who possess no talent or substance, rocket to prominence and a hectic, unstable will-o'-the-wisp quality colonizes the body politic with respect to issues of fame.[1] It is not that the world is heedless of the requirement for fame or for celebrity leaders; it is that the collateral of fame today is widely discounted as base, and celebrity attraction is often regarded as being hollow, nowhere more so than in the case of celetoids. On top of this, too many achieved and ascribed celebrities are dismissed as popinjays of the PR-Media hub and big-business interests. But this begs the question of why celebrity froth has become ubiquitous.

In economics, inflation is understood to be the consequence of a disequilibrium between demand and supply. When consumer demand for a favoured commodity exceeds supply, the dilemma of allocation is reconciled by a rise in price. This also holds good for celebrity culture. The public demand for celebrities, and the propensity of big business and the PR-Media hub to shower economic rewards and prestige upon stars, reflects a disequilibrium between demand and supply. But what, at root, is the nature of the disequilibrium here?

Celebrity is not like a physical commodity. When a bad harvest results in fewer apples being gathered, the price of apples will rise. Celebrity impact factors are more complex and issues of overexposure and underexposure are pivotal. However, other than at the extremes, the metrics of celebrity exposure are notoriously imprecise, and handling exposure properly is an art. The aim is to bring the public on the side of the celebrity to maintain or augment star power. But the relationships between celebrities, the media and the public consist of delicate, volatile forces. One wrong move can make public sympathy explode. Conversely, there are moments in a celebrity career when the public cannot get enough of the star. Rationing the right photo opportunities, press interviews and public appearances is the Midas touch in effective exposure management.

Categorically speaking, overexposure is the condition in which celebrity supply is greater than consumer demand. Underexposure is the reverse condition, in which consumer demand exceeds supply. It is not just a matter of the physical quantitative relationship between demand and supply, that is how many times celebrities or products authored by celebrities tangibly appear before the public. It is also a question of impact factors, which has to do with more elusive, esoteric qualitative relationships of image aggregation and image accumulation. As Bernays says, the challenge for the PR-Media hub is to 'know how to regiment and guide the masses' (Bernays, 1928: 127).

To come first to the issue of physical access, as a general rule, overexposure increases the propensity to diminish economic and cultural value. For example, Nicholas Cage and Anthony Hopkins are frequently scorned in the media for overexposure. By implication, they are indiscriminate about the film roles they accept. By appearing in too many films, they are held to weaken the star brand. On the supply side, too much access risks breeding a negative or nonplussed response from the public.

Celebrity endorsement, known as *celebrity vamping*, is the condition in which overexposure weakens public trust in celebrity product endorsement. Currently, in the industry, Kate Moss, David Beckham and Bono are often cited as leading examples of celebrity vamping.

Bono's reputation as a celebrity advocate and diplomat of good causes is legendary. He has been nominated for the Nobel Peace Prize three times. He is regularly presented as a mover and shaker with world leaders on questions of Third World debt relief and aid. In the charity world he is formally associated with no fewer than twenty-nine mainstream charities: 46664, ALAFA, Amnesty International, Charity Projects Entertainment Fund, Chernobyl Children's Project International, DATA, EDUN, Food Bank For New York City, Global Fund, Greenpeace, Keep A Child Alive, Live 8, Make Poverty History, Mencap, Millennium Promise Alliance, Millennium Villages, Mulago Positive Women's Network, MusiCares, Not On Our Watch, ONE Campaign, (RED), Simon Community, The Lunchbox Fund, UNICEF, UN Millennium Project, War Child, Wildlife Conservation Society, Witness and Zero Hunger.

Kate Moss has been an advertising representative for Burberry, Calvin Klein, Roberto Cavalli, Dior, Louis Vuitton, David Yurman, H&M, Rimmel, Bulgari, Longchamp, Virgin Mobile and Nikon.

David Beckham has fronted advertising campaigns for Vodaphone, Rage TV, Police sunglasses, Pepsi, Adidas, Gillette, Calvin Klein, Motorola and Marks & Spencer.

For many analysts of celebrity culture, in all three cases the result is overkill. The novelist Paul Theroux (2006), who taught in Africa before he became a renowned writer, tore into Bono for supporting the Bill and Melinda Gates Foundation in offering Africa 'prestige projects' and 'voluntary labour'. He contends that Bono possessed little more than a superficial understanding of Africa's real needs. Packages of debt relief and donating free computers and iPods to African villages have a high media profile in the West, but on the African continent they are soft targets for money laundering and fraud. For Theroux, the right priorities for aid money are the introduction of free and fair elections, husbanding principles of good governance and addressing the root causes of hunger and poverty. Theroux sees Bono as a well-intentioned, out-of-touch rock superstar, who steamrolls glamour relief projects into the developing world. In doing so he unwittingly disrupts the less attention-seeking, informed work of professional aid workers.

Doubtless, Bono and his entourage would object strongly to being described as ill-informed. His career as a celebrity diplomat is founded in intense data gathering and briefing by specialized advisers. However, it is one thing to gather data and be briefed as a field worker and quite another to rely on a team of advisers in the middle of a world concert tour while also managing an extensive and complex business portfolio.

It also exposes him to the charge of developing relationships with public figures that the rock world condemns as strange bedfellows. In 2008 the media carried reports of grumblings from band members in U2 about Bono's extensive charity work. Larry Mullen regretted Bono fraternizing with Tony Blair, 'a war criminal' in the drummer's eyes; and the band's lead guitarist, The Edge, was reported to wearily counsel Bono against risking subordinating music to politics.

Against this, Cooper (2008) maintains that Bono's charity work has been subtle and effective. Bono's skills of behind-the-scenes diplomacy and brokerage are pointedly contrasted with the direct, belligerent approach taken by Bob Geldof. Cooper (2008) portrays Bono as a realist, who can launch a charm offensive rather than knock heads together to get results.

Be that as it may, the sheer number of charities that Bono supports, raises questions about the depth of his knowledge and personal involvement. It leaves him vulnerable to the charge of overstretching himself and having a superficial understanding of aid, relief and Third World politics. This is not without public consequences. As a general rule, the wider the number of good causes that a celebrity supports, the weaker the public faith in celebrity endorsement.

In 2006 Beckham was dropped by Police sunglasses and replaced by Antonio Banderas. Sources at the company said that his star appeal had diminished following England's lacklustre performance in the 2010 World Cup. However, industry analysts also blamed overexposure.

Kate Moss was dropped by the Swedish fashion retailer H&M in 2005, and her contract with Chanel was not renewed. The H&M termination of contract was connected with allegations about Moss's cocaine use. The reasons for the Chanel termination were not publicly disclosed but are thought by analysts to be due to overexposure. The cocaine allegations tarnished Moss's public image as a carefree, independent modern girl. However, in the long run they did not significantly erode her appeal to advertisers. Moss dealt with the overexposure issue boldly by launching her own line of clothes with TopShop in 2007 and the release of a Moss set of fragrances with Coty.

Although celebrity vamping and overexposure are often condemned as the result of the sin of avarice, they are sometimes the outcome of circumstances that are beyond the star's control. In particular, when the breakthrough of a star follows a long period of public indifference, it increases the propensity of all copyright holders to clear their inventories. For example, when David Bowie became a cult sensation with the release of *The Rise and Fall of Ziggy Stardust and the Spiders from Mars* with RCA Records in 1973, Deram Records rereleased his kitsch, novelty single, 'The Laughing Gnome' (originally released in 1967), which was aimed at the infant market. The novelty song was an embarrassing contrast with Bowie's new bisexual, cutting-edge art image. But RCA and Main Man Records, the companies that represented him, were powerless to halt the progress of the single in the pop charts.

Just as commercial interests have inventories of product that may cause embarrassment to stars after they become famous, the pre-fame life of stars consists of an inventory of memories and folklore among friends and associates that may compromise the gloss of stardom. For example, Bill Clinton famously declared 'I did not inhale' when the media carried reports that he used marijuana when he was a student at Oxford University. The remark was a forerunner to his infamous comment in response to allegations of an affair with Monica Lewinsky: 'I did not have sexual relations with that woman'. Both comments damaged Clinton's presidency, because they suggested an untrustworthy, slippery leader.

On the other hand, the release of nude photographs of Madonna taken before she was famous did not damage her public appeal.[2] On the contrary, her reputation as a modern girl free from outmoded conservative hang-ups was enhanced. The prurient interest in these soft-core images may have been a factor in encouraging Madonna and her camp to launch her *Sex* book – a volume of nude photographs that was artful, but also calculating and explicit. By association, the pre-fame nude shots of Madonna evoked public memories of Marilyn Monroe's foray as a nude model. Madonna and Monroe appeared to be of the same mettle in courageously exploiting male-dominated media opportunities in search of deeper, more meaningful fame.

These examples again show that the fame formula is a deeply flawed doctrine. The formula exaggerates the power of cultural intermediaries to control image and impact factors, and it underestimates public literacy about celebrity brand construction and management.[3]

Achieved celebrities are the product of fame attainment and exposure management. Attainment and exposure management is what might be called, the prelife of the star. This contains an inventory of episodes and incidents before they were famous that can come back to haunt them. Inferior and ill-judged types of authorship and insalubrious conduct may produce challenges and difficulties for exposure management. Because cultural intermediaries have no outright power to control image inventory and stories that emerge from friends and associates, they do not genuinely have the capacity to regulate impact factors.

The problem is not restricted to copyright holders who have inventories that are authored or associated with celebrities before they entered the limelight. Copyright on images can be easily infringed by producers and bloggers. For example, Mario Lavandeira, the blogger behind the celebrity gossip website perezhilton.com was sued by Universal Pictures for featuring a topless photo of Jennifer Aniston on his site. Lavandeira's legal defence is that this and other celebrity photos on his website fall under the principle of fair use. That is they are used for commentary rather than for pecuniary gain. Further, the photos are edited. This supports the defence that parody is at play. In law, parody is understood to be a creative input that does not infringe copyright because a new cultural value is produced that is beyond the intention of the copyright holder. Thus, the photograph is transformed into an *original* work.

However, this is a grey area. It is one thing to maintain that the photos are not used directly for pecuniary gain. In contradiction, analysts note that the perezhilton. com site receives 2 million hits per month and charges $9000 for advertising space. On the question of parody, it is one thing to edit a photograph, but what is being infringed is copyright over the general image of the star. If I unilaterally put a topless photo of Jennifer Aniston on my website, I am not simply reproducing her image; I am making public an image that she and her cultural intermediaries have not given me permission to use and may reasonably wish to suppress. For my communication of the photograph may alter the relationship between the public and her general celebrity persona. Since this image is the foundation of her public impact factor, I may be deemed to be acting in a way that is detrimental to her celebrity value with authorized sponsors, PR-Media personnel and the general public.[4]

Image aggregation and image accumulation

This brings us back to the technical issue at hand, which is the measurement of the non-physical characteristics of celebrity value. Technically, celebrity impact factors are situated at the crossroads between image aggregation and image accumulation. Image aggregation refers to the total number of images that are produced and distributed by cultural intermediaries. The general purpose behind image aggregation is to build the brand. Into this category fall photographs, interviews, sound bites and press releases. The purpose of cultural intermediaries is to build a public image of the celebrity that ultimately carries high approval ratings with the public. This is not a simple matter of spreading good news and upbeat images. It is a complex, multi-layered process in which the distribution of data on celebrity foibles, vulnerabilities and partialities are used in a disciplined process of image factor enhancement.

But celebrity impact factor is not simply a matter of design; it is also a question of accretion. This is where the concept of image accumulation comes in.

The concept refers to the total number of images consumed, produced and exchanged by the public. By definition, this is beyond the capacity of cultural intermediaries to delineate and control. If you take a photo of Miley Cyrus or Nicole Richie and post it on your website you are adding to image accumulation.

This cannot be centrally controlled. To begin with, it involves multiple players who do not fall under the jurisdiction of a central authorizing agency. RCA and Main Man were unable to stop Deram offloading inventory of 'The Laughing Gnome' and I cannot be prevented, at least initially, from putting non-copyright protected snapshots of celebrities on my Flickr site for free exchange. In terms of exposure management, image accumulation amounts to a network without a centre. This complicates notions of authorized practice and protocols since exchange cannot be effectively authorized or policed.

In addition, while image aggregation is a matter of the star's subordination to designed exposure, image accumulation extends to unregulated practice and exchange. That is areas of social competence and social encounters that are beyond the reach of cultural intermediaries. In essence, this involves celebrities acting in their private lives in ways that are contrary to the public face assembled for them by cultural intermediaries. Examples are legion.

The TV presenter Fern Britton fronted the Ryvita Bikini Keep Fit Challenge (2008). During the campaign the tabloid press revealed that her weight loss was not the result of 'healthy eating and cycling', as she claimed, but gastric band surgery. Britton's campaign credibility imploded and Ryvita's brand took a trade hit.

Similarly, when Sharon Stone observed in a TV interview (2008) that the Sichuan earthquake was the result of 'bad karma', Christian Dior blocked advertisements in China that featured her and eventually cancelled her contract.

The Australian cricketer Shane Warne suffered the same fate when his contract with Nicorette chewing gum was cancelled after he was photographed smoking during the West Indies tour (1999).

Rather than attempt to provide an exhaustive list here, let us consider one recent, widely reported case to illustrate some of the issues and dynamics at work.

In 2009 Tiger Woods was reported to have earned $100 million from sponsorship deals with AT&T, Pepsi, Nike, Tag Heuer, Accenture, Electronic Arts and Gillette. At the end of 2009, following revelations of his multiple marital infidelities, the soft drink company Gatorade announced it was dropping a Woods endorsed product, but claimed this was unrelated to the scandal surrounding Woods's private life. Gillette cancelled a thirty-second advert featuring Woods that was due to be aired on US television. The management consultancy firm Accenture terminated its sponsorship of Woods, citing that the golfer was no longer 'the right representative for the company'. AT&T followed Accenture in dropping Woods from their campaigns. However, Woods also received steadfast support from other sponsors, like Nike and Electronic Arts, who pleaded to the public for 'understanding' during what was acknowledged to be a 'difficult' time in Woods's private life.

Industry analysts estimate that the top five sports-related sponsors of Woods underwent a decline in market value following the revelations about his private life. Accenture and Gilllete are reported to have suffered a 2 per cent fall. Electronic Arts, Nike and Gatorade lost over 4 per cent (Bhusnurmath, 2010). This loss is passed on to shareholders and while it may not be permanent it raises the question of whether the investment in Woods is worth the rate of return.

Cultural intermediaries around Woods have responded with a programme of concentrated exposure management designed to accomplish rehabilitation. Initially, Woods dismissed allegations of marital infidelities as malicious hearsay. This was misjudged.[5] Eventually, he was prevailed upon to give a scripted public apology admitting irresponsibility and unacceptable behaviour in his marriage. Interestingly, in addition to culpabilities of personality, his apology cited the vanity of celebrity culture in which an illusory belief that 'normal rules do not apply' is perpetuated. The effect was intended to be face-saving. In fact the conference compounded public disquiet about Woods because it involved him not only in confessing that he was an adulterer but also exposed him as a dissembler with the public. It will be a long road back to winning public trust and reviving the faith of sponsors. Gradually, he is being eased back into a low-profile role in golfing tournaments, with press access strictly controlled. However, the separation from his wife has now ended in divorce. The PR-Media hub will either decide that Woods has suffered enough or take the divorce as confirmation of his lack of fitness to endorse commercial brands.

At the time of writing, it is unclear if this exposure management programme will bear fruit. Woods was the first athlete to earn $1 billion from sporting tournaments and sponsorship deals. This extraordinary financial success was built upon a public image of clean-cut, moral rectitude. The revelations about Woods's private life have produced deep cracks in the public face of his celebrity. It remains to be seen if the rehabilitation campaign to restore corporate confidence in Woods as a prime marketing device bears fruit.

Celebrity cognitive dissonance

Cognitive dissonance is the enemy of exposure management.[6] When the public has expectations of celebrity character and practice that are not corroborated by celebrity actions, the result is friction and tension. For exposure managers, the challenge is to engineer realignment so that cognitive harmony between public expectations of celebrity and celebrity behaviour prevails. To quote Bernays again:

> In our present social organization approval of the public is essential to any large undertaking. Hence a laudable movement may be lost unless it impresses itself upon the public mind. Charity, as well as business, and politics and literature, for that matter, have had to adopt propaganda, for the public must be regimented. (Bernays, 1928: 53)

The same law applies to celebrity exposure management.

By the 1960s the PR company that dominated Hollywood celebrity culture was Rogers & Cowan. In his autobiography, Henry Rogers (1980) identifies building trust as the core of effective celebrity exposure management and PR realignment. The leverage of trust is based on a relationship between the media and the client. Central to this task is possessing accurate data about public expectations (gathered through various forms of market research) and completely frank and honest exchanges with the client. Effective PR work means building high trust relations with the celebrity and getting the media on the side of the client.

But this presupposes that the media will be steadfast in matters of probity. Rogers refers to an incident involving Frank Sinatra. In 1961 the *New York Daily News* reported that Sinatra was under the influence of liquor at John F. Kennedy's inauguration ceremony. Rogers, acting for Sinatra, demanded a retraction from the press on the grounds that twelve witnesses were prepared to state that Sinatra behaved in a proper manner. The newspaper refused to take this course of action on the grounds that they did 'not like' Sinatra. Following legal advice, Rogers determined that suing the *New York Daily News* would be fruitless since it would a) be too costly, b) highlight and pander to public concerns about Sinatra's character and c) prove too challenging to make a persuasive case (Rogers, 1980: 164–5).

According to Rogers, most relations with the media are smooth and sound (Rogers, 1980: 169–70). However, he acknowledges that press events, press releases and interviews with the client carry hazards. In the case of press events, the main risks are, first, that the media does not attend; second, that the client is asked a provocative question that creates a bad impression, leading to unfavourable reporting; and, third, that the media misinterprets the purpose of the press event by boosting an obscure element or ignoring the primary thrust of the meeting.

A similar range of risk issues arises with press releases. First, they can be ignored by the media; second, they are rewritten to provide a different slant on the intended message; and third, the release is invalidated by a change in circumstance which invalidates the original purpose of the document.

On the subject of interviews, Rogers notes five risks: first, the media does not attend the arranged interview; second, the client fails to attend the arranged interview; third, the interview takes place but does not produce copy; fourth, the press produces copy but the client complains that he has been misquoted; and, fifth, the article appears but is deemed by the artist and his retinue to be damaging (Rogers, 1980: 170).

Rogers uses the apt metaphor of walking the tightrope to convey the relationship of leverage between the client and the media. He writes:

> As a public relations man, my contacts with the media are crucial if I am to serve my client effectively. Our relationship is based on trust – that is the press, television, and radio must trust me as a reliable source of information ... There must be an open, reciprocal working relationship between me and the media. If there is a breakdown in that relationship, I can no longer properly serve my clients. It is in this relationship with the media on one side and the client on the other, that I am constantly walking the tightrope. (Rogers, 1980: 163)

Optimal exposure management involves walking the tightrope effectively. Basic to this is steering image aggregation in the direction of building the celebrity brand. As a corollary, the PR-Media hub must acknowledge and apply a gatekeeping function to image accumulation. When the PR-Media hub makes a judgement that matters of public record will erode the star brand, various forms of damage limitation can be initiated. Some of the strongest weapons are candour and timing.

Compare the Tiger Woods sex scandal with the course taken by David Letterman and his advisers following a blackmail attempt to release details of his infidelities. Woods and the cultural intermediaries surrounding him initially tried to stonewall press reports about his extra-marital sex life, condemning them as hearsay or groundless rumour. When the momentum of allegations became irresistible, Woods was forced to make a public apology, which eventually took the form of a confession to the media. As a result, what Gamson (2001) calls the 'institutionalized morality' backlash of the media came into play. The media reaction to the Woods sex scandal was amplified and remedial strategies were compromised. Woods was accused not only of proven martial infidelities but of lying to the press and the public. As it became disclosed that Woods's liaisons were overwhelmingly with young white women, racial overtones were added to the imbroglio.

In contrast, Letterman faced the allegation of marital infidelity head-on. Following a blackmail attempt to extort $2 million from him, he took a prime-time slot on his show to confess to the public about his infidelities. Letterman's candour, allied with his representation of himself as the victim of a blackmailer, defused the ritual media condemnation that follows a sex scandal. He took the hit of being publicly identified as an adulterer, but gained credit for openly and quickly confessing to his misbehaviour and gained public sympathy by citing the private anguish he suffered at the hands of the blackmailer.

The avid public interest in the private troubles of stars brings us back to the question of why celebrity culture is ubiquitous. Exposure is subject to laws of supply and demand. We must now come to the subject of the parts that supply and demand play in the inflation of celebrity culture.

6 Supply Side Factors in Celebrity Inflation

The biggest supply side factor in the development of celebrity culture is access. The most important instrument of access is the media. It follows that the expansion of the media with the development of cable, satellite and the Web, is frequently credited as the engine in the growth of celebrity culture. More channels require more content. TV programmers responded to this challenge by developing celebrity game shows, star quiz shows, celebrity interview programmes, celebrity makeover shows, celebrity panels, celebrity chef shows and reality TV. As a corollary, other branches of the media, notably print culture, developed publications like *Hello!, Heat* and *Closer* to feed the apparently insatiable public demand for supplementary data about the private lives of stars.[1]

The circulation figures for celebrity-lifestyle weeklies are astounding and have become an industry benchmark. While print publications have been suffering from the challenge posed by Internet delivery, celebrity-lifestyle weeklies have gone from strength to strength. *In Touch*, launched in 2002, grew its circulation by almost 50 per cent in the first half of 2005. *US Weekly* grew by 24 per cent to 1.7 million and *Star* reported a 21 per cent increase to 1.4 million readers. It is estimated that over 40 million Americans read *People* magazine each week. In the United Kingdom, 23 million people are estimated to read the top ten bestselling celebrity publications and ten bestselling tabloids (which have a heavy concentration of data relating to the stars). In France *Paris-Match* sells twice as many copies as the national newspapers. With the rise of cable, there are entire channels and dozens of programmes that focus exclusively on celebrity culture (Alexander, 2007; 2010b). In the face of such data, it is hard to ignore the cogency of the argument that celebrity inflation is supply-led.

There are several virtues to this line of argument. The supply of broadcasting has undoubtedly multiplied in the post-war years. The invention of television dates from the 1920s. By the outbreak of the Second World War, Germany, the United States, the United Kingdom and the Soviet Union ran television services. However, compared with today's provision they were skeletal, being confined to high-status echelons in metropolitan centres like Los Angeles, Berlin, St Petersburg and London.

The growth of terrestrial-based national television broadcasting began in the 1950s. The multiplication of public and commercial channels characterized broadcasting history in the 1960s and 1970s. This extended the repertoire of programmes and enlarged and intensified celebrity culture. For very rapidly, commentators observed that the medium of television affords a powerful sense of intimacy between audiences and TV stars. The relationship was described as being akin to a primary relationship, that is a face-to-face encounter between individuals who are related by blood or friendship ties and acknowledge a sense of progression in their social encounters. As we shall see presently, this led to an academic interest in what has come to be known as 'para-social relationships'. That is the culture and psychology of audience clusters relating to mediated (television) stars as if they are on first-name terms with them (Horton and Whol, 1956).

Increasing media access also catered directly to the desire of young audiences to see the new pop and rock and roll stars created by the reinvigorated post-war music industry. When Elvis Presley appeared on the *Ed Sullivan Show* in January 1957 it was estimated that 82.6 per cent of the American viewing public tuned in (Marling 1994: 180). This level of public interest was only matched in 1964 when The Beatles made their debut on the same show drawing an estimated TV audience of 73,700,000. This was the high-water mark of television's power to set public agendas and reflect popular sentiment. Since those heady days the power of television in making celebrity culture has receded. As the *Idol, Got Talent* and *X Factor* franchises richly demonstrate, it remains a considerable force. But it is now challenged by the domestic system of fame, especially the facility of the Internet to represent and dramatize events and personalities.

Television employed techniques perfected by the Hollywood studio system between the 1920s and 1940s to portray film stars as regular, attractive, humane representatives of the people. Staged interviews and winning photo-play spreads of stars relaxing, gave audiences the impression of continuity between the life of the celebrity and the ordinary lives of the people. Hollywood photo-plays were scrupulously attached to demonstrating that achieved celebrities were 'one of us' because the link between stardom and the ordinary public was recognized as the goose which lay the golden egg.[2]

This existed in some tension with the parallel view that stars live a frontier existence, blessed with dazzling opportunities yet prey to pressures that are absent in ordinary walks of life. For all that, it was an effective response to the hunger from audiences to know more about the secret lives of the stars. Staged presentations of off-camera celebrity existence reinforced audience identification by giving the impression that achieved celebrities had not forgotten their roots or their manners (Barbas, 2001).

The star system that emerged in the medium of television in the 1950s borrowed the same technologies of psychological identification and social reassurance. Programmers encouraged audiences to formulate and develop the impression that they were on first-name terms with stars and privy to details of their private lives. Interviews and photo-spreads in celebrity magazines and newspaper gossip columns reinforced associations of neighbourliness and intimacy. Audiences responded inquisitively about the private lives of these public figures. They missed them when they were absent, they identified with their reported moods and their romantic, business and medical challenges (Horton and Wohl, 1956). However, it was not until the rise of cable and satellite broadcasting that television became truly global.

The first satellite television broadcast via the Telstar satellite took place in 1962. But the real boom in satellite broadcasting occurred with privatization and deregulation in the 1980s and 1990s. In this period the British Sky Broadcasting Group (BSkyB), USA Network (owned by NBCUniversal), ESPN (owned by Disney and the Hearst Corporation), Nickelodeon and MTV (owned by Viacom) and TBS (owned by Time Warner) emerged and consolidated their position as primary global providers (McPhail, 2006).

Satellite, cable and the Internet proliferated celebrity culture. They produced round-the-clock international broadcasting. This ramped up the ratings wars. More channels meant more programmes and more intense competition for advertising revenues. As a result, niche programming based upon a menu of sport, soft news, music and lifestyle extended its hold over air time (Castells, 2009). Satellite and cable presenters like Georgie Thompson, Natalie Sawyer, Stephen Cole, Lorna Dunkley and Stephen Dixon became household names.

Today, satellite and cable are being challenged by the domestic system of celebrity production. In the last decade new stars have been created from their living rooms and private laptops. Amber Lee Ettinger developed a singing career on the strength of her Internet fame as the 'Obama Girl'. Perez Hilton (aka Mario Armando Lavandeira) is a celebrated Internet blogger whose site achieves millions of hits per day. Lisa Donovan used YouTube to promote her short comedy parodies and became an overnight sensation. Jack Conte has developed a successful singing career by releasing videos through YouTube. The *Back Dorm Boys* achieved fame by posting lip-syncing videos on the Internet and gained advertising work promoting Motorola Cellphones in China and the Beijing media company, Taihe Rye.

The Internet affords new avenues of fame acquisition. So much so that the phenomenon of the celebrity meme is now recognized in the literature. The term 'meme' was coined by Richard Dawkins (1976), to refer to compact units of cultural information or symbols that are accessible and have high impact factor ratings. The celebrity meme refers to catchphrases, dance moves, songs and entire persona unveiled on the Internet that has instant appeal. A case in point is the popularity of the lip-syncing routines of the *Back Dorm Boys* to the songs of the *Backstreet Boys* and other pop stars. Successful memes spread among global youth audiences like wildfire. They can generate high economic rewards and build a cultural profile for the Internet celebrity.

In some ways the celebrity meme is akin to the celetoid. The exception, and it is crucial, is that celetoids are generally created by the media, whereas celebrity memes emerge from the domestic system of celebrity which seize media attention from below.

But we should be cautious about reading too much into the celebrity meme phenomenon. In particular, the celebrity meme may lead to the inference that fame is now within everyone's grasp. The separation of acclaim from content was anticipated many years ago by Daniel Boorstin (1962) who proposed that the PR-Media hub, technology and visual culture contain an inherent propensity to manufacture 'pseudo events' (fabricated newsworthy items). For Boorstin, the celebrities who personalize these items are also fabricated. Thus, his famous definition of celebrity as 'a person who is known for his well-knownness' (Boorstin, 1962: 67). Despite being a tautology, the definition has rung down through the decades because it encapsulates the pivotal connection between technology, the PR-Media hub and the pre-eminence of visual culture in the social ordering of fame.

Since Boorstin's day, strides in technology have made the link between technology, visual culture and fame at one and the same time more essential and more accessible. The Internet certainly provides access to anyone with a computer and Web connection and, today, access is the foundation of fame. However, a good deal of cold water must be poured on the leap of fancy that the celebrity meme is the future of celebrity culture. It is one thing to see the *Back Dorm Boys* as an overnight sensation. But this is very different from explaining why celebrity culture is ubiquitous. Image accumulation is a phenomenon that accompanies every sensational event in the media. Susan Boyle's audition video for *Britain's Got Talent* was the most watched YouTube video of 2009, with 120 million viewings (Bunz, 2009). The business of transforming image accumulation into viable image aggregation is tricky. A celebrity meme requires the intervention of dedicated public relations staff to manage exposure. In the case of the *Back Dorm Boys* and Boyle, this happened but they are the exceptions to the rule. After the first pang of public interest abates, the overwhelming majority of celebrity memes sink without trace. Yet the celebrity meme approach ignores the social and technical roles of cultural intermediaries in favour of an unlikely biological model that purports to reveal the work of social genetics. This is not the place to go into the many criticisms that can be made of Social Darwinism.[3] Suffice to say that any approach to contemporary celebrity that fails to engage with the imperatives of the business/state interests behind celebrities and the skills of the PR-Media hub is problematic on grounds of credibility.

Observers like Cashmore (2006) subscribe enthusiastically to the doctrine that supply creates its own demand. But this grossly underestimates the cultural literacy of audiences. Television is undoubtedly a powerful means of image accumulation. But there is no iron law which states that image accumulation leads directly to image aggregation. The mere supply of images of fame is unable to account for celebrity worship syndrome, the negative public response to celebrity vamping or the current popularity of celebrity as a form of life-coaching.

What Cashmore's approach fails to grasp is the position of celebrity in relation to a search for meaning in the lives of both stars and stargazers. While it is commonplace to portray identification with celebrity as close and intimate, the culture of fame is properly described as second hand, since it consists of recorded data transmitted by the PR-Media hub rather than face-to-face encounters. Yet the prominence and durability of this culture suggests that the world of fame is fulfilling a public need that is not satisfied by traditional relations of family and community. This again may give pause for thought to all those who regard celebrity culture to be froth.

Branding

Another aspect of the supply side of celebrity inflation is branding. Here, a distinction must be drawn with reference to branding. The celebrity brand refers to the images, symbols and associations built around a celebrity. By strengthening the brand, the celebrity builds the fan base. When this is successful, it translates into high impact factors that, in turn, attract advertisers. It is estimated that 20 per cent of American advertisements now feature celebrities (Story, 2006).[4]

A separate meaning of celebrity branding refers to the use of celebrities to endorse products. Celebrity endorsement is the business of 'the brand building the brand'. That is the celebrity brand is applied to provide transferable glamour to other products. The most potent transferable elements are physical appearance, athletic competence, intellectual capacity, emotional intelligence and lifestyle. Optimal celebrity endorsements require compatibility between the brand and the celebrity in criteria of identity, personality and market positioning.

As we saw at the beginning of this chapter, the link between celebrities and brand endorsement is well established (Pringle, 2004). The list of successful celebrity endorsement campaigns is long and growing. For instance, Louis Vuitton has used Christina Ricci, Chloë Sevigny and Scarlett Johansson to endorse their products. Gap has used Willie Nelson, Kris Kristofferson, Marianne Faithfull, Natalie Imbruglia,

Sissy Spaceck and Isabelle Huppert to build an eclectic, edgy image. Nike has employed Lance Armstrong, Kobe Bryant, William S. Burroughs, George Foreman, M. C. Hammer, Dennis Hopper, Michael Jackson, Denis Leary, Spike Lee, Dennis Rodman, Cristiano Ronaldo, Wayne Rooney, Monica Seles, Maria Sharapova and Michele Wie to enhance the appeal of their commodities. There is no particular need to give more examples.

Corporations would not persist with celebrity endorsement unless they had proof that it enhances brand recognition. Brand endorsement extends the exposure of celebrities. That is why it is grouped under the supply side set of factors to explain the inflation of celebrity. From the standpoint of the corporation, the aim of endorsement is to transfer a measure of the glamour and prestige that the celebrity has achieved in one walk of life onto the commodity. As we have already noted, celebrity endorsement has the potential to humanize commodities. It invests inanimate objects with personal qualities. For example, an Omega watch carries enhanced associations of glamour, social honour, attraction and cultural cachet because billboard campaigns show George Clooney and Nicole Kidman wearing the brand. Even independent validation that a celebrity has touched, let alone owned, a commodity has market value (Newman *et al.*, 2011).

Gillette has used celebrity endorsements from David Beckham (football), David Chappelle (comedy), Dale Earnhardt Jr. (motor racing), Steve Garvey (baseball), Method Man (rap), Redman (rap), Telly Savalas (film/TV), Thierry Henry (football), Roger Federer (tennis) and Tiger Woods (golf). In addition to the success and glamour that they impart, these figures have been selected because they represent male independence, boldness, virility and daring-do.

In Marxist sociology, commodities are treated as things that are separate from humans, as things that satisfy human wants. But Marx himself refers to 'metaphysical subtleties' and 'theological niceties' that emerge only after close scrutiny of how commodities are produced, exchanged and consumed in market culture (Marx, 1977: 76–78). Commodities are inanimate objects, but the process of production and circulation bestows animate qualities upon them. They come to stand over us, persuading us to make this or that decision about how we use our time and spend our surplus income. Yet a commodity does not have legs or possess a brain and a voice. So how might it be said to 'stand over' us or 'persuade' us?

Marx calls this 'commodity fetishism', which he describes as a condition in which 'the products of the human brain appear as independent beings endowed with life, and entering into relation both with one another and the human race' (Marx, 1977: 77).

Interestingly, for Marx (1977: 77–8) commodity fetishism is primarily explained as the result of the lack of social contact between producers, which disguises 'the social character of each producer's labour'. Because people experience a connection with each other only through a world of things (commodities) and money, the social relationships that give rise to this world are obscured. Things and money take on a life of their own.

Celebrity endorsement constitutes a new stage in the process of exchange and a new benchmark in commodity fetishism. There is still a lack of knowledge about the social character of production. Hence, I do not know the producers of Omega watches and they do not know me. Impersonality, which is the core of the 'magical' qualities that Marx claims exist under commodity fetishism, remains intact. However, I do know who George Clooney and Nicole Kidman are. When they wear an Omega watch in an advertising campaign, the magazine photographs and billboards have a personal element based upon our wider, often intense emotional involvement with the star. Celebrity endorsement is designed to transfer the commodified magnetism of the star onto the product. Through the sorcery of celebrity associations, the social character of labour is substituted by the image of the star.

The extraction of an economic margin from the consumer is therefore not simply based on charging a price for the commodity that is greater than the cost of production. Now, for many corporations, it also entails sponsoring the cultural capital that celebrity endorsement brings to the exchange relationship between the retailer and the consumer. The cost of sponsorship is passed onto the consumer by increasing the price of the commodity. That some famous commodities are produced by sweatshop labour in the Third World is beside the point. In a fully developed consumer society what matters is exchange at the point of sale. A visible link between the commodity and the celebrity speaks volumes to consumers. By choosing the right celebrity match to endorse the commodity, the corporation produces an overwhelming positive message of glamour and prestige.

This is not an issue of enhancing the material qualities of the commodity. An Omega watch is an Omega watch is an Omega watch. It is about investing an Omega watch with what, today, we would call the powers of association, and in an older language would have been referred to as the characteristics of idealism. Thus, Omega watches have long held a coveted status in the marketplace. However, a new social status is invested in them when George Clooney and Nicole Kidman are appointed to provide endorsements in billboard campaigns. The human characteristics of physical beauty, integrity, intellectual capacity and emotional intelligence, with which the consumer is familiar through their acquaintance with the public face of the star, merge with the inanimate object to create the impression of a new, transcendent force. In short, there is what Newman *et al.* (2011) refer to as a 'contagion effect' between celebrity association and the value of the commodity.

The social character of labour is a non-issue for consumers, because the halo of star-conducted glamour and prestige cancels it out. In the eyes of the consumer, the watch is an extension of the star. So the consumption of the watch produces a living relationship with the star and a link with concomitant values of beauty, emotional intelligence, prestige and integrity. This suggests that celebrity culture is complicit with producing a much broader notion of value than is generally recognized by the laws of economics.

In a world dominated by images produced by the PR-Media hub, celebrity images have commodified magnetism. It is this quality that corporations want consumers to relate to when they sponsor stars to endorse their commodities. By identifying with the image of the star and buying the commodity, consumers acquire a layer of appropriated glamour and prestige and adhere it to their ordinary social relationships. It is not that you become George Clooney or Nicole Kidman when you buy and wear an Omega watch; it is rather, that in doing so you recognize yourself as belonging to a prestigious fraternity which, in turn, signifies common pedigree. It is of no consequence that the pedigree has no genetic basis whatsoever. Image is all.

To resume, we have already noted a few of the problems that arise with celebrity endorsement. Corporations select endorsers for their physical appeal, athletic competence, intellectual capacity, emotional intelligence and lifestyle. Where the audience experiences cognitive dissonance between the public face and personal behaviour of celebrities, the result may be a negative feedback loop. This is not confined to the celebrity brand. By association, it carries over to the brands that celebrities endorse. The market losses suffered by Gillette, Accenture, Electronic Arts, Gatorola and Nike after the Tiger Woods debacle, may be referred to as a case in point. This brings us back to the question of the cultural literacy of consumers and the public.

The cultural literacy of the public

In her history of fans in movie culture, Barbas (2001) notes that from the earliest days of Hollywood, fans were interested in two critical aspects of star culture. To begin with, public information about celebrities was widely understood to be rationed. Disclosure, revelation and exposure about the private details of the lives of celebrities rapidly carried high cultural and economic value. Fans who were in the know carried aplomb and exerted superiority over fans that were in the dark. By way of recognition, PR-Media hubs established a variety of official and covert means of digging into the secrets of the stars and making them public. Hollywood did not create the gossip columnist, the paparazzi, the celebrity photographer or the culture of informants about star secrets, but it aided and abetted their development.

If fans were acutely conscious of the politics of information rationing, they were also keenly inquisitive about the accuracy of celebrity data. In the 19th century, the hugely successful, somewhat infamous American showman, P. T. Barnum coined the adage, 'the bigger the humbug, the better the people will like it' (Fuhrman 1989: 16). This worked well with Barnum's circus of curiosities, which included mermaids, the 161-year-old wet nurse of George Washington, bearded ladies and, most famously, the dwarf General Tom Thumb. Barnum spun a web of deceit and intrigue around all of these show turns. He would have agreed with Bernays, who declared: 'The voice of the people expresses the mind of the people, and that mind is made up for it by the group leaders in whom it believes and by those persons who understand the manipulation of public opinion' (Bernays, 1928: 109).

Barnum was certainly adept at manipulation and has gone down in history as one of the greatest celebrity spin doctors of all time. By the age of cinema, blatant chutzpah was wearing thin. Endorsements from celebrity impresarios were subject to more rigorous press scrutiny and a more culturally literate public. To be sure, Hollywood studio bosses and publicists were not above publicity stunts. One of the most famous in the history of motion pictures occurred in 1910. The IMP studio head, Carl Laemmle, issued a press release stating that his leading female star, Florence Lawrence, had been killed in a streetcar accident. The news resulted in wide press coverage. However, it was a hoax. A few days after stargazers had been plunged into mourning, Laemmle issued a counter press release stating that initial reports were false. He capitalized on the resultant publicity by organizing a publicity tour for Lawrence, which drew huge crowds.

Notwithstanding this, the old idea of an omnipotent studio system moulding public opinion at will is untenable. What comes through most forcefully in Barbas's (2001) study is that, as early as the 1920s, movie fans exercised considerable discretion about the Hollywood publicity machine. They were accomplished in organizing their own information networks to extract nuggets about the private lives of celebrities and determine the truth. Through clubs and newsletters they bypassed the Hollywood studio system. Their information was not always solid gold. They were often victims of organized PR-Media misinformation and rumour-mongering.

Nonetheless, they were active agents in challenging Hollywood whitewash.

Perhaps enough has been said to reach some conclusions about supply side explanations of celebrity inflation. The proposition that an increase in supply produces greater demand is partly valid. But it emphatically does not tell the whole story. The post-war expansion of terrestrial, cable and satellite channels undoubtedly expanded the range and numbers of stars. This contributed to making celebrity culture ubiquitous. Not least because it supported an ancillary industry consisting of celebrity print and Internet cultures devoted to screen and TV stars. Given the enormous profile of media celebrities in post-war culture it is hardly surprising that the glamour and prestige of stars emerged as a magnet for corporation investment.

The evidence that celebrity endorsement can boost turnover and increase market value is corroborated. This lends credibility to the proposition that supply side factors are fundamental in explaining the rise of celebrity culture in the West after 1945.

But we would not be talking about fame attack and celebrity worship syndrome, unless we were responding to considerable public disquiet about the onslaught of celebrity culture. As with all supply-led programmes designed to increase value, increasing celebrity broadcasts and extending celebrity endorsements is subject to the law of diminishing returns. From the beginning of the 1920s the Hollywood studio system recognized that public scepticism about some PR-Media releases was a problem. This suggests that the suppliers themselves were wary about the argument that supply creates its own demand. They appreciated that blanket bombardment creates a public reaction that, if left unchecked, will weaken the celebrity brand.

Bernays characterized the public as being capable of nothing more than a 'herd' mentality. But, even in his day, it was cavalier of him to discount the cultural literacy of the public (Bernays, 1928: 126). The inflation of celebrity is not a matter of too many corporately produced celebrities chasing too few fans. At the heart of the matter is the increased propensity of the public to look for personal and group meaning in stars. Celebrity culture would not be ubiquitous unless it answered some need in the public. This need, or group of needs, may exceed the capacity of the PR-Media hub to supply suitable celebrity figures. This observation brings us to the question of celebrity demand, its true nature and its role in the inflation of celebrity culture.

7 Demand Side Factors

Demand side explanations fall into three categories: Articulation and the Culture of Display; Hero Worship and Narcissistic Idealization; Religion, and its Decline in the West. All three identify celebrity as the response to the recognition of some sort of emotional deficit in personal relationships and public life. Thus, briefly, Articulation and the Culture of Display arise from the demand for social acknowledgement; Hero Worship and Narcissistic Idealization are rooted in a lack of self-esteem; and Religion, and its Decline in the West, refers to the erosion of organized religion and the collapse of conjoining moral integrity that provides a coherent sense of stability and order.[1]

Supply-based accounts of celebrity inflation highlight the issues of leadership and manipulation. They provide a top-down perspective that portrays the enlargement of celebrity to be the result of the combination of the acquisitive motives of celebrity impresarios, the gigantic expansion of channels of communication, especially print, film, cable and satellite and the avaricious business interests of corporations. The PR-Media hub is analysed as the gatekeeper, employed by cultural impresarios and business executives, to ration exposure and stoke the fires of public interest. It applies a campaign of manoeuvre and calculated hearsay to make audiences receptive, and to position stars in a favourable light.

Vertical and horizontal sides to this strategy must be differentiated. In terms of vertical manoeuvring, the PR-Media hub is dedicated to making stars cultural skyscrapers in their field of activity. That is winning the best movie roles, writing the most discussed books, recording the best regarded music, triumphing in the most prestigious sports tournaments, championing the best fashion designs, and so on. Horizontal manoeuvring refers to positioning stars as celebrity diplomats, celanthrophists, celebrity environmentalists, celebrity endorsers, etc. When the PR-Media hub raises the celebrity upon the social horizon as the conscience of the public, their public appeal is maximized. They are portrayed as sharing the concerns and voicing the thoughts of the silent majority. Their highly visible acts of celanthropy provides a general substitute for the many, dispersed feelings and aspirations of ordinary people. The celebrity acts as a reed for public opinion and is the representative agent of public concerns. When George goes on a fact-finding mission to Darfur, Angelina visits Somalian refugee camps in Kenya and Haiti as UN Goodwill Ambassador, and Bono dines with Kofi Annan and Barack Obama to discuss debt relief in Africa, they stand in as 'big citizens' purportedly representing the will of the public.

With supply side explanations of celebrity inflation the accent is upon moulding public opinion through the strategic manipulation of celebrity associational values and the halo of prestige. This assumes that power is concentrated in the hands of the suppliers. Once again, to invoke the unintentionally disturbing phrase coined by Bernays (1928), it is the vision of 'the invisible government' in celebrity culture that drives the show.

In contrast, demand side approaches start with the proposition of want and vulnerability in the body politic. According to this line of argument, celebrity is ubiquitous because people hanker after, and, in some cases, obsessionally crave, larger, sanitized versions of themselves or idealized substitutes. That is versions free from insecure doubts about personal worth, disabling worries about social status and painful anxieties that life has no meaning. From this vantage point, it is the emotional loneliness, powerlessness and insecurity of the public that is the key to celebrity culture. In effect, stars are credited with therapeutic powers. Celebrity carries positive associations of action, drama, prestige and power. Identification with this culture affords ordinary people voyeuristic experience of heroic public impact and making a difference in the world. By wishing upon a star we move to the elusive land of the frontier, where old rules do not apply and everything is possible. Common experiences of estrangement from politics and isolation from glamour dissolve by empathizing with celebrity agents and their highly public interventions. Celebrities become public representatives of private troubles and anxieties. When Bob Geldof threw in his lot with the task of remedying famine in Ethiopia he did so not only as a rock star but as the representative of Everyman. Celebrities articulate and implement a 'can do' attitude that contrasts with a widespread public sense of impotence about approaching and solving public problems. Large sections of society project the emotions of compassion, beneficence and the desire for recognition onto stars.

Projection can elevate some celebrities into positions of political and social significance. Indeed some have gone down in history as class champions. When the Beatles achieved global celebrity in the 1960s, they were feted not only as talented composers and musicians, but also as 'four working-class lads from Liverpool'. Charlie Chaplin, who hailed from the South London slums, occupied the same class position in the silent film era. In the United States, the success of Clara Bow (the 'It' Girl), James Brown, Johnny Cash, 2Pac and Puff Daddy partly reflects their public position as warriors of class and ethnicity.

The role of celebrities in class battles, to say nothing of wars between the sexes and racial conflicts, is of historical importance. Celebrities not only represent private troubles and anxieties, they articulate general collective aspirations of class, gender, race and nation. In a world where visual culture is increasingly important as a medium of communication, and soft news is exchanged, first and foremost, by sound bites, the face of the celebrity is shorthand for powerful emotional connections and complex political arguments (Castells, 2009).

Demand approaches therefore bifurcate between analysing celebrity as part of the psychology of projection and viewing stars as agents of resistance and change. Although these traditions of analysis involve contrasting assumptions and lines of investigation, they share the hypothesis that celebrities are agents for problem solving. They are lionized and courted because they promise to supply answers to emotional deficit disorders.

It goes without saying that these solutions may be delusional. If personal and public problems were simply a matter of getting the right celebrity to articulate and tackle them, they would have been banished from the chart of human history long ago. However, without gainsaying the validity of this point, stars can assuage personal dilemmas and provide a sense of momentum for tackling public ills. This brings me to the question of the detailed differences between the three demand side explanations of celebrity inflation.

Articulation and the culture of display

What does articulation and the culture of display have to do with the inflation of celebrity culture? On the face of it, the question is eminently reasonable, because issues of articulation in class and race are based on collective experience. In contrast, celebrity culture revolves around individuals and groups. True, there is a collective dimension in the shape of the audience. Moreover, this may be influenced by distinctions of class and race. That is some celebrities may appeal more strongly to one class or race, or combination of classes and races, than to others. And yet, to propose that the audience for a given celebrity consists entirely of one class/race or class/race combination is implausible. The cult of modern fame is mostly blind to distinctions of this sort. However, on closer inspection, especially of the history of achieved celebrity, the links between class and race, the culture of display and fame become transparent and irresistible.

Over the last 250 years, the history of celebrity has been dominated first by the struggle, and second by the gradual, albeit incomplete, replacement of ascribed forms of celebrity with achieved types. Celebrity used to be chiefly about destiny. Those born into an ascribed status were meant to live life in the time-honoured way.[2] Today, in the age of the new aristocracy of fame, it is mainly about the distribution of chances of upward mobility that arise from democracy, industrial-urban development and the expansion and intrusion of the media.

Ascribed celebrity refers to the assumption of fame by dint of genealogy or marriage. For example, Prince William and Prince Harry are internationally famous because they are children of the prospective British monarch and therefore, heirs to the throne. Their mother, Princess Diana, was born into the aristocracy, but only acquired significant international fame via her marriage to the Prince of Wales. Ascribed celebrities may add or subtract to their complement of fame by virtue of their deeds. For example, Diana was indeed famous when she married Prince Charles. However, she only became a global superstar following her famous BBC television interview with Martin Bashir (1995) in which she revealed her husband's infidelity (which tacitly identified her with the plight of countless women in the world), and also fronted various international charity campaigns.[3] By these means, she added to her global fame as an ascribed celebrity. However, the concrete foundation of ascribed celebrity rests in the position in the social hierarchy assumed by reason of birth or marriage.

Ascribed forms of celebrity are paramount in traditional societies where patronage rules over accomplishment and custom over innovation. Modern societies are organized around industrial production, scientific and technological innovation and democratic government. Integral to modern civil society are the legal principles of individual freedom, equality and democratic justice. It follows that the kind of fame that is most highly valued here is the product of personal virtue, discipline and ambition.

Achieved celebrity is fame acquired by reason of talent, accomplishment and skill. Of course, the PR-Media hub can expand the profile of celebrities. But in a democratic society the high and the low are formally equal so that, outwardly, their fame is a measure of personal achievements. For example, Daniel Day Lewis and Leonardo DiCaprio acquired global fame because of their acting talents and accomplishments; Beyoncé, Shakira and Christina Aguilera are among today's most famous female pop singers because of their singing and performing abilities; and Lewis Hamilton and Fernando Alonso (motor racing), Rafael Nadal and Novak Djokovic (tennis), and Lionel Messi and Cristiano Ronaldo (football) dominate celebrity sports culture by reason of their natural gifts and dedicated training. In social conditions where civic honour is the reward for accomplishment, and where rule is governed by the principle of universal suffrage, it is perfectly normal for talented, dedicated people to spring forth from the rank and file to gain prominent cultural prestige and high economic rewards. At least, that is how it appears with hindsight.

In fact, the ascendancy of achieved celebrity was turbulent and protracted. The European Revolutions in the seventeenth and eighteenth centuries turned Oliver Cromwell, Maximilien Robespierre, Georges Danton and Louis Antoine de

Saint-Just into achieved celebrities overnight. More importantly, they irrevocably expressed the power of the people in challenging the authority of the monarchy. These were revolutions led, respectively, by the gentry and professionals and intelligentsia. They boldly rejected the *ancien régime* and paraphernalia associated with ascribed celebrity, but Cromwell became Lord Protector and was succeeded by his son Richard, while the people's revolution led by Robespierre, Danton and Saint-Just created the conditions that paved the way to the enthronement of Napoleon Bonaparte as Emperor.

Nevertheless, both the Civil War in England and the French Revolution fundamentally challenged the principles of immemorial hierarchy and ascribed celebrity in Europe. Nothing has been the same since.[4]

Further west, the American Revolution overthrew monarchical rule in the thirteen colonies and sought to establish a new republic based upon principles of liberty and equality. The very idea of revolutionaries supported the development of a new type of personality: intrepid, indignant about blind custom and superstition, bold and determined to be free from the inhibitions of the past.

Thomas Jefferson, Alexander Hamilton and Benjamin Franklin were not exactly new men. Thomas Rainsborough and Henry Ireton articulated similar doctrines of freedom, justice and republicanism during the English Civil War.[5] But the Revolution in America was part of the Enlightenment tidal wave that shook the *ancien régime* to its foundations.

Coming to the question of race, the nineteenth-century African American Frederick Douglass, who had been born into slavery and escaped, became a famous and feted abolitionist, lecturer and writer in America and Britain. Douglass's autobiography, *Narrative of the Life of Frederick Douglass, an American Slave* (1845), was an international bestseller. He regarded education as essential to social progress. He campaigned for the desegregation of American schools and the emancipation of women. Douglass was appointed chargé d'affaires for the Dominican Republic and in 1872 was nominated for Vice-President of the United States for the Equal Rights Party.

Douglass's conduct and repute were immensely important in serving the cause of building African-American prestige. The strength of his character stood as a permanent reproach to white supremacists, and his assimilation into the establishment as an African American of equal stature to white leaders, was a cause célèbre for civil rights activists. His emotional intelligence, strength of character, people skills and the clarity and fortitude of his political vision, humanized abstract principles of political oppression, intolerance and racial equality. As a leading African-American celebrity, he was a seminal figure in the business of racial integration and consensus politics in the era of Reconstruction and since.

The expansion of industry, commerce, science, the arts and the growth of colonization created innumerable new opportunities for achieved celebrity. New strategies of making a mark, getting noticed and claiming personal attention were struck, burnished and multiplied. The rising industrial classes borrowed motifs and styles from the theatre and applied them to the tasks of emotional management and public presentation. They developed attitudes of debating, forms of fashion, vocabularies of culture and industry designed to be noted and acquire acclaim. Bearing, grooming, hygiene, fashion and style became crucial aspects of impression management and self-promotion.

Several historians of celebrity culture have described the emergence of new public spaces in which personality could be expressed, exchanged and developed, notably cafes, dining clubs, arcades and public squares (Gundle, 2008; Inglis, 2010). Froideur and panache ceased to be regarded as God-given moods. They became resources of emotional intelligence and emotional labour, to be deployed in the business of making impact, getting a name, and being recognized as someone of note and repute. Economic success, cultural cachet and social power were no longer understood to be matters of family inheritance, as they had been in traditional society. Men were now regarded to be captain of their destinies.

This was fertile soil for the growth of celebrity culture. 'A society that attributed importance to front and performance,' writes Gundle, 'needed mirrors to hold up to itself' (Gundle, 2008: 66). Celebrities articulated winning styles of self-promotion and impression management. Viewed politically, this involved a double code of articulation. Thus, an African-American celebrity in the nineteenth century, such as Frederick Douglass, embodied the frustrations, aspirations and highest characteristics of an entire racial group. Douglass was a touchstone for much more profound questions of power and injustice. In this sense, individual celebrity articulation expresses deeper social, political and economic forces. It represents a cultural biography of certain elements in the time and place of their day. This is why, to refer back to the opening pages of the book, the death of such figures is a cultural supernova that momentarily brings the world to a halt.

The second meaning of celebrity articulation is the expression and refinement of self-promotion, impression management and people skills that were appropriated as social resources among large, aspirational sections of the ordinary population. Boswell's *Life of Samuel Johnson* (1791) broke the mould by comprehensively engaging with the subject. The use of anecdotes, asides and even the complete replication of conversations brought Johnson to life in a way that was widely noted and admired at the time and indeed, since (Sisman, 2000). This was a new approach to representing biography and history which was symptomatic of the growing importance of educated opinion, pointed comment, heartfelt sentiment, dress, grooming and visual culture in general. It conveyed the impression of getting to know the celebrity via all sorts of personal touches in prose style that made biographies before Boswell seem lifeless and stiff by comparison.

In the eighteenth century Adam Smith concluded *The Theory of Moral Sentiments* (1759), with an outline of the truly virtuous person. He held that such a person must possess prudence, justice, beneficence and self-command. Smith understood that it does not suffice to cultivate these personality characteristics as direct demands of virtue. It is also necessary to display them in the public conduct of life. To fail to do so exhibits a narrowness of soul. Smith's outline captured the honoured and desired features of achieved celebrity in the eighteenth and nineteenth centuries.

Needless to say, the articulation of achieved celebrity did not pass by without resistance and opposition. Self-promotion and impression management was associated with 'tall poppy syndrome', namely, the pruning or scything down of people who are above themselves or demand attention in ways that are regarded by others to be unreasonable. Achieved celebrities were awarded prestige and economic rewards, since they symbolized the break with the *ancien régime.* But they were also criticized and condemned if they placed the demand for prestige above the demonstration of talent and accomplishment. This carries over to the present day. The media and the public raise questions of a strident dresser like Lady Gaga on the grounds that her demands for attention precede and eclipse her talents as a composer and singer.

Performance and front are necessary characteristics of celebrity, but a surfeit of them breeds censure and, in some cases, revulsion. Achieved celebrities are properly celebrated as men and women who recognize and cherish their talents and accomplishments, and display them with the grace of prudence, justice, beneficence and self-command, as Smith's theory of moral sentiments outlined. But the danger that they could become *too* full of themselves, overly self-important and demanding, was present from the birth of the era of achieved celebrity. This is a matter of the proper balance of narcissism in the personality and public face of the celebrity. Modern men and women need a degree of narcissism to do anything in life. But when the mirror of celebrity culture held up to them shows preening, self-centred, selfish, intolerant, undisciplined stars, they become dismissive and wonder out loud if the public passion for fame has gone too far. But what is this narcissism that gets us so exercised, and what might be the right balance between the will to get ahead and outright narcissism? This brings us to the second main approach to explaining the inflation of celebrity.

Hero worship and narcissistic idealization

Hero worship is a condition in which deep sentiments are invested in a champion or warrior acclaimed with overcoming various adversities and difficulties. The moral code and rectitude of the hero is also referred to as a model for society. The hero is therefore regarded to be a more complete man, blessed with levels of fortitude, resourcefulness, vision and courage that other men conspicuously lack. Heroes are seldom merely self-interested. In addition, they are usually perceived to be blessed with powerful sentiments of magnanimous altruism that makes them believe that they are acting for the benefit of mankind. Hero worship is generally an aspect of charismatic rule. Interestingly, it often takes the form of identification with mythical constructs rather than real figures. For example in Ancient Greek culture, Hercules, Achilles, Theseus, Odysseus, Perseus, Orpheus, Jason and Cadmus waged daring deeds against human enemies, Minotour, Medusa and lesser gorgons. Similarly, in Celtic and Anglo-Saxon culture, the Arthurian legends provide a mythical resource of bravery, nobility and self-sacrifice. Today, the paramount concentration of this resource has switched from and oral and print culture to visual culture.

With the transition from traditional to modern societies most of the popular features of the hero myth have been appropriated from legend by media culture. The Hollywood studio system and the wider PR-Media hub produce heroic stars who comply with corporate commercial imperatives but rely upon elements of non-commercial myths and legends to achieve pronounced public appeal.

Stardom is not confined to film roles and media scripts. Rather, it involves constant slippage between the celebrity and the scripted role (in film and song), between real life and fiction that mimics the conceptual structure of myth. Thus, the Dionysian rock star (Jim Morrison, Mick Jagger, Jimi Hendrix, Robert Plant, Gene Simmons, Pete Doherty) and the Herculean movie hero (John Wayne, Charlton Heston, Sean Connery, Bruce Willis, Keanu Reeves) and the *Star Wars* system of noble and evil characters, consciously deploy elements from mythic genres and repackage them as aspects of celebrity culture.

For most people, hero worship is a second-hand sentiment. That is a reaction to constructs of the hero ideal that have been assembled and communicated by the PR-Media hub. Positive identification with the fictional characters Obi-Wan Kenobi, Luke Skywalker and Han Solo in the *Star Wars* movies is automatic because we relate to them as heroes in the battle for good and right against the forces of Evil represented by Darth Vader, Emperor Palpatine and Count Dooku. But the ground for these reactions has been carefully sown by George Lucas and his team through script conferences and audience research. The *Star Wars* audience reacts not to events, but to cues, leads and prompts supplied by the PR-Media hub. It might be surmised that our propensity to follow these scripts is entirely a matter of schooling. After all, in the television and Internet age the PR-Media hub has long been as much a part of the infant's world as contact with the family. But to account for this propensity in terms of PR-Media schooling is only part of the story. It helps us to understand how we read media scripts that communicate the hero ideal, but it leaves a bigger question unresolved. Namely, what are the reasons in contemporary society for the psychological demand for dramatic heroes? This is a complex matter.

Achievement famine and its discontents

A start to answering the question can be made by proposing that hero worship is the mirror of achievement famine. The latter may be defined as a condition in which the demand for fame is distributed more generally than the means of attainment. By definition, non-heroic life is clouded with routine, reserve and dependence. It may include courageous and eventful episodes but, in contrast with heroic life, these features do not constitute the hallmarks of existence. Non-heroic life waits, as it were, in the wings for heroes and leaders to make a difference and change the world.

Feelings of impotence and inconsequentiality are widespread in the West. If the President of the United States cannot solve global warming or the Israel-Palestine conflict or gun wars in America, what hope do ordinary men and women have to make a substantial difference? Little wonder that they moderate their dissatisfactions and feelings and project the desire for the heroic life on to celebrities. The PR-Media hub tirelessly encourages them to do so. Bruce Willis's heroic successes in the *Die Hard* movies or the triumph of Frodo Baggins (Elijah Wood) and Gandalf (Ian McKellen) in *The Lord of the Rings* film trilogy provide vicarious escapism from the treadmill of non-heroic life.

Frank Sinatra's 'My Way' (1969) and Gloria Gaynor's 'I Will Survive' (1978) are torch songs for people who possess the same sentiments but lack the public stage to articulate them to a wider audience. They afford escapism for people who feel indignant about injustice but are paralysed to act meaningfully on the national or global stage.

Additionally, the philanthropic work of stars provides an outlet for muffled, repressed popular sentiments for a better world and outwardly gives the comforting appearance of fixing things. Thus, to take some more or less random examples, Lady Gaga's vociferous protest about American military policy at a rally in Maine in 2010; Naomi Campbell's participation in the 'We'd rather go naked than wear fur' poster campaign in 1997; and the involvement of Cyndi Lauper, Whoopi Goldberg and Elton John in the *Give A Damn* (2010) campaign in support of LGBT (Lesbian, Gay, Bisexual, Transgender) rights, promote ordinary worries and concerns and provide a colourful release for popular tensions. For many, the gap between the demand for fame and the means of attainment is filled with the projection of unsupported desire onto celebrity objects. Media heroes are substitutes for the thwarted public passion to be heroic. The common notion that the lives of celebrities are packed with excitement, incident and emergency directly reflects and magnifies this wish.

'The engineering of consent,' wrote Bernays, 'should be based theoretically and practically on the complete understanding of those whom it attempts to win over' (Bernays, 1947: 114). The PR-Media hub caters to the widespread demand for the heroic life by exaggerating incident, emergency and risk in the lives of celebrities. In doing so it exploits and channels unsupported popular desires for achievement and recognition into commercially profitable ends. The commodified magnetism of stars exploits the slippage between their scripted roles and their status as contemporary heroes. There is an important aspect of governance to this state of affairs. The heroic life of celebrities relieves the burden of responsibility of ordinary people to cast aside the non-heroic life and challenge the status quo. Big solutions to the world's problem require large, high-profile interventions. Most judge the cards to be stacked against them. Most are only too conscious of living in a condition of achievement famine.

Celebrity hero worship is therefore explained as a means of handling the emotional impasse of this state of affairs. Vicarious engagement with the make-believe adventures of heroic stars provides escape from the non-heroic humdrum. It enables ordinary people to live out epic struggle through the heroic roles and humanitarian campaigns of celebrities. We govern our feelings of inconsequentiality and impotence by living through the on-screen and off-screen PR-Media recorded achievements of the stars. But the subject of modern hero worship is more complicated than questions of projection, vicarious engagement and tension release.

Celebrities are not alone in exhibiting symptoms of narcissism. The rewards of achieved celebrity may enlarge a sense of entitlement, superiority and vanity, but these traits are rooted in society at large. Large swathes of the population display the demands for acknowledgement and acclaim. It is not enough to be themselves, they demand an audience to recognize their qualities and attainments. The hunger for recognition precedes concrete achievement. The success of the *Idol, X Factor* and *Got Talent* TV franchises is one measure of how ill-judged many are in believing they have unique or noteworthy talents. But these neurotic delusions reach further back into parenting and schooling. Infants are taught not to be burdened by their weaknesses but to confront them and to accept them if they can't be overcome. Parents and teachers reward the demand for self-expression to be recognized rather than corked. The whole person must define himself or herself as emotionally alive and is therefore encouraged to vent their sentiments and aspirations. Reserve is often interpreted as a symptom of inhibition or introspection. From an early age we learn what the 60s counterculture preached: to let it all hang out, to be direct and transparent about our needs. Frankness about our emotions and inner life is regarded to be a character strength. To be sure, candour is interpreted as a sign of vigour and health in the personality, while modesty and reserve smack of an unseemly character defect. It is not enough to be bold and candid in one's self. Venting sentiment and letting it all hang out require an audience.

Narcissism and society

In traditional society, esteem and good opinion were matters of the personal approval of friends and neighbours. This involved the cultivation of personal worth through self-promotion and impression management. But in an age in which fame is a matter of public recognition by the PR-Media hub, there is a pronounced disconnect between esteem, good opinion and personal approval. This changes the nature of personal approval and the dynamics of achievement. As Christopher Lasch puts it:

> Today men seek the kind of approval that applauds not their actions but their personal attributes. They wish to be not so much esteemed as admired. They crave not fame but the glamour and excitement of celebrity. They want to be envied rather than respected. (Lasch, 1980: 59)

It is eerily reminiscent of the last days of ascribed celebrity, when some people behaved as if their reputation was transparent, inviolable and took precedence over their actions. In the modern age we behave as if the self speaks for itself and requires no justification for its authority.

Narcissism involves a strong propensity to be recognized as perfect. It goes without saying that perfection is notoriously elusive and requires considerable inner strengths of discipline and judgement. But in the age of self-promotion and impression management most narcissists settle for gaining the gloss of perfection in the eyes of the beholder. The portrayal of physical beauty, strength of character and special talents is a defense mechanism for personal unresolved insecurities. The psychological condition of narcissism is based in an unreasonable demand for admiration and entitlement.

Narcissists divide society into two groups: the meaningful and powerful, and the majority who is held to be defined by incorrigible mediocrity and emotional timidity, which might be called *the bus class*. The prestige of the first group is reinforced by the PR-Media hub. Through press events, domination of popular forms of entertainment, product endorsement and the like, celebrities provide footprints of commodified magnetism that draw a line between them and ordinary people.

In contrast the bus class is composed of people who are regarded to be going nowhere. The bus class inhabit the world of casual, low-paid labour, rented accommodation, poor education and general hopelessness that is tantamount to social and economic ground zero.

Narcissists want to be part of the world that consists of people who have made their mark and make a difference. They are drawn to these gleaming cultural edifices because they want to be associated with winners rather than losers. Narcissistic idealization consists of the transference and magnification of positive narcissistic traits of glamour, fortitude, resolve and courage on to celebrity heroes. The positive images of celebrities, carefully constructed by the PR-Media hub, are reinforced and enlarged by the devotional energy of narcissistic fans who seek to find idealized characteristics of humankind in their chosen stars.

The technical features involved in the promotion and management of narcissism are bolstered by historical and political forces. Post-colonial critics rightly condemn the West for cultural imperialism. Cultivating a self-image of racial superiority is part of this. But this self-image is also the product of the revolt against the *ancien régime* and the liberation of ordinary men and women which, in turn, has produced unparalleled levels of upward mobility and wealth. From the perspective of most Western citizens, the long march of Everyman is an heroic tale. It is made up of a patchwork of overwhelmingly courageous images of tumbrils rattling along the cobblestones carrying the greedy, corrupt, merciless rich to their well-deserved fate; science and medicine stripping away the mumbo jumbo of superstition and religion; education challenging and overturning prejudice and much else besides. In sum: the ideology of Western progress is steeped in the rhetoric of opposing dark forces to advance freedom, equality and justice. Among narcissists the sense of superiority in cultural struggle and achievement has become disproportionate. They may pay lip service to critiques of the blinkered nature of Western individualism. They certainly regard themselves to be on the side of the culture of achievement. However, they have permitted entitlement to replace tolerance and allowed self-regard to overshadow respect for others. They are denizens of the 'me' world where their way of defining things and going about their business must have unchallenged advantage. Their needs, insights and ambitions are contrasted with the untalented majority, the *bus class*, who are automatically defined as mediocre and insignificant.[6] A common defence mechanism includes cultivating the image of infallibility. This goes hand in hand with the demand for abject, unreserved apologies from anyone who dares to gainsay them. This is an attempt to create a culture of total control where the point of view of the narcissist is not only privileged, but possesses absolute priority. The rest of the world can go hang.

This aspect of the narcissistic personality is associated with irresponsibility and a front of invulnerability. It supports behaviour that is heedless of convention, contract or the law. For example, in the summer of 2010 Paris Hilton was faced with a lawsuit of allegedly $35 million from an LA-based hair extension company, HairTech. The company maintained that Hilton was in breech of a $2.2 million legal agreement that prohibited her from advertising hair extensions from rival companies. HairTech alleged that Hilton wore a rival company's extensions after signing a contract to exclusively represent HairTech's 'Dream Catcher' range of extensions.

Similarly, in September 2010 Lindsay Lohan was sent back to jail after a failed drug test. This followed her incarceration three months earlier for violating the terms of her probation. She joins a long recent list of stars who have served jail sentences. In 2001 Martha Stewart was sentenced to five months for insider trading. In 2007 Nicole Richie was sentenced to four days in prison for driving under the influence of drugs. In the same year Kiefer Sutherland spent forty-eight days in jail for repeated drink-driving offences. Robert Downey Junior was jailed for six months following drugs convictions. In 2008 O. J. Simpson was jailed for thirty-three years having been found guilty of criminal conspiracy, kidnapping, assault and robbery. In 2009 Boy George was imprisoned for fifteen months for falsely imprisoning a male escort. In the same year, the 69-year-old 'Wall of Sound' record producer, Phil Spector, received a nineteen-year sentence for the murder of the Hollywood actress Lana Clarkson in 2003. In 2010 George Michael was jailed for eight weeks after he admitted crashing his Range Rover in London under the influence of cannabis.

These criminal acts and misdemeanours point to personalities who do not see themselves as travelling bus class and regard themselves to be above the law and therefore unaccountable. For them, transgression is a weak concept. The line between the rules of ordinary life and infraction is purely academic. Early in their careers, most celebrities learn that they can have their cake and eat it. If society chooses to punish them, it is because society does not understand what they have had endure to acquire achieved celebrity and prestige. Celebrities are well versed in the doctrine that artists suffer for their art. They wear their heart on their sleeve because, in their mind, it is the world – not them – that has finally, made them objects of exhibition. If, in doing so, they partake of acts of exhibitionism to taunt the world. If this incurs the world's wrath, it is the world's problem. Fines and imprisonment are simply further proof of being misdiagnosed and misunderstood.

Narcissism certainly breeds bad behaviour traits. However, in most cases it has an Achilles heel: insecurity. The excess of emotion and extravagant selfishness disguises a profound lack of self-confidence and self-worth.

For celebrities, the spiral of stardom momentarily casts this problem in the slipstream of applause and goodwill. At first, acclaim and recognition are experienced as the reward for narcissistic courage and daring. However, the more celebrities harness and exploit these social reactions, the more they apply them to underwrite acts of narcissistic extravagance and irresponsibility, trapping the star in a spiral of excess. In the long run, the problem of insecurity, for which narcissistic behaviour is a defence mechanism, is intensified and may become disabling. In the words of the late Christopher Reeve: 'A famous person can be unkind, uncharitable, selfish, ungiving with friends, non-responsive and be indulged in it. Then the famous person loses self respect – and that can be very damaging' (Reeve in Berlin, 1996: 264).

If celebrity narcissists often suffer from a lack of self-confidence and self-worth the problem is compounded for ordinary people with narcissistic tendencies. For they do not even have the experience of the spiral of fame to sustain them. Their displays of omnipotence and personal significance mask an inner world beset with anxieties of impotence and inconsequentiality. The more their desire for acclaim and recognition is impeded, the greater is their propensity to transfer these unsupported emotions through narcissistic idealization.

It might be supposed that society would deal with this by encouraging people with narcissistic tendencies to face their inner demons. But this is not the case. The rise of therapeutic culture is one side of the respect that Western democracies place in the individual. There is the unshakeable insistence that no individual faces life alone. Yet just because of this there is an unprecedented public interest in the conditions that prevent or corrode the healthy development of individuals and, by extension, the responsibility to offer professional help. Narcissists may be beastly, but they are also commonly appreciated as deserving of our understanding, compassion and support. Their behaviour is lousy, but it is incumbent upon us to make allowances, to understand their pain and reach out.

It goes without saying that most narcissists do, in fact, have a history of difficult, failed relationships. They cannot build whole relationships because everything revolves around a perpetual zero-sum game that consists of strangers constantly admiring them, praising them and submitting to placing them on a pedestal. Their partners are required to be emotionally secondary. Equality is not the name of the game. On pain of dismissal and excommunication, partners must scrupulously refrain from probing questions into why a lack of self-worth and self-confidence is evident. So the partner joins the game of bluff, spin, avoidance and deceit.

It is no accident then, that celebrities, who in many cases are seriously, meaningfully narcissistic, often have a turbulent relationship with the PR-Media hub and the public. Their grandiose self-image, pressing demand to be admired by strangers and empathy deficit makes enemies. Although narcissistic celebrities behave as if they can have it all and get away with anything, they are often brought to heel by the police and the law. I have already mentioned the rash of celebrity jail sentences in the last few years. In addition, there are many other high-profile cases of celebrity brushes with the law.

In 1991, American comedian Paul Reubens, who created and played Pee-wee Herman on children's TV, was arrested after being discovered masturbating in an adult movie house. His conviction for indecent exposure sent his career into free fall, which took many years to turn around.

In 2001 the popular British comedian Michael Barrymore was accused by the tabloid press of holding drug-filled gay orgies at his house after a body of a male had been found floating in Barrymore's swimming pool. The mystery surrounding the death lead to the collapse and disintegration of Barrymore's TV career.

In 2002 the Hollywood actress Winona Ryder was found guilty of theft and vandalism for stealing goods worth $5,500 from an exclusive Beverly Hills department store.

Charlie Sheen was arrested in 2009 for menacing behaviour and criminal mischief, following a complaint of domestic violence. In 2010 police removed him from his suite in the exclusive Plaza Hotel in New York after he caused reputed damage of $7000. In 2011 after allegations of substance abuse, CBS dismissed Sheen from his starring role in the successful TV series *Two And A Half Men*. Sheen's subsequent attempt at rehabilitation via a live promotional tour met with mixed responses.[7]

Arguably, the most famous recent global case of celebrity brushes with the law is Mel Gibson. In 2006 he was arrested for speeding with an open bottle of alcohol in his car. This followed a long history of battles with drink. In 1984 Gibson crashed his car in Toronto and was banned from driving for three months. In 1991 his admitted reliance on drink forced him to attend AA meetings. Knowledge of his struggle with alcohol filtered through to the public along with his ultra-traditionalist Catholic outlook and reactionary opinions. The speeding offence became notorious for the anti-Semitic outburst that Gibson directed against the arresting officer. This led the cultural intermediaries surrounding him to organize an elaborate, staged apology on television in the form of an interview with Diane Sawyer and high-profile meetings with Jewish leaders to help him 'find the appropriate path of healing'. Gibson was sentenced to three years on probation for his driving offences and ordered to attend self-help meetings. Following his arrest, his publicist released a press statement to the effect that the actor had entered a recovery programme to cope with his drinking problem.

In 2010 Gibson was again involved in bad publicity after transcripts of tapes of his menacing rants against his girlfriend and mother of one of his children, Oksana Grigorieva, appeared in the press. Gibson was heard launching a verbal fusillade against Grigorieva. In the words of the *New York Times* op-ed columnist David Brooks:

> He pummels her honour, her intelligence, her womanhood, her maternal skills and everything else. Imagine every crude and derogatory word you've ever heard. They come out in waves. He's not really arguing with her, just trying to pulverize her into nothingness, like some corruption that has intertwined itself into his being and now must be expunged. (David Brooks, 2010)

Narcissists resist taking responsibility for their own behaviour. Lousy conduct is always presented as a matter of exceptional external pressures and nameless demons that society has unleashed upon them. So Winona Ryder explained her shoplifting as a reaction to misdiagnosed painkillers, and Gibson, in a public apology to the Jewish community for his anti-Semitic outburst, referred to his abusive behaviour as 'insane' and 'a drunken display' (as if getting drunk was something visited upon him by some anonymous malevolent force and not his choice). Gibson's apology includes reference to his faith and describes himself and the Jewish community as 'God's children' (Gibson, 2006, *timesonline.co.uk).* The acknowledgement of character flaws is reminiscent of the public apology that Tiger Woods (2010) issued in respect of his repeated adultery.

The PR-Media logic is the same. Public apologies by celebrities are ritualized forms of behaviour. The disgraced hero must plead sincerely for public forgiveness and understanding before taking his rightful place back on the pedestal of fame. Acknowledgement of personal failings, the invocation of the pressures of the frontier existence of stardom, followed by a suitable period of contrition, often containing high-profile charity work, are de rigueur. The formatted, operatic nature of public celebrity apology may be driven by an authentic need for forgiveness, but it leaves many doubting if the plea is truly heartfelt. Cynics dismiss it as a weapon in the arsenal of exposure management. Certainly, Gibson's public apology for his anti-Semitic barrage did not prevent him from contemptible behaviour against Grigoreiva four years later.

Yet, because celebrity public apologies highlight narcissistic traits that are widely distributed in the population, they often generate a compassionate response. In letting it all hang out and demanding understanding of the audience, celebrities walk the same line as many ordinary people in 'bus class'. The demand expressed here is urgent and apparently inexhaustible. Everyone wants to be recognized. It is entirely natural. But when the demand for admiration and sympathy is disproportionate and inexorable, it suggests a malady rather than health. In creating the ubiquitous demand for adulation and recognition in the midst of achievement famine, society contributes to the froth of celebrity culture. It also produces strong narcissistic tendencies among ordinary people that can only be supported fitfully and inadequately by fantasies of hero worship and narcissistic idealization.

Religion, and its decline in the West

In traditional society, organized religion provided a compass for life that was socially recognized and universally accepted. The Church gave purpose to life and extended a moral code that everyone comprehended. The word of God was the glue of society. To spend one's days faithfully and charitably observing the deity was God's will. The Church consecrated the word of God through the clergy and strict religious observance.

Christian religion in traditional society was organized around a divide between the sacred world of the deity and his holy retinue and the profane world of man. This division was so sharp and insistent that it led to the crystallization of various prohibitions and taboos against polluting the divide. In particular, representations of the deity and the sacred were closely scrutinized and policed to ensure the appropriate honour and respect due to them.

The modern concept of 'idol' has complex roots in the Greek terms, *eidos* meaning 'form'; *eidolos* meaning 'representative of form'; and *latreuein* meaning 'to serve, revere and adore'. *Webster's Dictionary* identifies five contemporary meanings of the term: a likeness of something; a visible form or appearance but without substance; an object of extreme devotion; a representative or symbol of an object of worship; a false conception or fallacy. Even in secular societies like our own, where religious belief in a divine creator is waning, the writ of monotheism runs right through many beliefs, opinions and practices.

Idols have traditionally carried a pejorative connotation in Western civilization. Christianity identifies them as prime battalions in Satan's army and contrasts them with the one true God. Judaism has a series of prohibitions against idolatry, with respect not merely to idolatrous objects, but idolatrous ideas and representations. It claims that to recognize idols is to deny the *Torah* or 'The Law of Moses'.

There are parallels in Islam. Muslims are enjoined to cleave to the virtue of *tawhid* (identifying with that which is 'one'). Here the sin of idolatry is not restricted to the worship of false gods. It extends to any urge or desire that deflects individuals and groups from practising *tawhid*. Lust, ego, the hunger for riches, fall under the sin of serving corruption.

Monotheism is the belief that the universe is created and governed by a single Supreme Being. It acknowledges no competitors with God, whether they be cast in the role of rival gods or mortals who see fit to emulate or, through their creations, symbolize the reverence due to God. The wrath that is often directed against idols derives from absolute belief in the divine creator.

Monotheism recognizes any deviation from the doctrine of one God, who has one voice and one purpose, as heretical. The system of education and law derives its authority from the system of religion that subjects the actions of individuals and groups to fundamental principles of divine judgement. There is a high degree of inflexibility around moral questions and legal rules. Matters of right and wrong may be widely debated but they are subject to the word of God and Allah, embodied in the Bible and the Koran.

In contrast, polytheism is a religious doctrine that acknowledges the existence of many gods. Worship is therefore associated with diversity, not only in the form of reverence imparted to the Deity, but also in the content of what the Deity constitutes. Polytheism respects religious difference. The system of education and law recognizes rights and demands responsibilities of different religious groups. Above all, it upholds the freedom to declare and practise many religious beliefs providing they remain within the letter of the civil law.

The secular alternative to theological models proposes that there is no God. Instead it encourages respect for various human qualities such as liberty, freedom, justice, vulnerability and mutual care. Secular societies are therefore associated with pluralism in culture and politics. The system of education and law is not based upon divine principles or theological dogma. Instead it is the expression of rational debate. Individuals are not obliged to obey cognitive or spiritual hierarchies based in divine or theological authority. They are at liberty to disagree with the law, and to change it if they so wish; they have an inalienable right to criticize elected rulers and foment opposition; and they have the right to think differently and make their thoughts heard providing that it does not involve injury to others.

Secular freedom is not without defects. It does not offer the comfort of believing that the world is subject to divine order or the moral belief that right unequivocally delivers might. Under polytheism, there is no belief in a universal divine order. Because of this, moral questions and legal rulings are often wrapped up in ambiguity, ambivalence and doubt. Unlike monotheism, there is always another point of view that might come into play. The absence of a strong dividing line between the sacred and profane means that religious belief is often parodied or recanted.

Monotheism breeds a kind of mono-mania that ruthlessly and simplistically divides the world into the sacred and profane with all of the divisions and rites of social inclusion and exclusion that accompany it. It is unable to tolerate difference or diversity. Certainly the censure directed against idolatry, the worship of idols, in monotheistic systems is generally out of all proportion to the threat they pose to the status quo.

The Biblical precedents of idolatry are unequivocal. According to Exodus (xxxii: 1–3), when Moses remained on the Holy Mount the people became agitated and petitioned Aaron to bring forth gods and make a calf out of molten gold. The people worshipped the molten calf for delivering them out of the land of Egypt, offered sacrifice and engaged in ludic pastimes. In Settim the people fornicated with the daughters of Moab and adored their gods (Numbers xxv, 1–3). After the death of Josue the children of Israel served Baalim and followed 'strange gods' (Judges ii, 11). Whenever Jehovah ruled that the children of Israel acted with evil intent he delivered them into the hands of their enemies.

Panics about idols and idolatry recur throughout Christian, Jewish and Islamic history. Religious art emerged in church decoration in the third century, and by the fourth century was widely established as a devotional accessory. The craze for holy images was an extension of the cult of the saints. Some early Christian theologians such as Vigilantius disapproved of the use of images in acts of worship. He argued that their expansion threatened to dilute the divine and weaken the channels for grace, mercy and salvation. Others, such as Augustine and Jerome, were more sanguine, holding that the desire for holiness in a locus such as a painting, carving or shrine, was a natural expression of devotion which the Church should gratify, albeit with the appropriate level of vigilance against a possible slide into idolatry. In the sixth century the cult of images developed massively, especially in the Eastern Church. In Byzantine culture, many icons acquired cult status provoking disquiet among clerics that culminated in the Iconoclastic controversy of the eighth century.

The crux of the issue was the nature of man's relation to God. Jews and Muslims rejected the use of visual images in religious worship on the grounds that they constituted blasphemous attempts to imitate God's will. Images, relics and cults around some saints threatened to intervene between man and God, thus offending the foundational principle of monotheism of the absolute, undefiled relation between the Supreme Being and his creations. Within Christianity a division emerged between those who embraced martyrdom rather than risk contamination from heathen gods and 'iconophiles' or 'iconodules' who cultivated the worship of images and cult objects.

The latter were doubtless influenced by the arguments of Pope Gregory I, who propounded the defence of icons on the grounds that they performed an educational function. For the illiterate, he maintained, icons were the *libri pauperum*. That is they afforded a tangible means to express devotion. On the whole, this defence was accepted by ecclesiastical circles who presided over the liberalization of devout belief about icons. For example, at the end of the eighth century, Charles the Great recognized the existence of sacred objects, the *res sacrata* (the eucharist, liturgical vessels, the cross, scriptures, relics of saints) but ruled that images could never be regarded as sacred.

In the twelfth century a *cultus divorum* developed around the saints who became objects of artistic veneration and popular devotion. This was expressed in the multiplication of images of the saints and representations of their deeds and a popular passion for holy relics, often manufactured and faked. The psychology of many believers became fixated upon representations and objects invested with holy reverence. For example, the Shrine of the Holy Cross at Tallard in France, which was believed to contain fragments from the saviour's cross, and which was purported to work miracles, became an object of pilgrimage. This provoked a degree of censure from the clergy and some scholars. Thus, Pierre d'Ailly's tract *De Reformatione* (1416) pointed to the abuses that followed from assigning exaggerated importance to saints and images. Likewise, Jean Gerson, in his *Expostulatio adversus corruptionem juventutis per lascivias imagenes* (1402), revived the anxiety that the craze around icons raised the serpent's head of idolatry. However, for the most part, the spirit of Gregory's *libri pauperum* was preserved in the Christian faith and a relatively relaxed attitude to religious icons prevailed until the late fifteenth and early sixteenth centuries when a new backlash occurred against 'false religions' and 'graven images'.

Historians of German evangelical reform in the sixteenth century have coined the maxim that Erasmus laid the egg that Luther hatched. Certainly, Erasmus disapproved of what he saw as the corruption of religious belief in the sixteenth century and argued for the revival of the values of the Apostolic Age. He held that pilgrims, veneration of the saints and worship of images and relics to be a deviation from the sacred culture of the deity. He advocated the cultivation of pietas, an orientation to religion that concentrated on inner substance and not outward show. In this he followed the gospel principle that 'it is the spirit that gives life, the flesh is of no avail' (John 6.63). His colloquies on 'Rash Vows' (1522) and 'A Pilgrimage For the Sake of Religion' (1526) repined the commercialization of piety. The pilgrimage, he maintained, was an occasion for irresponsibility and sin. It afforded the veneer of religiosity, but was really motivated by the vain wish to show off. Pilgrims desired to display their piety to others. If divine presence is universal, asked Erasmus, why should pilgrims believe Mercy to be concentrated in sites of pilgrimage such as Santiago and Walsingham?

Erasmus's fundamentalism offended the taste of many in the Church. As early as 1522 the Inquisitor of Louvain demanded the public burning of the Colloquies. The Theological Faculty of the Sorbonne also condemned them. But Erasmus's demand for the revival of pietas, and his rejection of religious ornamentalism, did not entirely fall on deaf ears. In particular, the poor and evangelical reformers among the clergy responded to his propositions that the culture of religious icons fragmented the deity and that the Church devoted excessive resources to the trappings of worship.

In 1522 Andreas Karlstadt (1480–1541), a colleague of Luther at the University of Wittenberg, published his tract *On the Abolition of Images*. It dismissed the *libri pauperum* by holding that the deity must be worshipped through spiritual engagement and not the material world. Karlstadt held that nothing belonging to God's divinity is to be transferred to relics, icons or the hosts of the Eucharist. He condemned the human imagination corrupted by the enchantment of material objects. These arguments produced social unrest in Wittenberg. Crowds smashed religious images, destroyed relics, overturned altars and fed consecrated hosts to dogs and goats.

At about the same time, in Zurich the reformist preacher Ulrich Zwingli (1484–1531) argued that man's love of created things produced 'strange gods' or *abgott*. Following Erasmus, he maintained that 'Christ alone' mediates between the deity and men. In his *Answer to Valentin Compar* (1525) he draws a sharp distinction between the creator and the created. The creator alone is acclaimed as the object of human worship. Created things exist only by the mercy of God. Therefore to venerate them is to turn against God. Interestingly, the argument acknowledges that false worship is often attached to abstract phenomena like money, glory and power. For Zwingli these inner wants are attractive because they contribute to men's sense of emplacement in the world. Idols are often the corporeal or spiritual representations of these wants. The argument moves from questions of religious doctrine to the psychological motivation behind idolatry. In Zwingli the proposition that the *abgott* is a manifestation of the perversity of the human imagination is born.

The attack on idolatry was given additional force in the sixteenth century by the writings of John Calvin. The essence of Calvinism is that men are created to know God and to contribute to his glory through worship and obedience. The argument in Erasmus and Zwingli that veneration of idols distracts men from the one and true relationship with the creator is repeated. Calvin rejected earthly or carnal conceptions of God on the principle that *finitum non est capax infiniti* (the finite cannot contain the infinite). The superiority of the spiritual over the material is the kernel of Calvinism. The spiritual is revealed to men only through Scripture. Man's knowledge of truth and divinity is impaired by the Fall, which deprived man of knowledge of the truth. Man retains a hunger for truth, but in the Fallen state can only grope blindly. The Fall then is crucial for Calvin. From it he deduces the sense of loss in human culture and the tendency toward corruption because men succumb to the temptation to fill the vacuum with idolatrous practice. In the state of sin man is drawn to the earth and the flesh as respite and diversion from the overwhelming loss of divine grace. In Calvin's view, idolatry reveals not faith in new gods but the depth of human desperation. Wrenched from God through original sin we cast about for man-made objects of worship. The honour due to God is therefore vitiated and the fallen state of humanity compounded. Hence, Calvin's proposal that the outward show of worship should be rejected, and his injunction that we must return to the truth of the Scriptures.

Monotheism, therefore, carries an integral tendency to wage war against idolatry. It compels us to reject false gods and it scorns human desire in the form of lust or avarice for affecting to replace God as the focal point of worship. More than this monotheism privileges original, primal authority in the creator in the constitution of culture and society. Upon this basis – the authority of the Supreme Being and his teachings to us in the form of Scripture – rests our earthly comprehension of right and wrong. The Manichean belief that the world is poised between absolute good and absolute evil reflects the belief in Christian monotheism of perpetual conflict between God and Satan. Idolatry does Satan's work because it deflects us from devoting our spoiled, fallen lives to the attainment of God's grace.

The fundamental questions in idolatry are therefore religious in character. They have to do with voluntarily replacing our quest for God's grace with the immediate gratification offered by false gods or the transfiguration of human desires into spiritual ends. Either way, the monotheistic case against idolatry holds that there is one true God and departures from this proposition are morally and spiritually unsound. Hence, the righteous nature of the indignation and censure that is directed against idols and idolatry.

For most people in the West, science and humanism have combined irresistibly to divest this entire cognitive and spiritual framework of a belief in the Deity. Organized religion is no longer the glue in society. Today, most people live without a religious compass. They have developed other means of direction, one of which is celebrity culture.

Incontrovertibly, for some time, in the West, organized Christian religion has been in transparent decline. In the USA 24.7 per cent of females under the age of 50 attend church once a week, rising to 37.7 per cent for the over 50s; for males the figures are 18.3 per cent of the under 50s and 32.2% of the over-50s. In Australia the figures are 5.4 per cent for females under 50, rising to 26.4 per cent for the over-50s; for males the figures are 11.7 per cent and 19.7 per cent respectively (Kirk et al., 1999). In the UK, the mean figure is 14 per cent (British Social Attitudes Survey, 2009). Of course, among ethnic and cultural minorities in these societies, such as the Islamic, Hindu or Buddhist communities, rates of participation in organized religion are much higher. This reflects the relatively marginal position of these communities in the power hierarchy and the related need to build strength through social inclusion.

However, if participation in Christian organized religion is falling, it does not follow that the cognitive and spiritual framework constructed around the belief in the Deity is now irrelevant. Sociologists have devised the term *religiosity* to refer to beliefs, dedication and practices that emerge via organized religion but are not, in all respects, necessarily, subject to its finite authority. For example, the modern belief in faith, hope and charity has its origins in the Bible, but it has outlived the death of God. In this it is not alone.

Today the strong tendencies of hero worship and narcissistic idealization refer back to the traditional religious binary divide between the sacred and profane. Demands for meaning that is greater than science, and more glamorous than humanism (which, after all, is based in the belief that men and women are cut from the same cloth), remain widely distributed. Without a religious compass to inform them, and still carrying fervour for a higher, dynamic direction, men and women have cast their nets around for various substitutes. Celebrity culture has filled the vacuum left by the waning of organized religion. The faith in fakes is an echo of idolatry which is bolstered by the realization that monotheism as a universal religion is dead.

The sheer illumination of celebrities via the PR-Media hub suggests larger than life figures who possess extraordinary powers. In the early days of Hollywood, the PR-Media hub described celebrities as 'gods' and 'goddesses'. It credited them with 'magic' and messianic 'spellbinding' power. Jean Harlow, Mary Pickford, Carole Lombard, Rudolph Valentino, Clark Gable, Gary Cooper and Cary Grant were celebrated, both as idealized representatives of the common man, who drew themselves up by their own bootstraps, and other-worldly figures in touch with higher forces. They were not called 'stars' for nothing. They showed people the way to brighter, more pure things and, as such, they were defined as inherently privileged.

In nearly all other respects, modern society prides itself on being gloriously free of primitive superstition and occult doctrine. Celebrity culture is the exception.

Dionysian, shamanic and demonic powers are often invoked upon their behalf. The concert performances of some rock stars are accredited by audiences with expanding consciousness, breaking down boundaries and engendering ecstatic emotion.

The parallel with religious transcendence has been drawn many times. Thus, Sylvan, commenting on the response of audiences to the West coast rock band The Grateful Dead, writes of the concert experience at its best in terms of 'epiphany, a visionary experience of mystical unity and identity much sought after in various esoteric religious traditions but seldom attained' (Sylvan, 2002: 96). This sounds like a manifestation of the gift of grace, and has prompted some observers to attribute charismatic power to the Dionysian rock star. In the age of philanthrocapitalism this claim is enlarged and reinforced as celebrities apply humanitarian political functions as fundraisers, charity spokespersons and campaigners. Bono, Annie Lennox, Bob Geldof, Michael Stipe, Sting and others, are not just pop aristocrats dominating the concert platform and creating a sensation whenever they are spotted in the streets. They are 'big citizen' deal-makers solving the world's problems in liaison with elected government leaders and charity personnel.

But all that glisters is not gold. The political power of celanthropists is limited and is not supported by electoral consent. Celanthropists make no special religious or occult claim for themselves. They are simply the recipients of abundant media interest and public acclaim. They cannot perform miracles, although the PR-Media hub sometimes uses techniques and hearsay to imply that the contrary is the case. Their conduct may raise consciousness, overturn received ideas and change public opinion. Their powers of revelation are limited. In short, they do not constitute a genuine revolutionary force.

The commodified magnetism that they possess is artfully tinged with religiosity. In applying it to fulfil commercial and humanitarian goals, they draw on the cognitive and spiritual framework of deistic society. They represent the popular demand for elevated meaning in life and the performance culture associated with them trades in motifs of unity, ecstasy and transcendence. Religiosity permeates the production, exchange and consumption of celebrity culture.

Elsewhere, I (Rojek, 2001) drew parallels between the cognitive and spiritual framework of celebrity culture and monotheism. Briefly, modern fans covet autographs, letters, cheque stubs, locks of hair, clothes, pens, keys, combs, glasses, cigarette butts, rings, cars, golf clubs, and other celebrity accessories with the same fervour as Christians in traditional society sought relics of the saints.

Modern fans are drawn to visit and pay homage to the physical settings of celebrity birth, life and death of celebrities just as pilgrims once came to reconsecrate holy places in the pilgrimages of the Middle Ages.

Believers adopted the dress, opinions and vernacular of the saints, just as modern fans copy the fashion, hairstyle and public pronouncements of celebrities.

Celebrities are not Messianic figures nor can they perform miracles. However, they are widely associated with special powers of healing and inspiration, People look up to them in private moments for strength, solace and guidance, just as God and the saints continue to fulfill these functions for Christians. While the media regularly condemns celebrity culture, the famous are widely and automatically twinned with the status of transcendence.

For many Christians the religious name day is of greater significance than their birthday. In celebrity culture popular recognition of the birthdays or dates of death of celebrities challenge the Christian precedent. Today it is an open question whether the anniversary of a celebrity birth or death means more to most people than the commemoration of their own saint's day. But the fact that the question is open at all reveals much about the change in popular loyalties and priorities.

Celebrities then are the 'Strange Gods', the *abgott,* of the secular day. Their ministry is pursued in the concert stadium, the TV studio and through the cinema screen rather than the pulpit, church or cathedral. Nonetheless, they answer to the popular demand for bigger truths and transcendence in life. Metaphorically, at their best, they clothe our naked fears that life is meaningless and that existence has no purpose beyond the Darwinian impulse to survive and procreate.

At bottom, the condescending attitude of the media to celebrity culture is a comment on the naivety and superficiality of people who search for bigger truths and higher meaning in post-religious society. Yet in making their case the media also reveal how compliant they are with the trappings of religiosity and the deistic cognitive and spiritual framework. For beyond the canard that people who search for bigger truth and higher meaning are naive and superficial is the defence that scientific, humanistic truth is privileged. The attack on celebrity froth is fundamentally a campaign against imposture. Celebrities are framed as idols who challenge the priority of science and humanism. They work their magic on audiences by alchemy rather than testable propositions. In setting themselves up as larger than life figures they offend the humanist principle that we are all cut from the same cloth. Since there are no valid truths other than those supplied by science and humanism, the popularity of celebrity culture must be strafed and blitzed. It must be subject to denial in order to preserve the rule of science and humanism.

Of course, it is right to observe that there are some contemporary celebrities who are partly famous for their public fidelity to science and humanism. Richard Dawkins, Christopher Hitchens, Noam Chomsky, Bill Gates, Bill Mather and George Soros come to mind. However, in modern achieved celebrity culture they are exceptions. Overwhelmingly, the majority of celebrities are famous not for their atheistic or democratic views but for their glamour, talents and accomplishment. These are the very qualities that are both acclaimed and scrutinized by the media. Gossip columnists, bloggers and show business reporters devote a good deal of time to the task of showing us that our idols have feet of clay. The keen media interest in questions of bribery, adultery, pride and excess is part of a more fundamental concern with the question of celebrity and imposture. Far from being 'modern', this question reaches back to the sacred and profane division in traditional society – in other words, the belief in the absolute division between ultimate truth and the flotsam and jetsam of human deceit and duplicity. It also raises older questions concerning the relationship between appearance and reality and performance and truth. These questions are intensified in a society organized around the PR-Media hub and visual culture. For in these conditions a significant proportion of personal experience is not structured around the social, but the para-social. But what is really meant by *para-social*?

8 Para-social Relationships

The inflation of celebrity culture owes much to the social context in which it emerged and flourished. How might we characterize this context? There have been numerous attempts to pin down the main features of modern life compared with conditions in traditional society. It would be laborious, and, to be sure, a needless diversion, to go into the details again here.[1] What emerges most forcefully is that modern life has many conditions that render it peculiarly susceptible to *intimacy between strangers.*

Richard Schickel (1975) gets it right, when he posits that this is the crux of celebrity culture. Our reliance upon truth and opinion through visual culture rather than face-to-face contact; the geographic and social mobility which tears us away from our roots; the strains of family life, reflected in high rates of divorce and the expansion in numbers of children with antisocial attitudes; the growth of flexitime, working from home, Web labour and flexible lifestyles, which multiply diversity and variation in everyday life and weaken the traditional notion of community – these are some of the chief conditions to which commentators like Schickel refer. They are associated with specific psychological and cultural effects. Geographic and social mobility slackens the hold of community ties and renders the extended family mostly invisible.

Ernest Gellner captured this condition of life very well when he wrote:

> Optional human relations in fluid sub-communities have become – at any rate for members of the white collar classes and upward in affluent liberal societies – the very centre of life, the area where happiness or misery is decided; and they are menacing, incomprehensible and uncontrollable. To face them without support or solace is unthinkable. Yet where can we turn? (Gellner, 1985: 36–7)

In Gellner's day, and to his evident aggravation, he judged the first important port of call for support and solace to be psychiatry. Gellner was a master thinker, albeit occasionally an unjust and cantankerous critic. His squib is designed to expose what he took to be the shallow pretensions of the psychiatric profession. Whether or not this is a worthy goal is beyond the scope of this book. What we can say is that we contemporaries do not necessarily turn to psychiatry as the first port of call for support and solace. In the wrap-around, 24-hour media world we look elsewhere: celebrity culture. The *abgott* offer escapism, life-coaching and presumed intimacy in lives floating in – to repeat Gellner's phrase – 'fluid sub-communities'.

The notion of presumed intimacy between strangers is enormously fruitful for understanding modern celebrity culture. We live in an era of para-social relationships. That is overlying the primary relationships of family and community, we inescapably enter into webs of intimacy with celebrities that are based on impersonal print, photographic and electronic systems of communication. If the conditions are amenable, we connect with these prominent media figures as people in the know, learned commentators, holy fools, victims who require our help (if only they knew), people who we would like to be, beautiful people, friends. The rub is that our knowledge of these stars is mostly second hand and, further, we are usually total strangers to them.

Celebrity power ultimately depends upon the acclaim of fans. However, despite participating in blog sites, interviews, fan conventions and press events, stars maintain considerable spatial and social distance from fans. The essence of the star is to be out of the reach of ordinary people. Characteristically, it is mostly a one-sided, non-reciprocal relationship. For all the inside dope, the tales of chance meetings, the bits and bobs from Web chat rooms that afford fans the secrets and low-down on celebrity culture, the balance of power in information and opinion shaping is overwhelmingly in the hands of the celebrity and the adjoining PR-Media hub.

In the period before electronic communication, print culture provided glimpses of neurotic and obsessional tendencies in fans. From time to time, celebrity authors and national politicians were certainly plagued by adoring fans who supposed that, by virtue of being familiar with their words in print, they were on intimate terms with them. Abraham Lincoln deliberately exploited this intimacy for publicity purposes in his meetings with ordinary people in Washington during the conduct of the Civil War, as did Charles Dickens in his famous reading tours of Britain and America in which he portrayed characters from his fiction to adoring fans.

But the transition to visual culture vastly enlarged and greatly intensified the phenomenon. The electronic media have normalized para-social relationships. Now, it is as natural for infants to solidify emotional and psychological attachments and seek role models in Britney or Paris, as it is to form bonds of love with their brothers and sisters and look up to their parents. Understandably, the situation breeds confusion about lines of authority, systems of truth and contours of belonging.[2]

The term 'para-social relationships' captures this complex set of developments. It was coined by Horton and Wohl and refers to 'the illusion of face-to-face relationships with the performer' (Horton and Wohl, 1956: 35). The power and clarity of Horton and Wohl's discussion of this branch of celebrity culture reflects an engagement with forms of televisual self-promotion and impression management that were brand new at the time. The 1950s decade was the moment of the birth of new public personalities like continuity staff, chat-show hosts, weather forecasters, newsreaders, as well as TV playlet, comedy and soap stars. For Horton and Wohl, the new presenters did not usually promote themselves as truly larger than life stars. These promotional devices were mainly employed in other branches of the entertainment sector, particularly the Hollywood film industry. Rather, the first wave of TV celebrities typically adopted the personae of peers. They used the model of direct address, which relates to invisible spectators by talking to them personally and confidentially. Building ratings depends upon presumed intimacy between the presenter and the audience. This often entails the audience amassing feelings for the presenter as a friend, a confidante or a trustworthy counsellor. However, unlike face-to-face (primary) relationships, the role of the presenter is formatted by managers to represent a specific public personality type. In other words, it is not an 'innocent' type of communication, but a type of exchange intended to mould public opinion.

Typical methods of interaction favoured by managers are to encourage presenters to engage in small talk and impromptu asides. Despite obviously having greater wealth and public influence than most of the spectators who watch them, presenters harp on the humdrum nature of their lives. The aim is to come over as a regular guy, just like you and me. These interactive methods contribute to the illusion of an unscripted, 'natural' exchange between equals and diverts the attention of the audience from the impersonality of the medium of interaction (the broadcast signal). By these means, affinity between the presenter and the viewer is engineered.

The public personality type of presenters is a facade that often bears nothing more than a loose connection with the private life of the 'real' person. However, because television permits para-social exchange in the home, and also because it allows interaction to carry a sense of evolution, it can result in unusually powerful emotional attachments between spectators and presenters. Spectators have no obligation or responsibility to presenters. They can withdraw at any moment. However, if they stay engaged they may become hooked. Isolated and lonely people are vulnerable to developing what Horton and Wohl refer to as 'extreme para-sociability' with certain presenters (Horton and Wohl, 1956: 45). That is fantasies of intimacy and solidarity that carry over into primary relationships. A slippage between the impersonal world of commercially organized television and ordinary day-to-day relationships occurs. As such, the authors provide an embryonic version of the fame attack thesis, since they plainly identify extreme para-sociability with entering a world of fantasy relations and delusions in which unhealthy neuroses and morbid obsessions may supplant primary relationships.

Typically, when people interact with someone playing a well-defined, formatted public role they experience discomfort. For example, when we engage with a judge, a policeman, a medical doctor or a social worker, we are conscious of a degree of formality, rigidity and inequality. This may make us guarded in what we say and watchful of how the exchange occurs. It is probable that we will not offer confidences and apply a measure of discretion in what we disclose. This translates into a degree of emotional separation from the people occupying these roles. We may be polite and up to a point, forthcoming, but the spontaneity and trust that obtains in everyday conversations is often reserved.

With para-social relationships involving a celebrity, most of this does not apply. The relationship is based upon presumed intimacy. A sense of fraternity is deliberately mustered and applied. The presenter may be direct, confrontational and outspoken in ways that we would wish to be given half the chance. In this sense it is reasonable to propose that some celebrities allow us to play out our fantasies for public recognition and advocacy. The chat-show hosts David Letterman, Graham Norton, Jonathan Ross, Conan O'Brien and Oprah Winfrey are adept in portraying themselves as substitutes for the man and woman in the street. Just as celanthropy has produced Bono, Bob Geldof, Madonna, Angelina Jolie, George Clooney, Annie Lennox, Michael Stipe, Leonardo DiCaprio, Mia Farrow, Jay-Z, Naomi Watts and others, as stars with a heart, ready to devote part of their fame to the achievement of humanitarian relief. They have the assurance to put to the media what is on the minds of Everyman. In this, they can assume a degree of common ground with the public.

Public acclaim is seductive. For some celebrities who are inured to being the subjects of narcissistic idealization and hero worship it may produce a dangerous sense of invulnerable assurance and vigilante law. In 2009 Kayne West swept on stage at the MTV Music Video Awards as 19-year-old country singer Taylor Swift was accepting the award for Best Female Video and proclaimed that Beyoncé would have been a more deserving winner. The intrusion was widely condemned as rude and insensitive. West was forced to go on the Jay Leno show to issue a public apology. It is an example of a celebrity who believes himself above the rules, someone who has the confidence to believe that he speaks for the public despite being unequipped with a formal endorsement to do so.

A primary conduit of knowledge about common ground is focus group research sponsored by chat show producers into the concerns and opinions of the audience. Via the PR-Media hub and informal chat networks, the public is supplied with morsels of knowledge about the private lives of celebrities. On the other side, the PR-Media hub schools the celebrity to engage in formatted, closely manicured presentations that are designed to mould public opinion in predetermined ways. Chat-show and talk-show hosts appear to occupy the middle ground, between the star and the stargazer. In reality, the thrust of their questions is also mostly pre-determined with the input of specialized PR-Media personnel and they have been coached in mannerisms and television patois designed to produce presumed intimacy.

Today, star chat- and talk-show hosts like Larry King, David Letterman, Jonathan Ross, Oprah Winfrey, Conan O'Brien and Graham Norton may cultivate a regular guy persona. By identifying with the ordinary man and woman, and using unscripted, impromptu asides as people do in ordinary conversation, they stress their unity with the public. They are non-politicized 'big citizens' who on television and elsewhere strive to give the impression that they speak and behave as the ordinary citizen would if they had the means to occupy the public role.

Celebrity icons

This is a qualitatively different type of para-social relationship from that between a celebrity who presents the formatted role of a fame icon based upon presumed intimacy with the public. Celebrities like Britney Spears, Jay-Z, Beyoncé, Paris Hilton, Jodie Marsh, Simon Cowell and Kanye West, are often portrayed in the media and perceived by the public as divas and prima donnas. Although they may engage in impromptu asides and occasionally cast themselves as regular guys, the locus of their fame resides in being more glamorous, wealthier, having more glitzy appeal, business opportunities and being free of normal social conventions.

These are the celebrities who present a public image of living a frontier existence in which emotional and psychological pressures are greater than for the ordinary person. As a result, the normal rules of everyday life do not apply. Theirs is the world of private airplanes, helipads, chauffeur-driven stretch limos, maids, personal chefs, bodyguards, tantrums, enormous performance fees and heedless consumption. The PR-Media hubs that work for them want the public to know it. For celebrity icons the nucleus of fame is a public image of exoticism. They are the rare and colourful birds of the jungle. They fly higher than other celebrities and the rest of us. So their demand for public attention knows no limits. They are stellar.

The term 'celebrity icon' has interlaced meanings. It refers to an exotic star, whose life may act as a cultural biography of the times. In addition, celebrity icons often attract and represent sectional, devotional interests and these are commonly rooted in generations. Thus, Pete Townshend, Bob Dylan, Joni Mitchell, Johnny Rotten, Boy George, Kurt Cobain, the late Michael Jackson, Lil Kim, Rihanna and Jay-Z are iconic figures for emergent youth subcultures who define themselves in opposition to dominant and residual cultures.[3]

It is an error to assume that cultural icons are confined to generations. They also represent separate social, political and religious sectional interests. Thus, Bob Marley remains an icon for postcolonial black rights; long before his untimely death, the singer Nusrat Fateh Ali Khan became an icon for Sufi devotional music (*Qawwali*), which is closely identified with Islam and Muslim rights, and 2Pac and

The Notorious B.I.G. symbolized the inequality and injustice in American society that was meted out to large sections of the Afro-American community.

Celebrity icons are like living artworks in that they are designed to vividly portray and often, through their dress and mannerisms, deliberately exaggerate, wider social, political and religious values of specific human groups. The exoticism of the celebrity icon is therefore not confined to the self-interest of the star. It represents sections of the public who regard themselves as being, in some sense, oppressed or thwarted and seek a resplendent figurehead. So celebrity icons are frequently linked with gay interests, animal rights, racial minorities, prisoners or religious sects.[4] In representing one stratum of society, celebrity icons adopt forms of dress and public mannerisms that distance them from dominant and residual cultures. However, while their role as living artworks heightens the aesthetic dimension of their appearance, it is frequently connected to a broader domain of political, cultural or religious preferences. Through adornment and public appearances, celebrity icons use fame to speak for others who are too powerless and dispersed to have a coherent public voice in the media.

Lady Gaga: Gay icon

Lady Gaga, whom *Forbes* business magazine (May 2011) currently rates as the most powerful woman in the entertainment business, is an interesting case in point. She is notorious for her provocative music and outrageous fashion. The famous meat dress that she wore to the MTV Music Video Awards (2010) gained gigantic media attention. Yet celebrity commentators were quick to suggest meanings that go beyond the common reaction of personal attention-seeking behaviour.

Andrew Groves, course director of a degree in fashion design at the University of Westminster, maintained that the dress was an anti-fashion statement. At an historical moment when unauthorized downloading is undermining the music industry, he argued, the dress symbolized that the public interest in music stars today is not about music but about appearance. Because this fashion statement was made at a high-profile music awards ceremony, it was subversive. It used fashion as politics.

More conventionally, other commentators interpreted the dress as a feminist statement that female singers are treated by the industry, and regarded by large sections of the public, as pieces of meat, rather than artists. Other commentators regarded the dress as a comment on ageing, since meat is only fresh for so long. Thus, Richard Noble, an art academic based at Goldsmiths College, speculated that the dress was a reference to a meat sculpture by the Canadian artist Jana Sterbak (Winterman and Kelly, 2010).

Some of these interpretations seems somewhat laboured and, in the case of the comparison with Jana Sterbak, downright far-fetched. Lady Gaga is also a celebrated gay icon. A more tenable interpretation might pursue a more thorough examination of this connection. Hence, Lady Gaga wore the dress in the same month as she made a public speech in Portland, Maine and issued a *YouTube* video against gay discrimination in the US military. In the speech she stated that 'equality is the prime rib of America.' This is a pretty big clue which relates the dress directly to her attack on homophobia in the military and to enhance her status as a gay icon.

Celebrity icons are very often the public face of wider social movements. In the 1970s, the glam rock stars David Bowie and Marc Bolan were poster stars for the movement of bisexuality and gay liberation. Through their dress, use of cosmetics, spoken values and mannerisms, they challenged not merely heteronormative domination, but all types of established cultural rule. Elton John, who in the television documentary 'Tantrums and Tiaras' (1997) exemplified the larger than life, frontier existence of the celebrity icon, is also a famous spokesman and symbol for gay rights.

The dress and public attitude of Madonna in the 1980s performed a similar function. Madonna has a substantial gay following, but her larger fan base is the so-called 'new woman'. This generation defined itself partly in opposition to 1960s and 1970s feminism, by adopting cosmetics and fashion designed to signify sexual attraction and power. Rather than dressing down, they dressed up. Madonna represented this social movement and through her music and stage shows proseltyized the image of the sexy, clever new woman who was aware of her sexuality, conscious of, and sympathetic to wider forms of injustice and intolerance and fully savvy with the necessary tricks of forcing the media to play to their tune.

There is no special need to add to the list. Celebrity icons occupy a pedestal in celebrity para-social relationships. They symbolize not merely glamour but sexual assertion, generational difference and the promulgation of much wider rules of social inclusion and exclusion. Madonna's hit single 'Papa Don't Preach' (1986) was not just a female affirmation of generational freedom and responsibility, it artfully counterposed the values of the new woman with the baggage of old, discredited models of female submissiveness and dowdiness.

Analogously, Lady Gaga's meat dress is more than a fashion statement to publicize gay rights, it is part of a structural landscape that is intended to absolutely distinguish one system of cultural values from others that are regarded as dominant and prejudicial. Celebrity icons act as dramatic shorthand for complex social divisions and fissile cultural distinctions.

Totemic celebrity

One might even say that cultural icons have a totemic significance in celebrity para-social relationships. What is meant by this? In Sir James Frazer's classic account, *Totemism and Exogamy* (1909: 4–5), totems are not idols or fetishes. Rather, they are representational symbols portraying 'an imaginary brotherhood' that conveys meaning, ritual and unity to the group. Totems establish lines of demarcation that enable one group of people to separate themselves emotionally, politically, psychologically and culturally from other groups. Social inclusion and social exclusion follows demarcation lines and is automatically recognized by groups on both sides of the divide.

Anthropologists have regarded totemism as a characteristic of the earliest, most impressionable societies. Because life was so uncertain and mysterious in these societies, certain groups developed a propensity to seek meaning and solidarity in symbols of semi-fathomable superhuman forces (Levi Strauss, 1968).

We like to think that modern society has moved on from the world of the earliest peoples. However, semi-fathomable worship of incoherent, powerful forces is surely at the heart of celebrity worship syndrome and narcissistic idealization. These forces require the celebrity to be spatially and culturally remote, just as totems in the earliest societies were symbolically separated from the people. If, through emulation or physical propinquity, the people came too close to the totem, its power was held to be polluted.

Modern celebrities use conspicuous consumption, outlandish behaviour, outspoken views and outrageous fashion to signify distance and immunize themselves from pollution. Very few people would exactly want to dress like Lady Gaga. By dressing outrageously she minimizes opportunities for social encounters that are not on her terms. Would you really want to mingle with a woman wearing a meat dress? The more common response is to ogle. As a modern cultural totem, Lady Gaga and the meat dress establishes immediate lines of demarcation. You instantly know which side you are on. The exoticism of the fashion translates into being above the mundane considerations of ordinary life. Lady Gaga does not live with Zeus. But her dress and mannerisms powerfully articulate complex social and cultural distinctions that place her as an inhabitant of a latter-day Mount Olympus, categorically separate from life in the lower territories.

Totems are striking, notable representations. For this reason they are likely to figure prominently on the radar of the media, and generate opinion and discussion. Whatever else one might say about Lady Gaga's flamboyance, it certainly, currently receives intense media coverage. This raises her personal profile and, as such, it may be interpreted sarcastically as a cynical method of self-promotion. Conversely, her public profile enables her platform statement criticizing discrimination against gays in the US military to be widely reported. So her status as a totem for gay rights has a demonstrable publicity dividend. It classically executes Bernays's advice to leaders to use drama and incident to generate leverage with the media (Bernays, 1928, 1935).

Syndicated fraternization

The relationship between celebrity icons, celebrity totems or what have you, and an 'imaginary brotherhood' is based in the idea of fraternization. In the digital age the fraternization at issue here is very different from ordinary face-to-face encounters (Castells, 2009). Crucially, it is mediated through a system of communication (a television screen, a computer interface, a mobile phone), it does not require focused attention and it is sponsored by a commercial or public service broadcasting organization. I can watch Oprah Winfrey live, but I can detach myself from the flow of conversation and ignore large sections of the transmission. If I did this in an ordinary face-to-face encounter, it would produce conflict. So celebrities use various strategies and techniques to create the protocol of fraternization with the audience in order to stimulate relations of closeness and intimacy. The aim is to build amity and solidarity through the personal touch. By virtue of their appearance, mannerisms and public statements, the celebrity expresses brotherhood with structurally specific emotional preferences, cultural values and lifestyle predicaments. This may take the form of knowing asides, tactful observations, jokes or political statements that the celebrity uses to establish rapport with the viewers. Building and sustaining confidence is a prerequisite of fraternization.

The celebrity icon is not the achievement of direct, co-present, collective organization and collective action. True, there is a sense in which a live TV broadcast is a collective, co-operative enterprise. The TV presenter addresses the studio audience. Questions and comments from the floor are part of *Oprah, Jerry Springer* and other popular TV talk shows. However, the audience at home is not strictly speaking co-present since they are at liberty to ignore most or all of the conventions that apply to ordinary face-to-face conversations. Celebrities and the studio audience do not directly monitor the audience at home (although the views and other responses of the latter may eventually be gleaned by focus groups, telephone surveys and the like). Likewise, the audience at home is under no obligation to engage with the studio exchange. Yet of course, the awareness of the celebrity host and the studio audience that they are participating in a live event, and that there is an invisible audience at home, influences the forms of talk, mannerisms and style of live exchange (Livingstone and Lunt, 1994: 55).

Of course, sponsorship influences the structure of communication. Public service and commercial broadcasting syndicate different cultures of fraternization. The former encourages affinity around values of education, impartiality, probity and artistic merit. These values are also cultivated by commercial broadcasting, but the latter operates in a context in which ratings wars and advertising revenue exert greater influence on programme-making and scheduling.

Fraternization requires the PR-Media hub to provide consumers of celebrity culture with prep-talk. The term prep-talk refers to personal information, planted gossip, potted histories and psychological insights that relate to the celebrity. This may be achieved through a variety of means, of which trailers, magazine interviews, gossip columns and entertainment pages, are central. Prep talk prepares consumers to interact with celebrities as known quantities. Fraternization emerges around personal data which seems to be shared but is mostly strategically placed by the PR-Media hub. We know that Oprah is today one of the richest and most influential talk-show hosts in the world. She is so famous that she is immediately recognizable by her Christian name alone. This is a distinction achieved by only a handful of celebrities. But most of us also know that hers is a rags to riches story. Born illegitimate in poverty in Mississippi, her ascent is often taken as a textbook example of the American dream. The release of personal data is rationed and accented by the PR-Media hub in order to achieve social impact. Despite the immense differences in wealth between her and the general public, we see ourselves on the same team as Oprah because we know that she was born on the wrong side of the tracks and made it by willpower, talent and hard work. Fraternization then is syndicated around a celebrity brand with a view to promoting celebrity affinity and idealization among the public.

The word 'syndicate' is used to emphasize the controlled, goal-driven nature of the communication. The PR-Media hub aims to build the celebrity brand as an icon or artefact that achieves general public recognition and scores a high impact rating with the public. The release of private data, particularly celebrity 'secrets', is essential to this process. It creates the preconditions for presumed intimacy with the audience.

It can be easily appreciated why this relationship is often conceived in terms of inequality and manipulation. Stars have great cultural power. This power may certainly be used to manipulate public opinion in ways that enhance the economic and cultural power of the star and the commercial interests that the star represents rather than the common good. But there is nothing intrinsic in the communication process that is predisposed to manipulation. The physical and social distance between the star and the stargazer is now so immense that strong brands are required to organize emotional identification and commercially meaningful fraternization with audiences. The trick for the PR-Media hub is to develop iconic messages and dramatic symbols that are communicated in the blink of the eye. The more that the ratio of contact is predisposed to instant identification rather than thought, the greater will be the initial investment of advertising and public relations. If this is achieved, physical and social distance is suspended, and a sense of fraternity with the celebrity icon ensues. The aim is not to hoodwink the audience, but to create a mainline route to their attention.

Fraternization is the key because it denotes the impression of friendship, shared understanding, common ground and other features of reciprocity between the celebrity icon and the audience. In this way, the audience is encouraged to 'know' the celebrity without ever physically meeting them. Bernays wrote: 'Today's leaders have become more remote physically from the public; yet, at the same time, the public has much greater familiarity with these leaders through the system of modern communications' (Bernays, 1947: 114).

In the United States and Britain this has long been apparent in electoral politics. Presidential and prime ministerial candidates with a strong message, and a clear, uncomplicated image, get elected and re-elected. Think of Ronald Reagan, Bill Clinton, Margaret Thatcher and Tony Blair. Candidates with a complex message and a fuzzy image fall by the wayside. Who now remembers Walter Mondale, Michael Dukakis, John Kerry, Iain Duncan Smith or Michael Howard?

The personal element provided by celebrities and the PR-Media hub is the key to the 'imaginary brotherhood' of syndicated fraternization. But the promotion of, and reaction to, this personal element is different in kind to everyday encounters. The imaginary brotherhood is based on remote physical and social relationships and is organized around facades that limit opportunities for spontaneity.

For example, Lady Gaga is an image. More than this, she is an image formatted by the cultural intermediaries that she works with to produce a facade to produce a calculated range of impact factors with the public. Her concerts are advertised as genuinely live on stage without miming – a point that she often highlights by breathing heavily into the on-stage mic when she finishes her numbers. In relating to the facade, we do not refer to the real person. For how can we know who the real person (Stefani Joanne Angelina Germanotta) is behind the Lady Gaga persona? Lady Gaga obviously performs in public and attends public events. Unauthorized data about Lady Gaga that might run counter to the facade, may be produced and exchanged through blog sites, chat-room sites and other mechanisms. Unquestionably, there is an interplay between the airbrushed, manicured image of a cultural icon and unregulated communication. In certain conditions data and opinions from unauthorized sources can provide a counter-image with sufficient strength and momentum to dent or transform the iconic facade. It is not a zero-sum game between authorized and unauthorized sources, but it is an unequal one. Exposure to the brand is continuous, ubiquitous and high profile, whereas unauthorized exchange networks typically operate on a disorganized, dispersed and episodic basis. It is the brand that hogs the limelight and, if properly managed, seizes public opinion.

If it is right to propose that the brand is contrived and the celebrity icon is an artifact that has no necessary relationship with reality, our relationship is not really with a person but with a thing, This may lead to intense levels of emotional connection between the audience and the celebrity, but it also carries limitations. Strong brands breed tunnel vision. Once a celebrity icon is established, the expectations of the audience are quite set. Variations of radical transformations of the facade of the celebrity icon are risky. Once you expect Lady Gaga to be the meat-dress lady, you feel short-changed or cheated when she dresses down.

The thing-like facade is intended to produce programmed responses, but this often carries over into a condition of estrangement in which the celebrity feels at growing odds with the public persona.

If the celebrity icon is a facade that is powder-puffed and blushed-up to achieve commercially meaningful syndicated fraternization, it may become an iron mask that the celebrity is forced to wear in order to gain acclaim. The public face of the star, which may be defined as the facade constructed by the PR-Media hub, is often privately experienced by the star as a prosthetic device that ceases to have a positive value after social impact is launched and achieved. Privately, the star may come to feel engulfed and suffocated by the public face of the celebrity icon. This often produces the urge in some celebrities to subvert the para-social relationship with the audience.

The list of stars who have attempted to step out of the mirror of para-social illusions is a long one. One thinks of John Lennon and his attempt to demythologize the public face of *The Beatles* (Wenner, 1981); Kurt Cobain's suicide in 1994, which, according to his suicide note, was prompted by a strong sense of being trapped by a phony show biz image; Britney Spears's decision in 2007 to shave her hair, which was widely interpreted as an impulsive, emotional bid to shed her glitzy Hollywood image; and, of course, the list of child stars who had well-documented, agonizing problems in struggling with their adolescent public celebrity face as they grew older, which I discussed in Chapter 2.

Para-social relationships, then, enable recognition and reciprocity. However, because they are based in the representation of a facade (a thing), not a person, they are not quite the same as connections and conversations that we have in ordinary life.

Ordinary conversations: The value of access, utility and labour

Of course, it would wrong to infer that the conversations in ordinary life are not formatted. Effective social life depends upon scripted roles. But in everyday relationships the scripts are not ordinarily well defined. Even among primary relationships, exchanges carry latitude for spontaneity and departure from scripts. There is much less latitude in conversations between a star and a stargazer because each has expectations of the other based on structural inequality.

If we think of social connections and conversations in structural terms they consist of three elements: access, utility and labour. The combination of these elements determines the value of the relationship.

Access refers to the ease and flexibility of contact. Continuous, engaged, relaxed feedback in multiple settings is the cornerstone of getting to know someone. This implies recognition of co-presence and respect for personal space. Usually it entails the acknowledgement of vulnerability since this builds trust in the relationship. If I have a fear of swimming and you acknowledge it, a toehold of emotional rapport is likely to follow. If you scoff at my fear, I may take this as a callous or out-of-tune response and become emotionally withdrawn. Acknowledging mutual vulnerability is one of the ways in which we build trust with one another, just as exploiting vulnerability is one of the most serious ways of overstepping the mark and breaching trust.

The prototype of ordinary access is the conversation in which we focus on interaction with another person and have a sense of mutual development.

If we interact with someone who seems emotionally wooden, narrowly intent on the business at hand, irrespective of other relevant considerations, such as our feelings or point of view, we withdraw. Access may be relatively open in term of time, but the scripted character of the exchange is experienced as off-putting. In everyday life, emotional commitments usually develop from unscripted exchanges in which we have the impression of getting to know the real person.

Access may, of course, produce the opposite effect. Even when we feel that we have gotten to know the real person, it may be that extended, focused interaction creates resistance, opposition and terminates in rift. However, limited access prejudices the evolution of the relationship and typically induces emotional withdrawal. This applies to the rationing of encounters. There may be some truth in the adage that absence makes the heart grow fonder. It is certainly true that relationships can persist and even develop (through Internet, phone and letters) without face-to-face contact. However, ordinarily prolonged rationing culminates in emotional disinvestment. Achieving access is one reason why people live together. It is a precondition of primary relationships and extends to relationships between parents and children, siblings, kinship networks and friendships.

Utility refers to the uses that we amass and apply from the relationship. If someone makes us feel good about ourselves and we develop the reciprocal sense of being good for them, we form close ties that enhance our mutual attraction and emotional security. Utility is a key resource in self-promotion and impression management.

If a relationship establishes a sense of positive use, it is life enhancing. The greatest utility of all is the state of love, in which the relationship 'naturally' fulfils our intellectual, spiritual, emotional and erotic needs. When we are in love we are conscious of an equilibrium that extends beyond the confines of personal psychology into our social relationships. Everything seems to flow.

Utility is perfectly compatible with extreme pragmatism. We may need someone to care for us, or listen to our troubles or enhance our personal status, but this can lead to one-sided, negative loops of behaviour. Gaining satisfaction from someone may be achieved by exploitation and abuse. We may seek to play a zero-sum game in which we take but never give (or vice versa). In some relationships, utility works like this. So it is right to say that utility is not always a matter of positive experience. Indeed, the seat of utility is emotional need and this may be expressed in irrational, harmful types of conduct.

Labour refers to the quantity and quality of physical, mental and emotional energy expended in a relationship. To achieve access and utility requires work. Not only do we make ourselves available for focused encounters, we monitor the quality of the exchanges. Emotional labour involves developing and applying the relationship and people skills that bring the best out of people and help us achieve our goals. Labour is a means of accessing utility. The more effort we put into doing something, the more chance we have to learn and assimilate transferable skills.

There is a lot of misunderstanding about emotional labour. It is often applied to putting people at their ease and making them feel good about themselves. But it is not intrinsically about caring for others. Emotional labour may be mostly driven by narcissism, dedicated to getting one's own way and enhancing self-esteem. It may be a life strategy that goes with narcissistic idealization and hero worship.

If labour makes us closer to another, it also exposes us and increases our obligation to create time and space and produce systems of monitoring that protect and enhance the relationship. The strength of the relationship is directly related to judgements about the competence of the labour used to sustain it. If we feel that the person talking to us does not really understand where we are coming from or misreads our intentions, we become emotionally ruffled and may disinvest and eventually disengage. Ordinarily, making relationships work is not just a matter of labour, it is a question of the recognition of labour. If this recognition is absent in face-to-face encounters it requires other forms of reward, such as gifts, treats or public statements.

Para-social conversations

Celebrities obviously respect issues of access, utility and labour in para-social conversations. Talk and chat show hosts go to some lengths to express their availability and solidarity with the studio audience during airtime. By presenting themselves as the unelected spokesman of the audience, a clear message of affinity with the group is established. In addition, the use of apparently impromptu asides, off-the-cuff jokes and tactful remarks is designed to make the studio audience and the audience at home feel that they are in the know and are trusted inquisitors.

Celebrities who give unscripted live performances and press events engage in similar types of behaviour to emphasize access and solidarity. For a time, Peter Gabriel, Iggy Pop and Bono made hand walking or diving into the audience a feature of live performance. They attempted to break down the barrier between stars and stargazers by making an issue of their vulnerability and dependence. When a star literally places him- or herself in the hands of a concert audience, there is no one else to catch him if he falls. Similarly, when film stars attend the Oscar ceremonies or a film premiere they often make a point of dramatically leaving the red carpet and reaching out to the crowd, signing autographs and shaking hands.

In these encounters access, utility and labour are present, but subject to the laws of structural distance that are at the heart of para-social relationships. Rock stars who mix with the audience during live performances always go back on stage having served notice of their availability, empathy, affinity and solidarity. Similarly, film stars who shake hands with the crowd and sign autographs at high-status metropolitan film premieres always tread back onto the red carpet. These encounters humanize the celebrity. For a brief interlude they appear to be just like us. They are willing to joke with us, pass the time of day, touch us and share a moment in our company. Then they resume the dizzy, cultural remoteness that makes us recognize them as true stars.

But there is something peculiar about access, utility and labour in para-social encounters. Unlike ordinary conversations, the recorded nature of celebrity makes access ubiquitous, utility infinite and labour inexhaustible. The labour theory of value proposes that workers are employed by employers to create value by adding utility to the resources of Nature and Society. Thus, in being employed as a professor my labour power is employed to add value to students by using my training, knowledge and experience to enhance their talents and expand their powers of comprehension. My employer employs me because so long as my classes are big enough and my research is published and recognized, I generate a surplus. That is for the university, the numbers enrolled in my classes generate a margin of profit, and my publications add to the cultural capital of the institution (allowing them to raise fees and increase margins if they are so minded). My work is partly recorded, in that my thoughts are contained in books. I receive a royalty for each book that I publish. In that sense, I am a recorded person. You can have a para-social relationship with me despite never having met me, and this relationship has the capacity to continue even after my death because part of my existence is now print based.

This is indeed a para-social relationship, but it is small beer compared with the para-social relationships that revolve around stars. MC Lyte and Matt Damon are recorded people. The data that is encoded in their records, videos and films is more complex than the words committed by me to the printed page. It is like the DNA of a genome.

A book written by me gives a limited data set of who I am. A DVD or film file of *Good Will Hunting* (1997), *The Bourne Identity* (2002) or *The Departed* (2006) is a much broader data set because it conveys information about embodiment, voice, thought and emotion. That this data is an expression of acting adds a new layer of complexity to questions of access, utility and labour. The issue then becomes: who is the real Matt Damon compared with the characters inhabited and played by the actor on film?

The labour theory of value treats access, labour and utility as bound by time and space. Thus, the value that I add as a professor reflects the time I spend in student contact and writing books and articles. The value produced by recorded celebrity is quite different. For there is no time or space limit on the exchange or reuse of Matt Damon DVDs or film files. As cultural commodities they can be perpetually re-engineered, to add values that were never envisaged by the actor or the producers that employed him.

It might be objected that cultural commodities have always had these qualities. A painting by Titian or a tune by Gilbert and Sullivan is subject to constant reinterpretation. Plagiarism and parody have always been the name of the game with cultural items. But what is new is that digital technologies permit rather more than copying or parodying a film or a song. They allow the complete overhaul and rearrangement of coded material.

This requires us to rethink not only what a para-social conversation means, but also the conventional premise of exploitation contained in the labour theory of value. To take the second issue first, the labour theory of value argues that the creation of additional value produced by the labour power of the worker is appropriated by the employer. The difference between the cost of labour power (wages) and the added value produced by labour power (surplus) is appropriated by the employer in the form of profit.

It might be said that this theory of value still applies to the production of cultural commodities. When MC Lyte releases a rap song or Matt Damon is employed to star in a film the employer assumes that the worker will add value that will eventually be accumulated as profit. But in the era of instant, weightless consumption there are several caveats that need to be added to this assumption.

To begin with, unauthorized downloading drives down profits. So employers can no longer assume that their investment in MC Lyte or Matt Damon will produce an acceptable return. More profoundly, from the point of view of our considerations here, the labour of MC Lyte or Matt Damon is now subject to the law of inexorable exploitation. But the exploiter is now the consumer, not the producer. With low-cost digital technology, the consumer can appropriate copyrighted recordings for free and re-engineer music and film files to engage in perpetual rearrangement. Old cultural theories based around the labour theory of value portrayed consumers as passive and culturally illiterate (Adorno, 1991). Today, the digital revolution combined with the increased cultural literacy of the consumer produced by higher numbers of the population going to university, require us to revise these old assumptions. It might be said that it was always a gross exaggeration to portray consumers as passive and culturally illiterate. But leaving that aside, what is quite certain is that in the field of culture it is now more accurate to speak of the active, literate consumer.

Looking at this matter from a different angle, the balance of power between the celebrity and the consumer has shifted. Obviously, star power still exists. But while we have been aware for some time that the recorded nature of star power influences patterns of consumption, it is only now that we are beginning to fully appreciate the consequences. It is not just a matter of access becoming ubiquitous, utility becoming infinite, and labour transforming into an inexhaustible resource, all of which greatly empowers the consumer, it is also a matter of the radical expansion of the cultural capital of celebrity to provide what might be called life-coaching. Ubiquitous celebrities do not merely sell music, film, television or the fashion of the catwalk; they provide free advice about grooming, impression management, self-promotion and even 'correct' social, political, cultural and environmental values. That this advice is unsolicited by the audience is neither here nor there. It is a feature of the facade of celebrity, which is layered onto the emotional connection, that is the heart of para-social conversations. Crucially, it carries over into ordinary life as a resource that equips individuals to present themselves as more relevant, competent and capable. Thus, star power provides cultural capital of lifestyle-coaching that is directly transferable to everyday life. Para-social relationships are important in culture, not merely as vehicles for narcissistic idealization and hero worship, but they are also used practically to enhance the presentation of personality, refine lifestyle skills and expand social appeal.

For Horton and Wohl (1956) para-social relationships are theorized as regimented, since the perception is that such encounters are usually organized around programmed live appearances or broadcasts. This radically curtails spontaneity. Unscripted access, which is often the key to getting closer to someone in everyday life because it requires us to be more inventive about conversational labour, is at a premium with stars. In addition, the contours of interaction are governed by the formatted facade of the celebrity. Since the facade is formatted, it follows that exchanges are limited to finite tramlines of communication. Fans are made to feel uncomfortable if they overstep the mark and intrude on the carefully protected privacy of the star.

The connotation of formatting is less powerful in societies organized around multimodal systems of mass communication. Para-social relationships are integral to television, film, mobile phone messaging, popular music and the Internet. Flexible accumulation is now the order of the day. Celebrities set out their stall, but consumers have far more power in selecting image accumulation. This is not to deny the fantasy relationship that is the axis of the celebrity-fan relationship.

For celebrities, the utility of the audience resides primarily in the acclaim that they mete out to the star. This is the cultural capital of the celebrity, which translates directly into financial reward and cultural influence. For fans, the utility of the celebrity lies in fantasy relationships with the star and social network engagement with other stargazers. Although the celebrity facade is an artefact constructed by the PR-Media hub, it can be appropriated by the audience as the basis for developing highly personal, aesthetic, intellectual and spiritual relationships. The imaginary quality of para-social relationships with celebrities is a common source of emotional support and coaching resources for stargazers. However, as we have already noted, Horton and Wohl (1956) recognized that in the case of isolated, vulnerable individuals caught-up in para-social encounters, the character of the relationship may become extreme, resulting in what we now call the symptoms of fame attack.

Para-social conversations are unusual in that they are simultaneously centred in the facade of the celebrity and also decentred in the inches devoted to them in gossip columns, entertainment news sections, chat rooms, websites and blog sites. Because representations of celebrity now occur on multiple fronts, regulating the unity of the celebrity facade through exposure management is a greater challenge for the PR-Media hub. The personal touch, which is the foundation of syndicated fraternization, is subject to mistiming and misreading. An intended personal remark designed to exchange utility with the public may be read in ways that suggest schisms or frictions in the public facade of the star. Rearguard actions by the celebrity to apply access and labour to correct public misreadings often have the effect of compounding the problem. Mistiming in para-social relationships can get the star into hot water. Kayne West acted like a highwayman in seizing the spotlight from Taylor Swift at the 2009 MTV Video Awards; and Mel Gibson's anti-Semitic tirade in 2006 and his menacing leaked phone calls to Oksana Grigorieva (2010) have tainted his celebrity facade with images of racism, sexism and domestic violence. In both cases, the stars conveyed an air of entitlement and invulnerability that is typical of some forms of narcissistic behaviour. West's public recantation of the act took the form of a straightforward TV apology.

Gibson's recantation is more complex. His denial that he is a racist or an abuser is wrapped up in a convoluted defence of frontierism. The pressures of stardom mean that stars like Gibson are forced to live on the edge, and therefore the restraints on verbally abusive behaviour that are second nature to ordinary people are less well-developed. In Gibson's case, this defence is intertwined with references to a history of needing professional treatment to deal with problems of alcohol abuse.

The psychology of invulnerability is interesting. Certainly, it goes with being accustomed to public acclaim, financial rewards and all of the confidence in expressing emotional labour that follows. But it also smacks of the tendency of self-destruction. Celebrities are not omnipotent, despite living in a culture that presents them as supremely talented and glamorous creatures. Mistimings suggest a devil-may-care attitude to public opinion. They are certainly seized upon as such by the media who clearly relish celebrity 'gaffes' and 'meltdowns'. The Greek playwright Euripides wrote, 'Those whom the gods wish to destroy they first make mad.' Para-social conversations are just as dangerous to some isolated and vulnerable stars as they are to isolated, vulnerable ordinary people. For they make the star look into the mirror of public adoration and media applause and see the reflection of an untouchable being. But this reflection is a mirage. Stars who are consistently heedless of public opinion or engage in recorded narcissistic outbursts walk on the edge of a cauldron. They are like Icarus, blind to the truth that his wax wings will burn if he flies too close to the sun. People who regard themselves to be untouchable write an open cheque for self-destruction.

9 The Icarus Complex

The myth of Icarus is the most powerful Ancient Greek parable of hubris. In a bid to escape exile in Crete, Icarus uses wings made from wax and feathers made by his father, the Athenian master craftsman Daedalus. But the sin of hubris causes him to pay no heed to his father's warnings. He flies too close to the sun, so burning his wings, and falls into the sea and drowns.

The parable is often used to highlight the perils of pride and the reckless, impulsive behaviour that it fosters. The frontier nature of celebrity culture perpetuates and enlarges narcissistic characteristics in stars and stargazers. Impulsive behaviour and recklessness are commonplace. They figure prominently in the entertainment pages and gossip columns of newspapers and magazines, prompting commentators to conjecture about the contagious effects of celebrity culture upon personal health and the social fabric. Do celebrities sometimes get too big for their boots and get involved in social and political issues that are beyond their competence? Can one posit an Icarus complex in some types of celebrity behaviour?

This chapter addresses these questions by examining celanthropy and its discontents (notably Madonna's controversial adoption of two Malawi children); celebrity health advice (Tom Cruise and Scientology); and celebrity pranks (the Sachsgate phone calls involving Russell Brand and Jonathan Ross). Frontierism involves many superstars in sincerely believing that they are living at the cutting edge of existence, beyond the experience of ordinary mortals. When this is allied to megalomaniacal tendencies of celebrity inflation to save the world, proselytize or engage in brinkmanship, the result can end in the pratfall of the star.

Celanthropy and its discontents

There is no reason to doubt that people in need have benefited from the humanitarian labour of superstars like Bono, Michael Stipe, Annie Lennox, Madonna, Naomi Watts, Angelina Jolie, Bianca Jagger and George Clooney, to name but a few. But celanthropy has also generated criticism that celebrities are often ill-informed and overstep the mark with their can-do attitude.

We have already referred to Paul Theroux's (2006) condemnation of Bono's African aid programme for privileging publicity-sensitive relief over more durable reforms of infrastructure. Geldof and Bono are portrayed as blinkered modern-day

Robin Hoods, taking from the rich and giving to the poor, but fleeced in the process by unscrupulous criminal elements in the developing world. Geldof and Bono have strongly denied these allegations, insisting that aid money has been properly distributed to target groups. But, given their many other artistic and business interests, it is not difficult to see why charges of absentee management are regularly laid at their feet.[1]

There is also a criticism in the undertow surrounding the 'one world' ideology that supports Third World relief. Critics regard it to be spurious, alleging that the relationship repeats old colonial patterns of affluent countries imperiously imposing solutions upon native peoples. In sum, who are white, privileged superstars to speak for 'the world'?

That the economically advanced world produces celebrity know-alls and celebrity aid packages that are insufficiently informed about local conditions is a familiar complaint. In 2007 such a complaint was levelled at Oprah Winfrey following allegations of sexual abuse at the Oprah Winfrey Leadership Academy for Girls, which she founded for underprivileged children in Johannesburg. Oprah, who herself came from a background in which abuse figured, invested £22 million from her charitable foundation in the school.

The Cape media carried local complaints that unemployed labour was prevented from cleaning and kitchen jobs at the school, and the police objected to security being provided by private firms. The insinuation was that Winfrey, who is known as 'Mama Oprah' in the region, had unwittingly created a gated community in which unscrupulous individuals might easily shield sexual misconduct from public scrutiny. The dorm matron at the centre of scandal was eventually dismissed. But Oprah suffered similar complaints of absentee management in 2009 when seventeen girls in the school were suspended after charges of sexual harassment.

The involvement of the celebrity elite in education programmes in the emerging and developing world is particularly vulnerable to the accusation of cultural imprinting. Subjecting native pupils to principles of Western education, even if it takes account of sensitivities to local conditions, is regarded by some commentators as being colonialism in modern dress. The issue is complex and full of contradictions and ironies.

Oprah's academy would not exist without funding from her charitable trust. It provides opportunities for the empowerment of pupils and social mobility that the South African state does not afford. More widely, her involvement creates publicity for aid to Africa that has a multiplier effect in terms of charity donations and government aid funding. However, when celebrity benefactors based in the economically advanced Western world get involved in the affairs of the Third World, it is inevitably seen in some quarters as the intrusion of privilege. For every one that welcomes the investment as pure, disinterested chivalry, others smell the scent of pampered narcissism and naked self-glorification.

The same could be said of celebrities who adopt children from the developing world, which raises some very thorny issues. Take the contrasting cases of Angelina Jolie and Madonna:

1. Angelina Jolie and multinational adoption

Angelina Jolie's charity work is legendary. In 2001 she was named a UNHCR (United Nations High Commissioner for Refugees) Goodwill Ambassador. This has involved her in field missions to more than 20 countries, including Sierra Leone, Tanzania, Cambodia, Pakistan, Ecuador, Thailand, Kosovo, Kenya, Namibia, Sri Lanka, North Causcasus, Jordan, Egypt, New Delhi, Costa Rica, Chad, Syria, Iraq and Haiti. Jolie has a reputation for personally bearing all of the costs of UNHCR missions and sharing accommodation with UNHCR staff.

The Jolie-Pitt Foundation is dedicated to eradicating extreme poverty, protecting natural resources and conserving wildlife. It has provided financial support for *Doctors Without Borders,* a humanitarian organization founded in France in 1971, to help victims of neglect as a result of circumstances such as catastrophes, epidemics, malnutrition and exclusion from health care.

Jolie also chairs the Education Partnership for Children of Conflict, part of the Clinton Global Initiative dedicated to provide support for children affected by conflict. Since 2006 the Clinton Initiative has brought together over 100 former heads of state, fourteen Nobel Peace Prize winners, scores of major global CEOs, prominent philanthropists, directors of non-government organizations and leading members of the press.

In addition she has also supported the Clean Streets project of Wyclef Jean to improve conditions in New Orleans after the hurricane and Haiti after the earthquake.

In 2003 she was the first recipient of the Citizen of the World Award given by the UN Correspondents Association to those who have made a significant contribution to global relief. Two years later she was awarded the Global Humanitarian Award by the UN Association of the USA for her work with UNHCR and with refugees.

The strength of the charity contribution made by Angelina Jolie is not in doubt. It is significant and most commendable. The critical issue lies elsewhere and it has to do with the charge of overstepping the mark by allegedly using fame to create 'designer families'.

In 2002 Jolie adopted her first child, seven-month-old Maddox Chivan. He was born as Rath Vibol in Cambodia and lived in an orphanage. Jolie decided on the adoption while filming *Tomb Raider* and making a UNCHR field trip.

Three years later she adopted a six-month Ethiopian girl, Zahara Marley (originally named Yemsrach by her mother), from an orphanage in Addis Ababa.

In 2007, she adopted a three-year-old abandoned child from Vietnam, Pax Thien (initially named Pham Quang Sang).

The media has criticized Jolie for overstepping the mark between humanitarian work and motherhood. It is one thing to work tirelessly on behalf of the races of mankind, but it is another to seek to combine these races, with their different histories and cultural traditions, in one family unit. Jolie's role as a mother to her adopted children is not an issue. It is the ambition of creating a multicultural mix in one family unit that is regarded as the ill-judged expression of star power. But the criticism directed against Jolie pales into insignificance when compared with the media furore over Madonna's ventures in adoption in Malawi.

2. Madonna, Raising Malawi and adoption

Like Jolie, Madonna is widely celebrated as a major celebrity humanitarian. She has supported the Afghanistan Relief Organization, American Foundation for AIDS Research, BID 2 BEAT AIDS, Bony Pony Ranch, Charity Projects Entertainment Fund, Children In Need, Children of Peace, Live Earth, Make-A-Wish Foundation, Millennium Promise Alliance, Millennium Villages, MusiCares, Partners in Health, Raisa Gorbachev Foundation, Sentebale, Sweet Relief Musicians Fund, Treatment Action Campaign, UNICEF and the UN Millennium Project.

Her most high-profile campaign is Raising Malawi, a non-profit organization she founded in 2006 with Michael Berg. The charity is dedicated to providing vulnerable children and caregivers with nutritious food, clothing, secure shelter, formal education, targeted medical care, emotional care and psychosocial support. Madonna matches every dollar raised through corporate, community and academic support.

In 2006 she adopted one-year-old David Banda from Malawi. Human rights organizations objected on the grounds that that Malawi law forbids inter-country adoption. But Madonna's legal team dismissed the residency requirement of petitioning adoptive parents as 'archaic'. They argued that in a globalized world these requirements are invalid because the rights of the child living with non-domiciled parents can be guaranteed by bilateral agreements. Further, the lifestyle that Madonna was offering David was so manifestly superior that it nullified local protests that the adoption law was being willfully circumvented.

Three years later the Malawi Supreme Court approved her application to adopt four-year-old Chifundo 'Mercy' James. Her original application was again rejected over residency issues. But on appeal, the ruling was rescinded. Madonna's legal team portrayed Madonna as a humanitarian committed to the nation and demonstrated that her parenting of David had fulfilled the requirements of the two-year mandatory probation period set by the law. Patricia Kaliati, the Malawi Information Minister was reported to back the appeal because Madonna had been 'good' to the country by donating millions of dollars via her Raising Malawi charity (Singh, 2009).

The adoptions of David Banda and Chifundo 'Mercy' James raise the same difficult questions as Angelina Jolie's adoptions of Maddox Chivan, Zahara Marley and Pax Thien. Four points must be made.

First, there is the question of celebrity parenting overriding the rights of the surviving biological parents and extended family. The traditional defence of celebrity parents petitioning for adoption in the developing world is that adoption is the salvation of the child. Thus, Madonna is quoted in the media as justifying the adoption of David Banda on the grounds that it 'helps one child escape an extreme life of hardship, poverty and, in many cases, death' (Lamont, 2006). Putting aside the vexed question of arbitrarily 'saving' one child while leaving thousands at risk, it is one thing for wealthy celebrities to adopt children from orphanages in developing countries in the grip of famine and disease. However, this does not mean that the child is exactly being rescued from surviving biological parents and the extended family, who often live below the poverty line.

Africa News reports figures from the Ministry of Information which indicate that Malawi has nearly 2 million orphans, 500,000 of which are roaming the streets surviving on donations and child prostitution: http://www.afriquejet.com/news. africa-news/madonna-sparks-adoption-law-changes [03.04.2009]. In this context, the press quotes from the biological father of David Banda that he never relinquished parental rights over David, but was concerned above all, to protect him, seem perfectly rational. He maintains that he put his baby son in an orphanage because he did not have the means to care for him. His intention was to fetch him and take him back when his employment circumstances changed. However, this defence did not carry the day in the courts. Similarly, Madonna's adoption of Chifundo was opposed by the child's biological father and grandmother, but their objections were overruled.

Given the differences in wealth between a petitioning celebrity of Madonna's stature and the poverty of the surviving biological parent and extended family, it is difficult to view celebrity adoptions in the developing world as anything other than a David and Goliath battle. Madonna's high-profile Raising Malawi charity is clearly appreciated by the cash-strapped government, not least because it massively raises global awareness of Malawi's plight. It may not provide children with the same material opportunities that Madonna provides for David Banda and Chifundo 'Mercy' James, but it undoubtedly gives relief and support to thousands of children in need. Against this, the impoverished biological parents have only the hand of natural justice to play, i.e. that the laws of nature dictate that it is right for the child to remain with their biological relations.

Second, there is the issue of the rights of the adopted child. Western countries have a strict code of conduct that prohibits the media from using the fame, notoriety or position of a parent as the sole justification for publishing details of a child's private life. In the United Kingdom, the Press Complaints Commission protects children under 16 from being photographed on matters concerning their welfare without parental consent. These considerations were observed when David Banda was taken to Heathrow Airport in London. His face was covered and he was guarded from the press by a nanny and security staff. In Malawi the situation was very different. Madonna was photographed carrying the child on her back, apparently indifferent to the intrusion of photographers (Lamont, 2006). The inference is that the photographs in Malawi were material in influencing legal and press opinion in favour of the adoption process.

Madonna's adoption of Mercy also involved the questionable use of photographic propaganda as an adjunct to the legal proceedings.

Martin Parr (2009) describes Madonna's release of a photographic image of herself in sepia with soft pink hue brushed onto the image of her skin in contrast to the audience of black Malawians in the background, holding Mercy, as 'a soft version of propaganda'. Comparing it with the use of black and white photographs to heighten consciousness about famine and hardship in the colour supplements, Parr contends that the image was designed to make Madonna look romantic and idealistic. The photograph conveys a saintly iconic image of Madonna, which indeed seemed to exert a positive influence on the judicial adoption process.

Stars have an international publicity machine that helps them get their own way. This breeds disquiet among the media and the public that star power produces quick fixes with states that want aid and publicity, which override due legal process.

Third, there is the question of the precedent set by celebrity adoption in developing countries. Many human rights organizations object to the relaxation or elimination of residency requirements in adoption on the grounds that it inadvertently paves the way for trafficking in children. High-profile celebrity adoptions may be exploited by traffickers as the pretext for the clandestine induction of children into trafficking routes. UNICEF estimates that up to 1.2 million children are trafficked each year. The majority are bundled into cheap labour activities or sex work (http://www.unicef.org/protection/index_exploitation.html). The crux of the objection of human rights organizations is that celebrity insistence on challenging residency requirements privileges the interest of the celebrity over the interests of the majority of children.

Fourth, there are the related issues of judgement and proportion. If celanthropy is truly dedicated to providing concrete solutions to the problems of Africa and other developing regions it should concentrate its resources in campaigning Western governments on questions of tariff restrictions with the Third World. Persuading the EU and the United States to drop domestic farm subsidies and introduce trade barriers to protect fledgling industries in the developing world would do more to solve the problems of hunger and global inequality than adopting a child or opening a school for disadvantaged girls or an orphanage for homeless people.

Admittedly, it should not be considered in either/or terms. Angelina Jolie is a regular attendee at World Refugee Day in Washington DC, which campaigns for raising public awareness of the condition of refugees. Even so, effective political campaigning is a full-time job. It follows that the balance between high-profile field trips and adoptions, and behind-the-scenes process of winning the hearts and minds of policy makers in Brussels and Washington, is regarded as being out of kilter. In short, celanthropy is seen to be overinterested in the limelight and not interested enough in the less visible, grinding process of lobbying.

To give to the Third World is at the heart of the humanitarian enterprise. Celebrities who donate time, money and engage in fundraising make a contribution. When celanthropists are criticized for taking too many field trips and not lobbying enough, they must despair that they are in a no-win situation. For even if critics contend that in many cases the latent goal of celanthropy is self-glorification, the manifest achievements of providing help and relief are indisputable.

But, to take, is another matter. Even if celebrities act with the best intentions, adopting children and raising them in the affluent industrial world inevitably leads to separate, difficult questions of colonial privilege and cultural indifference. In adoption, these questions are centred on the most defenceless, namely the adopted child. Celebrities and the cultural intermediaries that surround them inevitably appear to adopt a 'we know best' policy in the eyes of the biological relations of the child and the local media.

The idea of wealthy celebrities riding in from a clear blue sky into desperate conditions to save children who are in mortal peril, revives the old, discredited colonial notion of 'the white man's burden'. To argue that the children will have a better life in the West is oversimplistic. It trivializes the relations between the child and the biological family, is heedless of cultural distinctions and it smacks of the patronizing imperial belief that it is the duty of white people to save native Africans from themselves.

High-profile celebrities who adopt and parent children from the developing world may object that this line of argument has all the hallmarks of stellar paranoia. Yet it also exposes a cocksure, superior take-it-or-leave-it-attitude in celebrity culture. Taking a child from the developing world is regarded locally as a matter of cultural assertion quite as much as an issue of legal adoption. The global para-social facades of Madonna and, to a lesser extent, Angelina Jolie (because she adopted from countries where domicile requirements were not a major legal issue), have been tarnished by the media mill running stories about 'selfish superstars' and 'carry-out babies'.

Tom Cruise: Scientology, postnatal depression and Oprah

Fame is not for the faint-hearted. While every human perspective is partial, superstardom gives many celebrities the confidence and licence to behave as if their word is the universal law. This can result in an outspokenness and inflexibility about private and public issues, which many see as strident and insensitive. In some cases, media criticism produces defensive obstinacy so that the word of the celebrity comes across as belligerent, intemperate and mule-headed.

As an example, consider what analysts take to be a rash of serious para-social mistimings during the last eight years by Tom Cruise. It is commonly assented that by the mid 1990s Cruise was the leading film star in the world (Johnstone, 2006). It was a position built upon a string of box office triumphs: *Top Gun* (1986), *The Color of Money* (1986), *Rain Man* (1988), *Born on the Fourth of July* (1989), *Interview with the Vampire* (1994), *Mission Impossible* (1996) and *Jerry Maguire* (1996).

Until the peak of his stardom his public image was founded upon the public persona of an easy-going, accessible superstar. *Risky Business* (1983) and *Top Gun* (1985) established his reputation as the premier Generation X film star. His co-starring roles with Paul Newman in *The Color of Money* (1986) and Dustin Hoffman in *Rain Man* (1988) labelled him in the public mind as a serious young actor eager to hone his craft by learning from Hollywood elders. His marriage to Mimi Rogers in 1987 was life changing. Although the marriage lasted for only three years, Rogers is generally understood to have introduced him to Scientology.

Darker roles followed with *Born On The Fourth of July* (1989) and *Interview With The Vampire* (1994). At the time, critics interpreted these as diligent choices by the actor intent upon extending his acting range. However, they also reveal a new assurance and sense of entitlement of belonging to the Hollywood Pantheon. It would be quite wrong to suggest that, at this time, Cruise became indifferent to his public image. He retained a public relations management team, dutifully attended film premieres and engaged in humanitarian activities with the Hollywood Education and Literacy Project (H.E.L.P.), Children's Hospice and Palliative Care Coalition, Jackie Chan Charitable Foundation, Mentor LA and Stockings With Care. He also participated in the *America: A Tribute to Heroes* charity telethon for victims of 9/11.

However, he was also more assertive, less deferential and more conscious of his status as a Scientologist and superstar. What went with this was a new attitude in the presentation of his public façade. If Cruise spent the first part of his acting career being comparatively reserved, unassuming and guarded in his public pronouncements, his superstardom was marked by what many critics took to be ill-judged and ill-timed candour.

The new century witnessed some high-profile para-social mistimings that are widely regarded to have seriously damaged Cruise's public image. For example, on *Larry King Live* (2003) Cruise frankly rejected psychology, psychiatry and prescription drugs. He reiterated these views in *Access Hollywood* (2006), where he claimed to have saved a child from prescription dependency for attention deficit hyperactivity disorder and put her on the road to healthy food and vitamins.

At the time, the actress Brooke Shields had recently published a harrowing account of postnatal depression, entitled *Down Came The Rain: My Journey Through Postpartum Depression*. Shields climbed out of her depression through psychiatry and the drug Paxil. In the book she gives credit to both. As a rookie cinema actor, Cruise had a minor role in the Brooke Shields movie *Endless Love* (1981). However, in the interview he did not permit personal acquaintance to moderate his strong opinions. He denounced Paxil as 'lethal' and made the ad hominem remark that Shields's movie career had slumped since she used the drug. Cruise has no recognized medical training. So, not unreasonably, Shields publicly attacked him for being out of order and ill-informed.

The main source of Cruise's strong opinions is his belief in, and practice of, Scientology. This controversial system of beliefs has attracted many Hollywood stars, including John Travolta, Kelly Preston, Kirstie Alley and Tom Arnold. None of them has been more vociferous in their public advocacy than Cruise. He has used the media platform to proselytize Scientology, has required interviewers to spend part of the day at the Church of Scientology in Los Angeles before meeting him, and made it a condition of filming to have Scientology tents erected on the filmset.

Scientology is a much-disputed body of belief. Created by the science fiction author L. Ron Hubbard, it has been under federal surveillance in Germany.

It has the reputation of being cranky, over-assertive and intolerant. A US District Court Memorandum of Decision ruled that it had sought to 'destroy' opponents and accused it of 'malicious', 'wanton' and 'oppressive' conduct (Central District of California 1993).

Cruise responds to these criticisms as misguided and presents Scientology as beleaguered and slandered. However, many people find his defence inflexible, and his advocacy of Scientology as redolent of old-style salvationism. It has raised separate questions about his judgement and the use of his fame as a pulpit to evangelize.

These came to a head in a TV interview on the *Today Show* with Matt Lauer that was broadcast in 2005.

TC: I've never agreed with psychiatry, ever. Before I was a Scientologist I never agreed with psychiatry. And then when I studied the history of psychiatry I started realizing more and more why I didn't agree with psychology. And as far as the Brooke Shields thing, look, you got to understand I really care about Brooke Shields. I think here's a wonderful and talented woman. And I want to see her do well. And I know that psychiatry is a pseudoscience.

ML: But Tom, if she said that this particular thing helped her feel better, whether it is antidepressants or going to a counselor or psychiatrist, isn't that enough?

TC: Matt, you have to understand this. Here we are today, where I talk out against drugs and psychiatric abuses of electric shocking people, okay, against their will, of drugging children with them not knowing the effects of these drugs. Do you know what Aderol is? Do you know Ritalin? Do you understand that?

ML: The difference is –

TC: No, no Matt.

ML: This wasn't against her will, though.

TC: Matt, Matt, Matt, Matt –

ML: But this wasn't against her will.

TC: Matt, I'm asking you a question.

ML: I understand there's abuse of all things.

TC: No, you see. Here's the problem. You don't know the history of psychiatry. I do.

ML: Aren't there examples, and might not Brooke Shields be an example, of someone who benefited from one of those drugs?

TC: All it does is mask the problem, Matt. And if you understand the history of it, it masks the problem. That's all it does. You're not getting to the reason why. There is no such thing as a chemical imbalance.

ML: So, postpartum depression to you is a kind of a little psychological gobbledygook –

TC: No. I did not say that.

ML: I'm just asking what you, what you would call it?

TC: No. No. Abso – Matt, now you're talking about two different things.

ML: But that's what she went on the antidepressant for.

TC: But what happens, the antidepressant, all it does is mask the problem. There's ways [with] vitamins and through exercise and various things ... I'm not saying that that isn't real. That's not what I'm saying. That's an alteration of what I'm saying. I'm saying that drugs aren't the answer, these drugs are very dangerous. They're mind-altering, antipsychotic drugs. And there are ways of doing it without that so that we don't end up in a brave new world. The thing that I'm saying about Brooke is that there's misinformation, okay. And she doesn't understand the history of psychiatry. She doesn't understand in the same way that you don't understand it, Matt.

ML: But a little bit of what you're saying Tom is, you say you want people to do well. But you want them to do well by taking the road that you approve of, as opposed to a road that may work for them.

TC: No, no. I'm not.

ML: Well, if antidepressants work for Brooke Shields, why isn't that okay?

TC: I disagree with it. And I think that there's a higher and better quality of life. And I think that, promoting – for me personally, see, you're saying what, I can't discuss what I wanna discuss?

ML: No, you absolutely can.

TC: I know. But Matt, you're going in and saying that, that I can't discuss this.

ML: I'm only asking, isn't there a possibility that – do you examine the possibility that these things do work for some people? That yes, maybe there are abuses. And yes, maybe they've gone too far in certain areas. Maybe there are too many kids on Ritalin. Maybe electric shock –

TC: Too many kids on Ritalin? Matt.

ML: I'm just saying. But aren't there examples where it works?

TC: Matt, Matt, Matt, you don't even – you're glib. You don't even know what Ritalin is. If you start talking about chemical imbalance, you have to evaluate and read the research papers on how they came up with these theories, Matt, okay? That's what I've done. Then you go and say where's the medical test? Where's the blood test that says how much Ritalin you're supposed to get?

The interview produced a hugely negative reaction from the media and an enormous mixed, but largely hostile, postbag from the public. Cruise was accused of dogmatism and eccentricity. His remarks on psychiatry, Brooke Shields and pharmaceutical companies were condemned as ill-informed and inflammatory. The American Psychiatric Association issued a statement censuring him for being 'irresponsible' in promoting 'ideological' views that might dissuade people with mental health issues from seeking professional care.

The question of Cruise's eccentricity recurred in the same year during an infamous interview on *The Oprah Winfrey Show.* Cruise, who declared himself to be in love with Katie Holmes, jumped on the couch and engaged in zany, child-like behaviour. This was a highly public instance of cognitive dissonance in which the public were presented with a facet of the star's personality that conflicted with the regular, disciplined, restrained, nice guy facade that Cruise had cultivated for twenty years. Together with the *Today Show* interview it left many people in the public with the impression of an out-of-control celebrity who had lost touch with reality.

There is no law against a celebrity acting as an ombudsman for the public. People are free to agree or reject Cruise's case against Ritalin, psychiatry and the rest. The question is, should celebrities employ their pedestal in para-social relationships to make contentious pronouncements that may influence the medication and parenting practices of uninformed audiences? The techniques of advocacy and persuasion that he uses apply the standard techniques of demagoguery. Thus, he plays upon public fears of being powerless in the face of professional and big business manipulation. The psychotherapists and pharmaceutical companies are portrayed as targeting the most defenceless group in society, namely children. Cruise presents himself as a lone ranger, backed by the authority of Scientology, to defend public interest.

Three years later, as part of the promotional campaign for his new film *Valkyrie* (2008), Cruise returned to the *Today Show* with Matt Lauer, and described his remarks in the 2005 interview as 'arrogant'. He stopped short of recantation. When pressed, he maintained that he had *not* ceased to talk in public about Scientology. However, he now acknowledged that there is a proper time and place to air his views on the subject.

The question of how Cruise uses the personal element in para-social persuasion is pivotal and we shall come back to it at the end of this chapter. For the moment, the time has come to move on to a third example of celebrity behaviour that may be construed as revealing invulnerability, undue self-regard and hubris.

Russell Brand and Jonathan Ross: Sachsgate

Cruise may have made slighting remarks concerning Brooke Shields and the medical profession, but he was not guilty of invasion of privacy. In some cases celebrities have developed a powerful sense of omnipotence and untouchability that allows them to treat anything and any one as fair game. Chat- and talk-show hosts are especially prone to this because their stock-in-trade is to try to get behind the persona of a celebrity interviewee or social issue and, in the name of public interest, tease out the true facts. Comedians are also used to calling a spade a spade and making a gag out of embarrassing information or delicate circumstances. Matching a comedian with a chat-show host can be a turbulent combination in which all bets are off.

Sachsgate refers to the British scandal in 2008, involving two prominent British broadcasters, Russell Brand and Jonathan Ross, who, on Brand's BBC Radio 2 show, made tasteless comments about 'obscene' messages that they left on the answerphone of the *Fawlty Towers* actor and septuagenarian Andrew Sachs. The messages involved lewd remarks about Sachs's granddaughter, Georgina Baillie. In no uncertain terms, Brand informed Sachs of his former sexual relationship with Baillie, and Ross lent raucous support from the sidelines.

The prank backfired. It produced a storm of public complaints, including criticism from a number of MPs and the Prime Minister of the day, Gordon Brown. Ross, who, at the time, was the jewel in the crown of BBC chat- and talk-show hosts, was suspended without pay for twelve weeks. Brand and Lesley Douglas, Controller of BBC Radio 2, resigned. The incident was investigated by the BBC and the public regulator Ofcom. The BBC was eventually fined £150,000 by Ofcom. In 2010 Ross was forced out of the BBC after the Director-General, Mark Thompson, made it clear that his three-year contract – reputed to be worth £18 million – would not be renewed.

Ross, interviewed two years after the scandal, appeared to be nonchalant. In a newspaper interview he was reported as saying:

> Can I be quite honest with you? In a way, the whole experience was fun. Life can sometimes potter along in the same direction, and then something comes along over which you have no control ... It became almost like I was watching it happen to someone else ... It was weird watching people get themselves into a lather over something so intrinsically unimportant as that. It was just silly. Silly people writing silly things. (http://www.telegraph.co.uk/culture/tvandradio/bbc/7572792/Jonathan-Ross-Sachsgate-was-hilarious-and-I-cant-wait-to-leave-BBC.html)

In 2010 as part of the publicity round for his new autobiography, Russell Brand was interviewed on the BBC radio cultural flagship show, *Front Row*, during which the interviewer, Mark Lawson, brought up the Sachsgate affair.

ML: When you wrote the book you knew you were going to have to deal with the Jonathan Ross/Andrew Sachs incident in some way. What a lot of people will pick up on clearly is that Jonathan Ross tried to persuade you to remove those phone calls. And that again is the streak you have. You just thought 'I want to go with this'.

RB: Yeah, I just become – needlessly – also I am not good in confrontations. If people confront me with something I become more steadfast and more deliberate in my position. It fortifies my beliefs. It wasn't like I madly believed they (the messages) were incredibly funny, I just thought I hadn't considered it from any other perspective other than comedy and as content for a radio show. And when people said, 'Maybe we should remove that, you know, because it is sort of left on his answering messages', I was, 'No that's alright, I think it'll be OK'. I was sort of flippant about it and Jonathan, when Jonathan called, he said, 'Do you think we should be leaving them on? Maybe we should move it?' I said, 'Er, yeah. I think it's funny really, Jonathan', and it took up quite a lot of the radio show. It seems peculiar now, but of course at the time it was not subject to such scrutiny and hadn't been inflated to that degree.

ML: Well that's the other thing you say, there's a lot of remorse in this book about what happened, and you say that when it happened you were thinking of him (Sachs) as Manuel the waiter from *Fawlty Towers* rather than an old man with a family.

RB: I had no image of a grandad in my head. I wasn't particularly close to – well, one of my grandparents I was kinda close to, but like sort of, I didn't have – that's not a reference I really have. But the reference of Manuel from *Fawlty Towers,* that's really a prominent, archetype in my mind. I knew the words to *Fawlty Towers* from when I was five. And for me, yeah, I didn't think, I was just ... it was a peculiar ... I was peculiarly, single-minded about ... oh no, it's just a funny thing to have done, you know, I thought that – do you know what I thought? I thought 'I am going to have to end up apologizing to Andrew Sachs'. It is definitely rude, but I didn't think there would be consequences beyond that.

ML: And one of the things that struck me, I mean I know from other people that I know who have been through it, er, rehab, that one of the things that is encouraged is that you have to face up to what you've done and take responsibility for it. And that I guess, that is one of the ... very quickly you did, you resigned from Radio 2 and you did take responsibility.

RB: Yes, I think that's part of my programme for living, is taking responsibility for my actions and making amends where possible. And, it was – to tell you the truth – in this particular instance, I didn't feel that I had ... I felt that my options were limited. I only really wanted to make people laugh. I was only trying to be funny. Then I thought, well, that's definitely not what's happening now. This is not making people laugh. It's not funny. You've got no option but to stop.

The public pronouncements by Ross and Brand are revealing. Ross obscures the question of the invasion of privacy by concentrating on the public reaction to the prank. The attitude of the media is portrayed as frenzied and that of the BBC as exaggerated. He passes off the incident as an enjoyable diversion from routine.

By implying lofty distance from the reactions of the media and the BBC, he boldly signals notification that the phone messages were inherently trivial. Hence, his use of the term 'lather' to describe the response of BBC management and op-ed columnists.

Turning to Russell Brand, it is interesting that he takes responsibility for resigning but continues to see the obscene phone messages as justified by comedy value. As with Ross, the question of the invasion of Sachs's privacy is scarcely acknowledged. Brand uses the common-or-garden argument that there is nothing intrinsically wrong about having a laugh. That in this case the joke involves informing a grandfather about the private sexual life of his granddaughter seems to be regarded by Brand as a reasonable jest.

Again, these celebrity interviews are noteworthy for their use of the personal element in scandal management. Ross and Brand portray themselves as much maligned, awfully misunderstood ordinary Joes. The name of the game is fraternization with the ordinary man and woman. By mocking the sanctimonious who cannot see the joke, Ross and Brand identify with the people against authority in all its forms. Their twinning of sex with comedy is offered as droll compared with the stuffed-shirt attitude of critics and lily-livered do-gooders. In this way Ross and Brand carry off the invasion of privacy as an act of defiance. A private ill is magically transformed into a public good.

The personal element in para-social persuasion

Bernays presents what we now call syndicated fraternization in purely technical terms. According to him the big practical problem in large urban-industrial society is to furnish the masses with a sense of direction that they are unable to generate for themselves (Bernays, 1928, 1947). The public-relations solution is to construct political and business leaders who articulate progressive, popular sentiments.

Nowadays, celebrities are increasingly enlisted to achieve the same ends because they are known quantities, popular with the public. For Bernays the construction of successful policies is a matter of combining the conviction of leaders and celebrities with various scientific quantitative and qualitative methodologies, including questionnaires, focus groups and interviews. Part of optimizing leadership is winning hearts and minds. The logic of Bernays's position is that the various techniques of syndicated fraternization are merely the right tools for the communication age. They get the job done.

Bernays constantly stresses the idea that ethical restraint by PR-Media professionals pre-empts manipulation against the public interest. But this is hard to swallow. Even in Bernays's own day, the manipulation of public opinion between the 1920s and end of the war, by Fascist leaders and their PR-Media hubs in Germany and Italy, clearly demonstrated that the new technologies of mass persuasion were perfectly compatible with a sinister battle for the public mind. The use of celebrities and the organization of programming to bait opponents and encourage a paranoiac attitude in audiences was a tool of the Nazi party. Para-social relationships were clearly constructed around myths of authoritarian salvation, built around a leader who is projected as a worthy object of hero worship, and a means of racial purification.

Para-social relationships afford ample opportunity for para-social persuasion by allowing the celebrity to apply the common touch and invoke solidarity with the public. Stargazers are flattered by glamorous, adored stars who appear to share their most important values, even if they are not exactly sure what these values are, and talk directly to them. Presumed intimacy is the cloak for smuggling in contentious statements and passing them off as facts. Confiding with the public on air is intended to win approval because it demonstrates to invisible viewers that they are worthy of celebrity trust. Presumed intimacy is the badge of unity because it conveys the impression that the invisible viewers would act just like the celebrity if only they knew the real state of affairs and had the power to make things better.

In *The Today Show* interview, Cruise uses the personal element at several junctures. He presents himself as being on the side of the underdog. That is the ordinary man and woman who are presented variously as being either misinformed or ignorant about the details of psychiatry and the harmful effects of drugs like

Aderol and Ritalin.[2] He stereotypes the *Today Show* interviewer as 'glib' and scapegoats his opponents (psychiatrists and the pharmaceutical companies) as 'pseudoscientists'. He claims that his controversial views about psychiatry and the use of antidepressants are supported by history and science. They aren't. As the public statement issued by the American Psychiatric Association makes clear, the track record of psychiatry in dealing with mental illness is not in scientific doubt. It is one thing to propose that this record is far from spotless. It scarcely needs to be added that psychiatry can be used to harm people as well as to help them.[3] But Cruise does not make this perfectly reasonable submission. Instead he dismisses psychiatry *tout court* as a pseudoscience. This is not an objectively credible argument. It is built upon prejudice and invective.

Cruise weaves the veneer of democratic unity with the little man by ridiculing 'highbrow' attitudes. He uses the authority of the interview to exploit general feelings of impotence and resentment in the audience. On several occasions he resorts to shock statements to win over the viewers. The innocence of children is threatened by 'drugging' them with 'mind-altering' potions and ignoring other, safer ways of intervention. Antidepressants are the easy, false way out. There is a 'better', 'higher' quality of life solution. Firm decisions are required. Again, the appeal to strong leadership for the good of the people is reiterated. Scientology has the answers.

The build-up of propositions continues apace. Throughout, it is supported by anecdote and assertion, not scientific proof. Cruise's superstar glamour, which he is magnanimously putting to the service of the little people, and his lone ranger willingness to act as the public advocate against psychiatry and the pharmaceutical giants, invites approval and hero worship. Cruise is making a stand from which lesser men and women flinch. He presents himself as putting himself on the line for the public good.

Ross and Brand exploit and develop the personal element in a different way. In general, they adopt 'little boy lost tactics'. They are unable to see what the fuss about the obscene phone calls is really about. Ross brings the public into his confidence by giving them a scoop on what was really going in his mind in the aftermath of the scandal. He conflates having a sense of humour with holding a sense of common justice. The implication is that in transforming a jape into a matter of public censure the world has lost all sense of proportion. 'It's just a funny thing to have done, you know', agrees Brand in the *Front Row* interview. Their remorse is not focused on Andrew Sachs or Georgina Baillie, the victims whose privacy has been violated. It is concentrated on the media furore and the negative public reaction. Only when Brand decides that he cannot weather the media storm and the lashing of public disapproval does he concede, 'This is not making people laugh. It's not funny.'

The downfall of Icarus was that he flew too close to the sun. The mechanics of fame, hero worship and narcissistic idealization in today's celebrity culture result in some celebrities following the course he set. Thus, they develop and express strident, inflexible opinions about their beliefs or their entitlements, which produce cognitive dissonance in the public and indignation in the media. This is the result of the huge prestige and financial rewards that society showers upon them. Superstars live in gated properties, blanketed from the public by security staff and cultural intermediaries. In rarified conditions like these it is easy to lose touch with the public and live in a bubble of mindless acclaim and sycophancy.

Generally, the defence applied by cultural intermediaries for this behaviour is well worn and predictable. Celebrities are presented as living lives filled with emergency, risk and incident. Their frontier existence is contrasted pointedly with the routine, financial limitations and impotence of backwoodsmen and the para-social audience. The risky borderline existence that society requires of them, seduces some celebrities into believing that they have the right to behave just as they please without a by-your-leave for the consequences. Hence, Mel Gibson's anti-Semitic tirade against policemen on a Los Angeles freeway; Lindsay Lohan's repeated violations of restraining court orders; Winona Ryder's episode of shoplifting; and Boy George's menacing intimidation of a male prostitute. Although in each case this behaviour resulted in legal convictions, its source is the mental outlook that the star is above the law.

To some extent this is a perfectly sober, realistic attitude for celebrities to have. Historically, they may be damaged by allegations of invulnerability and imprisonment. But a variety of devices of rehabilitation, such as the ritual of a public apology before the media, voluntary community work and high-profile cash donations to charity, go a long way towards restoring public approval. In truth, there are comparatively few cases where public disapproval of behaviour brings stars down for good.

O. J. Simpson's persona of a polite, amenable and glamorous sport star and light comedy actor was destroyed by the trial in which he was controversially found not guilty of murdering his ex-wife and her associate, and his subsequent imprisonment for robbery. The career of the British glam rock star Gary Glitter imploded after his conviction as a child sex offender. Phil Spector, the highly eccentric 1960s and 70s record producer and Hollywood recluse, was found guilty of murdering the actress and nightclub hostess Lana Clarkson and sentenced to life imprisonment in 2009.

However, cases of the total annihilation of the celebrity facade are comparatively rare. In some cases celebrities take the threat of fallout and retribution into their own hands. For example, in 2009 the fugitive reality TV contestant Ryan Jenkins hanged himself after the murder of his ex-wife, the swimsuit model Jasmine Fiore. But episodes like this are exceptional.

This raises the separate question of how acute the emergencies and incidents of celebrity life really are. The frontier existence of celebrity involves stridency, narcissism and entitlement, but it is also compatible with self-correction and learning. The probability that Tom Cruise will ever engage in the childlike, zany antics he displayed on *The Oprah Winfrey Show* (2005) or make public denunciations of psychiatry and antidepressants, is low. His cultural intermediaries have advised that the publicity fall-out is too severe. Hence, Cruise's more measured comments on *The Today Show* in 2008 during an interview promoting the film *Valkyrie*, and his concession that his 2005 interview might have contained remarks that might be construed by many as 'arrogant'.

Yet celebrity expressions of invulnerability and hubris are constant challenges to exposure management. As the proliferation of media outlets conspire to support celebrities, in slipping between the public facade and private opinion they risk exposing aspects of personality or points of perspective that dent social impact factor ratings and trigger cognitive dissonance. The trend towards celanthropy increases these risks because it directly pits celebrities against sensitive personal, environmental and geopolitical issues. In expressing relevance, balance or responsibility for national or world issues, celebrities run the gauntlet of inadvertently revealing incompetence and arrogance. The acclaim that is habitually given to celebrities can seriously distort their judgement. Only superficially does commanding a concert auditorium or filling a movie theatre involve the same knowledge and skills as dominating the stage of world opinion. However, to refrain from celanthropy, serves notice on a literate media public of celebrity self absorption and downright selfishness. Celebrities are damned if they do, and damned if they don't. As Big Citizens their glamour and prestige may act as peerless private catalysts in fundraising, networking and consciousness raising. But in publicly taking on questions of global diplomacy and Third World debt that the world's political leaders have failed to solve, celebrities invite the unflattering comparison of being like turkeys voting for Christmas.

10 Reality TV: The Return of the Fool

The fool is the elephant in the room of celebrity culture. Generally, questions of fame attack put the celebrity and the PR-Media hub into the foreground. The analysis of stargazers brings up the rear. The investigation of the dynamics between ascribed and achieved celebrity, celetoids, PR strategists, media corporations and the audience may reap enormously rich findings. But it is not enough for someone to be a star, or for others to construct, glaze and wax the facade of celebrity, or for still larger numbers to be in thrall to celebrity worship syndrome, narcissistic idealization and hero worship. Celebrity culture also demands an absolute foil, a butt. The star at the pinnacle of the pyramid requires a negative force at the base to legitimate celebrity prestige and sanction levels of economic reward that would otherwise be regarded to be excessive. The star signifies capability, decorum, glamour, intelligence and authority. The fool is an anti-star. He signifies, among other things, incompetence, ineffectuality, indignity and weakness.

The concept of the fool has a long history in folklore, literature and drama among the Greeks, Romans, Chinese, Japanese, Semites and Christians. Most of us are aware of the Shakespearean fool, but in Indian drama there is also a stock comic character, called the *Vidushaka* who is often represented as a hideous dwarf and is the standard accompaniment of the royal hero. The fool is twinned so thoroughly with the concept of the hero as to be reasonably categorized as part of a symbiotic relationship. Regardless of culture and history, human groups appear to need their fools no less than they require leaders.

Nowadays, polite society does not take kindly to the word 'fool'. The inclination to use the term in public, and even in private, carries warning lights that automatically flash social disapproval. There is a touch of hypocrisy in this. While Bernays (1947) makes great play of the requirement to 'engineer consent' by matching 'desirable' leaders with public opinion, and the need to practise eternal vigilance against 'demagogues' and 'authoritarian' figures in democracy, it is perfectly obvious that he regards the public to be fundamentally passive and directionless. Hence the need for the PR industry to provide the 'service' of equipping powerful leaders with the people skills and desirable policies to keep society on the right track. Plainly, it would have been *bad* PR for him to use the word 'fool' with reference to the public. However, it is there in each iota and syllable of his rationale for PR in modern democracies.

Nowadays, we like to suppose that the word 'fool' is confined to the rhetoric of party politics. A right-winger may call a left-winger a fool in the debating chamber, but we know that the term is not really meant and only used for rhetorical effect. It is part of the rough and tumble of party politics. Elsewhere, to call someone a fool in private nearly always promotes indignation and controversy, while to use the term in public is generally accepted as unwise and even slanderous.

The restraint and inhibition that we feel about using the word fool to describe someone reflects the rise of therapy culture over the last century. The practice of making allowances for the conditions that shape behaviour and the lottery of natural dispositions over which the individual has no control are cardinal principles in this culture. According to this logic, nobody is born a fool. On the contrary, the condition is conceptualized as a matter of genetics, family, society, power, inequality or a combination of the above. To label someone a fool is therefore to confuse the consequences of social, economic and political forces for the causes, hence the reluctance today to apply the term to an individual. It is the context around the behaviour of the individual that is usually regarded to predispose and sustain the qualities of the fool. It is these conditions that dispose an individual to be, so to speak, more 'fool-like'. A characteristic formerly assigned to the person is now piloted into the Himalayan vocabulary of abstract forces and obscure origins.

The practical result of this is that individual is seen as blameless and society is called to book.

But therapy culture is, in some respects, brain-blind. We do not notice, or have forgotten, the unabashed use of the term in celebrity culture. In the fields of sport, film, television, pop music and literature, a star who is an angel one day is brought down to earth as a fool the next. Look at Tiger Woods, Tom Cruise, Sharon Stone or Kanye West. Celebrity is Janus-faced. The frontier, volatile, Wild West qualities of celebrity culture are conducive to the rapid transfer of emotions between strong positive and negative opinions. This transfer of strong reactions and powerful sentiments only occurs when there are no slips, and the contradictions only seem to be 'natural' to us, because the structural relationship between the star and the fool are two sides of the same coin.

Here, in the Christian world, perhaps there is some echo of the religious campaign against idolatry. Fame (not notoriety) inspires automatic respect, extravagant devotion and massive economic reward. So the questions about the worth of these social relationships and the talent and accomplishments of the celebrity become insistent. No sooner does someone acquire fame, than the public and media take steps to establish that celebrity worship is bogus and expose the idol as a charlatan.

The figure of the fool, then, is an essential part of the facade of celebrity. It can no more be discarded than the face of the celebrity can be ignored.

The fool and reality TV

But lately, there is another, arguably more interesting and revealing application of the fool in celebrity culture. Makeover shows, confessional talk-show formats, docusoaps, talent contests and other genres of reality TV explicitly label ordinary people as talentless, brainless, buffoons and morons. By implication the presenters and the audience are judicious and right-thinking. TV makeover shows label the ordinary people who participate as persons of bad taste and what might be called, lifestyle bafflement. The ordinary people who appear in these shows are depicted as grossly unable to live well. They are uneducated about effective impression management, sensorily dull about questions of appearance and domestic design. In one word, they are *uncool.*

That is why the TV presenters on these shows have licence to throw out the wardrobe, change the hairstyle, transform body posture, bin the lipstick, ditch the shoes, trash and rebuild the wallpaper and furniture. It is no exaggeration to propose that these shows present the ordinary people that appear in them as failed citizens. They are portrayed as being unable to negotiate even the most elementary presentational rules necessary for achieving social impact – hence, the need for a complete 'makeover'.

The *Big Brother, Idol* and *Got Talent* franchises turn the predicament of the fool into a melodramatic set piece of the format. Think of the initial *Got Talent* appearances of Paul Potts and Susan Boyle. They were presentations designed to produce a calculated effect in the audience. The aim was to portray the performers as fish out of water. Dressed unsympathetically, plain-featured, perspiring and awkward in gait, the first impression they created was of ill-placed, naïve, impudent, no-hopers – until they began to sing. Then their voices made a silk purse out of a sow's ear and turned their stage presence into reality TV sensations. This was no accident. Potts and Boyle were *positioned* to confound para-social expectations. Their appearance before the camera was not naturalistic, but ritually staged.

The stock-in-trade of reality TV is the celetoid. Most of the ordinary people that it elevates into the public eye do not achieve durable fame. In terms of the conventions of para-social communication Potts and Boyle were set up to provoke reactions of disbelief and scepticism in the audience. They lacked the camera aplomb and conversational ease of seasoned performers. Stage lighting and camera panning stressed their ordinary demeanour, reinforcing audience expectations that these apparently unimpressive amateurs were about to make fools of themselves.

But their abilities and accomplishments have made them achieved celebrities. Each of them has a successful recording and international touring career. For the audience, one of the pleasures of this form of reality TV is the overturning of expectations, what the Victorians and Edwardians called the collapse of stout party.

Potts and Boyle are bona-fide achieved celebrities. However, occasionally, reality TV produces celetoids who possess durability. This seems like a contradiction. After all, the essence of the celetoid is to be here today and gone tomorrow. The reason for this is that their abilities are negligible and their accomplishments are not amenable to career development. The essence of achieved celebrity is possessing talents and accomplishments that have a career. In contrast, celetoids typically have nothing going for them except their cocky impudence. Additionally, they are dependent upon single platform outputs, like the *Big Brother, Idol, X Factor* or *Got Talent* shows. This means that when celetoids switch to another platform, such as a rival show, the stage or some other form of public performance, they cannot get beyond the hurdle of their initial public image as merely impudent performers so that, gradually, public interest fades away.

There is nothing surprising in this. The short life of the celetoid is a precondition of most reality TV formats. As Graeme Turner observes, much reality TV is driven by 'the exposure, humiliation and shaming of its contestants' (Turner, 2010: 37). The blatant focus on controversy and embarrassment is, of course, intended to ramp up ratings. The content of shows like *Wife Swap, How To Look Good Naked* and *The Apprentice* is often sensitive and offers private disclosures. The para-social conversational setting encourages disclosure and can act as the basis for developing loyal sympathies between the celetoid and the audience.

For example, the diagnosis of Jade Goody's cancer was broadcast live on the Indian version of *Celebrity Big Brother* (*Big Boss*). The development of her condition defined the structure of subsequent para-social conversations that surrounded her until her death. The durability of her fame was extended as the audience dutifully followed the ravages of her illness, which was relayed in regular television broadcasts, much as parents of siblings would follow and support the illness of a child. The para-social conversation into what was, when all is said and done, a life and death issue, was presented as an extension of the para-social care and support network, rather than an intrusion. That is the media audience assumed the role of semi-invisible carers, ministering to the stricken star. Superficially, this can be read as the triumph of para-social democracy in which remoteness and distance are erased, as the audience pulls up their chairs to sit at the deathbed of the star. Conversely, and perhaps more accurately, it can be interpreted as a form of emotional labour engaged in by the moribund celebrity that ultimately benefits broadcasting channels to boost ratings. That is this form of private disclosure is more properly seen as a type of para-social exploitation rather than a 'conversation'. The conventional language of exploitation and the theory of surplus value are more relevant in explaining this state of affairs than fancy talk about the media-enhanced extension of democracy. The celetoid does not select which programmes to appear in or how to edit recorded interviews, documents of illness and the like. This is the remit of the TV production company, which also ultimately stands to gain the maximum financial benefit from the televised proceedings.

This is not the place to go into the question of the social functions of the reality TV genre (but see Andrejevic, 2004; Hartley, 2008; Hill, 2008). The point that needs to be made here is that the colonization of reality TV formats in programming schedules produced the conditions in which some ordinary people attain more durable types of fame. This requires the concept of the celetoid to be modified.

Jade Goody in *Big Brother* and William Hung in *American Idol* have been recognized and publicly rewarded for their lack of talent. To date, Goody is Britain's greatest reality TV star. Her stupidity was legendary. She was reported to believe that a ferret was a bird, Pistachio painted the Mona Lisa, Rio de Janeiro is a person and Saddam Hussein was a boxer. She was not adept at singing, dancing, acting or comedy. Yet she dominated British reality TV news and was a major figure in popular culture for seven years from her first appearance on the *Big Brother* show, until her untimely death from cervical cancer in 2009. As Stuart Jeffries (2009) wrote in his obituary of her, 'she had no perceptible skills and was ordinary looking, but still thrived in showbusiness.'

Turning to the United States, William Hung's (2004) infamous audition for *American Idol* displayed chronic self-delusion and ludicrous ineptitude. His performance of Ricky Martin's *She Bangs* was so dire that it prompted Simon Cowell to remark, 'You can't sing, you can't dance, so what do you want me to say?' Yet far from disappearing without trace, Hung marched on to develop a cult following. He has a dedicated Web fan site, a record deal that produced three albums between 2004 and 2005 and has pursued a successful career in TV chat shows, commercials and movies.

The success of Goody, Hung and others requires the revision of the concept of celetoid. In particular, it is necessary to make a distinction between short-life and long-life celetoids. A short-life celetoid is the familiar one- or three-minute wonder. It is a person with no perceptible talents or disciplined accomplishments, who has celebrity for short, concentrated periods of time and then ceases to be famous. A long-life celetoid is also devoid of perceptible talents and disciplined accomplishments. Despite this, they achieve durable or semi-durable fame. Goody and Hung are no Susan Boyle or Paul Potts. They are not distinctive for anything except their impudent ordinariness. It is correctly described as impudent because, despite having no recognizable talent or disciplined accomplishment, they act as if they have an entitlement to airtime and the media lens.

This raises a separate question and that is: why should impudent ordinariness be a sufficient basis for accumulating fame today?

The structure of the fool

The answer to the question lies in the power of broadcasting channels and the web of para-social relationships created by the media. Before we look at this in more detail, it is important to say a little about the character of the fool as a social type. For in positioning short- and long-life celetoids before the contemporary public, the PR-Media hub unwittingly draws upon character types that have a much longer social and literary history.

As long as there have been records of human groups there are references to fools (Welsford, 1935; Klapp, 1949; Shuttleworth, 1998). The Greek historian Xenophon describes the antics of Philip, who was a gatecrasher at the dinner party of Callias and engaged in horseplay with Socrates. Philip is remembered for providing diversion, parody and comic relief from weighty philosophical table talk. The fool appears in literary works by Athenaeus, Plautus and Lucian. He – and, in the overwhelming majority of recorded cases, the fool is a man – was a staple at the courts of Philip and Alexander the Great.

With the fall of Rome, the fool seems to vanish from the pages of history and literature, only to return in the late Middle Ages and Renaissance at the courts of the rising class of Italian despots. The fame of buffoons like Popolo d'Ancona, Ribi, Dolcibene, Gonella, Fra Mariano, Hans Clawert, Goring and Finit has come down to us in the writings of Sacchetti, Aretine, Humphrey, Kruger and Weldon. The court fool was an institutional feature of fourteenth and fifteenth-century courts in England. Martinetto de Vasconia fatuo played at the court of Edward I. Edward II kept a fool called Robert whose pay features as a standard item in the Wardrobe accounts, suggesting that he was a staple of court culture. Some fools were provided for in old age. The French monarchs Charles le Sage, Charles VI and Louis XII also had a fondness for fools. The names and deeds of their court jesters Piculf, Grant-Jehan, Haincelin Coq Coquinet and Jehan le Fol have come down to us through history.

From early times the distinction between 'natural' and 'artificial' fools seems to have been common. The former were men and women of obvious, and in some cases, severe mental and physical handicaps. Their defects, ungainliness, simplicity of character and physical deformities placed them outside of ordinary society. They occupied a place in which normal civil rules did not apply.

In contrast, artificial fools employed absurdity, innocence, naivety and ribaldry in their manner and are more properly described as recognized players, buffoons and jesters. They turned human shortcomings and the folly of mankind into an art form and sought to entertain for the purposes of instruction and diversion.

In both cases, the court awarded licence to the sayings and doings of the fool that were not granted to others. Court life revolved around jockeying for recognition and currying favour from those of superior rank. It was often a social cauldron of intrigue.

In these circumstances, the fool was the naïve voice of home truths. He exposed the gross human failings of court life and acted as a reminder that pomp and circumstance was part of the mystique of power. The fool occupied the bottom rung of the social hierarchy. In occupying this position he is beyond Good and Evil, or pretends to be. He absents himself from the race to be honoured and celebrated and paradoxically, by refusing – or not knowing how – to play the rules of the game, he turns himself into an object of note and even veneration. Although not directly involved in production, government or warfare, he was appreciated and valued. He was a mascot in battle and a life-charm in everyday relations.

Natural fools were commonly held to possess special powers and to have the gift to ward off evil. The court of Dadkeri-Assi, a Pharaoh of the Fifth Dynasty, included a legendary pygmy, one Danga, purchased in the Puanit region located on the mysterious, semi-explored borders of Egyptian society. Danga was plucked, so to speak, from the mists of Egyptian consciousness. He appears to have been respected by the court for mystical and even supernatural intimations. Upon this basis, his utterances, dances and diversions were granted not merely tolerance but privilege.

Dwarves, simpletons, halfwits and other physical and mental abnormal types were common at the court of the Ptolemies and Roman Empire. In Rome they were known as 'fatui', 'moriones' and 'stulti'. They were greatly prized, and commanded high prices at market. They were seen as links between the known world and the World of the Unknown.

In the Christian and Muslim worlds there are long-standing associations between the fool, prophecy and clairvoyance. Ibn Khaldoun, in his book *The Muqaddimah*, grants the mad with powers from the Unseen. He explains the reason for these in the weak integration between the body and soul in the mad. In not being fully formed, the mad are less able to defend themselves from the unscrupulous interference of non-human powers. Unseen forces find it easier to possess the mad and speak in their tongues (Khaldoun, 1989).

In Muslim society such people were frequently employed to adjudicate between disputants. The Arabs believed in supernatural beings called *djinn*, who were believed to reside in secret places and possess the spirit of human beings endowing them with supernatural knowledge. They fell into various categories of potency; the *shair* (the poet prophet), the *kahin* (the soothsayer) and the *arraf* (a lesser diviner). For many centuries Muslim literature recounted stories and verses about Buhlul al-Madjnun (Buhlul the Madman or Buhlul the 'Djinn Inspirer') who resided at the court of Harun ar-Rashid. He is portrayed as a comic hero blessed with such bountiful insight and pious divination that he was proclaimed to be saintly.

Later, in the Renaissance, the artificial fool becomes dominant. His deliberate interruption of decorum and taking liberties with precedent and rank became appreciated as arts. The fool is revered for courageously revealing the emptiness of procedure, the affectation of posturing, the vanity of pretence and the tragedy of the human condition. By virtue of departing from the rules of normal group life, appearing in a bedraggled state and speaking in an unselfconscious way, the fool occupies a space beyond the law. An interesting inversion in the status of the fool occurs at this time.

In pre-Renaissance society, the fool possesses low status and is the butt of many indignities. To be called a fool is to suffer disgrace. The fool has no responsibilities and no honoured function. His sole value is to be the naïve spokesman of misrule. In this capacity, nature or the *djinn* has equipped him to speak from the world beyond the fringes of Reason.

With the Renaissance, the status of the court fool changes. He becomes the accomplished liberty taker and ready scapegoat. He acts as the knowing catalyst of the management of emotions in court society, allowing aggression and laughter to be expressed. The fool continues to occupy a lowly social status. But his art in highlighting the common lot of mankind is recognized and savoured.

Must we impute sadistic motives to the co-option of natural and artificial fools into court society? Perhaps there was an element of taunting and ridiculing the misshapen, ugly, lamebrained and deformed. But there is more to it than that.

The purpose of the fool was to constantly remind the powerful that fame is arbitrary and influence capricious. The fool reminds the high and mighty of the low, bawdy, common world. In doing so, he offers the important lesson that social order is fragile. Power can be removed at once. The man of fame and decorum can be plunged into the moronic abyss in a trice.

Egyptian, Roman, Indian, Medieval and Renaissance society did not seek to escape from social and economic realities. Rather they imported them into the court. There was a reason for tolerating the fool. Licensed derision and abuse exposed the pretence of status. The airs and graces of the rich and powerful were brought down to earth because no one was so respected as to avoid the tongue of the buffoon. Fools were tolerated parasites at the courts and the rich family homes of Western European society because they provided constant reminders of the contingent nature of the society of the powerful.

Modern men and women find it hard to comprehend why the rich and powerful condoned the ridicule of the fool and even valued rebuffs, insults and scorn at his hand. They cannot understand why the acid tongue of fool was protected and revered. The main reason for this is that, in spite of all of their anxieties and worries that speak to the contrary, modern men and women are largely insulated from the world of slavery, famine and the carnage of battle. Many of us go through life without ever seeing a captive, a person suffering from incurable pain or even a dead person. Yet, in the court society that tolerated the fool, these experiences were seldom exceptional.

The fool provided a bridge between two worlds. On one hand, he was thought to conduct the judgement of deities and the insights of the spirit world into the world of court society. As we have noted, the Arabs believed that the *djinn* possessed the fool and used him to communicate with ordinary mortals. Just as importantly, the fool symbolizes caprice and waywardness. He bespeaks the *natural* world and therefore provides a contrast with the cultured, manicured relations of court society.

Welsford submits that the fool is essential in court society because he acts as an agent of shame release:

The Fool is an unabashed glutton and coward and knave, he is – as we say – a *natural*; we laugh at him and enjoy a pleasant sense of superiority; he looks at us oddly and we suspect that he is our *alter ego*; he winks at us and we are delighted at the discovery that we are also gluttons and cowards and knaves. The rogue has freed us from shame. (Welsford, 1935: 318)

The notion of managing shame by using another seems abhorrent to us today. Where it occurs, we seek help and recommend counselling. But in court society aggression, shame and impatience are managed by courtiers. Individuals who previously gained the ear of the monarch by virtue of their capacities as warriors or producers of wealth, gradually became valued for their tact, intelligence and point of view.

The fool was the lowest rank of courtier. His value lay in his apparent lack of guile or tact. By calling a spade a spade and not speaking in the tongues of preferment, the fool imparted unmarinated wisdom, home truths, untainted by the artificiality of court protocol and political intrigue. In the case of the artificial fool this contribution was largely symbolic. Yet having someone in court playing the part of the fool suited the need of the monarch to remind himself and his often devious, higher courtiers, to stay grounded. The luxury of keeping the fool at court was a means of monarchical and aristocratic self-assertion. It conspicuously displayed the wealth, power and confidence of high rank. For as a warrior or a source of economic wealth the fool was plainly useless. But as a bar to contrast with the afflatus and pomp of courtiers and as a link with the Unseen World and the world and the people, the Fool was invaluable.

The fool in the court of reality TV

Reality and talent TV shows like *Queer Eye, What Not To Wear, Extreme Makeover, Ambush Makeover, The Apprentice, Big Brother,* and the *Pop Idol, X Factor and Got Talent* franchises, are one of the few areas left in public life where treating an individual as a fool is regarded as entirely legitimate. It is even justified as a responsibility to correct the imprudence of the performer for venturing to go on to the show in the first place and the sorry state of the media in validating the audition and the broadcast. When the dress, grooming, deportment and manners of an ordinary person are ridiculed in the makeover show format, or the *Pop Idol* or Got *Talent* judges lambast a performer, or the audience votes off an unimpressive contestant on *Got Talent*, the panel are mocking the flaws of individuals and stridently expressing their inner sense of worth. *Reality* and *talent TV* figures like Jade Goody and William Hung became famous both nationally and internationally for their ineptitude and impudence. The public did not stint at decrying bad taste, foolishness and vulgarity in Jade Goody, until news of her cancer broke and she was transformed from a dim-witted *Big Brother* virago into an innocent victim.

The structure of these shows is based in rituals of judgement, punishment and reward. The responses of the panel are not just about judging, but also about social ordering. That is, they directly and tacitly position players in a hierarchy of IQ and moral worth. So allowances are made for performances from players who are labelled as having low IQ and a naive self-image. In the *X Factor/Pop Idol/Got Talent* franchises the panel is constituted as a sort of mini-court. They are not quite monarchs, but their prominence in the media affords them authority to make sweeping judgements that are, in career terms, life and death. The facework of the four individuals clearly evinces a variety of emotions from joy to anger and social reactions from approval to indignation. They do not simply communicate with the contestants, they impart sentiments through para-social conversations with the audience at home. Sometimes the panel acts as a team, conferring their collective assessment of the virtues of this or that act. However, as individuals they also employ techniques of jockeying, sparring, gamesmanship and playing to the gallery. They convey unspoken support to some contestants and Pontius-Pilate-like disdain for others. The panel operates like a court, registering the visible performance and hidden intents of contestants, indicating preferences and staging indignation for vote-getting.

Just as the leadership of the monarch is judged by the court and ultimately the people, so the airtime practices of the panel of the judges are evaluated by the media and the audience watching at home. The judges can be criticized for their arrogance and insensitivity. When she was a judge on *American Idol (2006–9)* Paula Abdul generally cultivated a compassionate, sympathetic response to contestants that was widely interpreted as a reaction to the blunt manner of Simon Cowell. Similar frictions were reported on *The X Factor* in 2009 between 'hardliners' Simon Cowell and Cheryl Cole on one side and the more restrained, sympathetic style of Louis Walsh and Dannii Minogue on the other. As in court society where the actions of the court were ultimately judged by the people, so the conduct of the TV panel is subject to the metrics of rating wars and popular opinion.

Of course frictions and tensions between the judges make for good television. They are controversial and provide a spike in social impact, which is an asset in the ratings wars. The inter-judge conflicts and social skills with contestants are part of the para-social conversations that the judges conduct with the invisible audience. The purpose is to influence the standpoints of other members of the panel, mould public opinion and, more concretely, the circumjacent media and audience of voters. By stimulating and building loyal enthusiasms, the judges try to sway other members of the panel and the audience. Para-social manipulation is consistent with the principles of mass psychology followed by Bernays and the PR-Media hub:

> Men do not need to be actually gathered together in a public meeting ... to be subject to the influences of mass psychology. Because man is by nature gregarious he feels himself to be a member of a herd, even when he is alone in his room with the curtains drawn. His mind retains the patterns which have been stamped on it by the group influences. (Bernays, 1928: 73)

The job of the judges in reality/talent TV shows is to gauge these patterns and seek to exploit and develop them in winning over members of the panel and the audience. This involves directly pandering to the repressed impulses of the group mind. When Simon Cowell launched into William Hung in the *American Idol* (2004) audition, he was articulating negative emotions that members of the audience screen out from ordinary public life. If we call someone ugly, incompetent and talentless in everyday life, we incite the popular reaction that we are being insulting and acting like a bully. If the same thing happens on the *Got Talent, X Factor* or *Apprentice* shows it is passed off as plain speaking.

The impact of the judges is enhanced by arousing emotions and making reactions that are disguised or adulterated in everyday life. To quote Bernays again:

> Men are very largely actuated by motives which they conceal from themselves ... It is evident that the successful propagandist must understand the true motives and must not be content to accept the reasons which men give for what they do. (Bernays, 1928: 75)

Just as subconscious motives are attributed to the audience with respect to their susceptibility to the lead of the judges, it is easy to detect the hand of the subconscious in media representations of the fool in reality/talent shows. The fool is not given a chance to excel. The producers of the show already know he has no real talents, accomplishments or skills. The fool is strategically positioned to earth the repressed popular reactions and prejudices expressed in the mob judgements of the studio. He allows us to feel better about ourselves and bathe in the belief that society is going to the dogs by permitting the media to make the *Pop Idol/Got Talent/X Factor* and *Big Brother* franchises prosper. His clumsy ineptitude makes us feel a little bit superior and his celebrity confirms this because, paradoxically, it demonstrates the privileged nature of achievement famine. You and I may not be celebrities. In this sense we are located in a (relative) state of achievement famine. But would we really wish to behave like William Hung or Jade Goody or subject ourselves to the barrage of media interrogation, in order to acquire fame?

The return of the fool is therefore a function of the supply side of celebrity culture.

Yet it echoes premodern demands for cosmic certainty and social order, in which the highest rung in society is built upon the lowest rung. We are made from these premodern histories. The spread of cultural literacy has not freed us from them. The religious beliefs and rituals that consecrated them in the past survive in our own day as pseudo-religious beliefs and degenerated rituals. The fool belongs to this category.

The media gives a platform for ordinary people that it positions as fools in reality and talent TV shows. The purpose is to win ratings wars by generating publicity. The fool on the media stage is condemned, rebuked and humiliated in ways that would be censured or prohibited in ordinary life. The fool is there to both confirm the democratic impulse behind reality TV and to promote the lie to the adage that anyone can make it. True, some fools prosper in reality and talent TV genres. They become long-life celetoids, but their careers are fatefully constrained by the label that they wear around their neck. The essence of the natural fool is not to develop but to remain the permanent, misshapen naïf. They are not 'anybodies', they are fools. They are ritually defined and culturally confined. This is the immoveable straitjacket of their celebrity existence.

11 The Sphinx of Celebrity and the Idolatry Funfair

The early Victorian essayist William Hazlitt (1930) published a piece, originally in the *New Monthly Magazine* in 1826, on 'Of Persons one would have wished to have Seen'. It is an interesting document for our purposes because it directly addresses the question of celebrity, before the emergence of the fully developed PR-Media hub. It is a light piece that takes the form of a meandering, after-dinner table talk between Hazlitt and others, over cake and brandy, on the subject of famous historical figures whom one would wish to have encountered. Predictably, most of the figures nominated are writers: Dante, Sir Thomas Browne, Fulke Greville, John Donne, Dr Johnson, Geoffrey Chaucer, Alexander Pope, William Shakespeare and John Dryden. Although Oliver Cromwell is also mentioned for 'his fine, frank, rough, pimply face and wily policy' (Hazlitt, 1930: 532), there are surprisingly few requests to meet political leaders, military campaigners, actors, actresses and the like. This reflects the high status assigned to fiction, poetry and belles-lettres among the arts in Hazlitt's time.

Dante apart, the list strikes us today as narrowly British. At this time, national traditions of cultural appreciation, no less than artistic production, were clearly ascendant. Western nations were beginning to define themselves by the perceived threats to domestic interests. These interests were not necessarily common or, still less, shared in any conscious way (Colley, 2009). Inter alia, they referred to the preoccupations of the monarchy, the aristocracy, the landed gentry and the rising industrial-urban propertied class, rather than to land labourers and the industrial working class.

This is in sharp contrast with the contemporary perspective on celebrity. Today celebrity culture is global and ecumenical. National traditions are not necessarily privileged. Recognition of glamour and achievement is drawn from around the world. Celebrity culture resembles an enormous, global washing machine in which different data from the world swirl around in perpetual motion. Altogether, it reflects a massive expansion in the arc of cultural appreciation that would have seemed amiss and unpatriotic in the eyes of Victorian and Edwardian cultural critics.

Hazlitt and his party were culturally literate men, active at a time when education was available to only a few. So cultural literacy was scarce. Hazlitt himself, and one of his guests, Charles Lamb, made their living by their pens. Their reading and debates equipped them with ample knowledge of literature, philosophy, science, history and the disciplines devoted to studying the mind and human relationships. It follows, that there is little reason to be surprised that the names submitted should consist largely of famous, long-dead British authors. These would be exactly the writerly ideals and role models for culturally literate people of Hazlitt's day.

Strikingly, Hazlitt discounts John Locke and Isaac Newton as worthy candidates since 'beyond the contents [of their writings] there is nothing personally interesting in the men' (Hazlitt, 1930: 524). This suggests that celebrity is not just about deeds, but also about *personality*. Tzvetan Todorov argues that a characteristic of Enlightenment thought is that it sought to understand individual men and women in 'particular situations' (Todorov, 2010: 9). Instead of pursuing the classical ideal of revealing the 'eternal laws' of human conduct and the 'exemplary character' of each action, Enlightenment thinkers were interested in the 'ordinary gestures' of exceptional and unexceptional human beings. Personality was slowly being acknowledged as the key to celebrity.

This interest in personality was not truly modern. Educated people in ancient and traditional society were interested not only in the deeds of Alexander the Great, Caesar, Cicero, Cleopatra, King John, Queen Elizabeth and other ascribed celebrities. They were also interested in them as people with particular attitudes, emotions, quirks, strengths of character and failings. What made the Enlightenment different is that these interests were transferred and expanded to refer to men and women from ordinary backgrounds, who, through their exceptional achievements, became objects of fame. There was a pedagogic element in this.

Ordinary men and women could study the character of Caesar or Queen Elizabeth. But they had no chance of ever becoming either an emperor or a monarch. However, in studying what made Rousseau great or how Thomas Paine came to formulate his views, ordinary men and women could assimilate personality traits and character strengths that would make them better, more effective, rounded personalities. Ascribed celebrities in ancient and traditional society were distant role models. Achieved celebrities after the age of the Enlightenment were role models *and* life coaches, equipping stargazers and members of the ordinary public with the people skills that enabled them to make a practical difference in their own lives. What *works* for celebrities could now be used to work for any Tom, Dick or Harry in their own walks of life.

Again, in this regard, the importance of Boswell's *Life of Johnson* (1791) cannot be underestimated. It provided a benchmark for biography by using private impressions and personal anecdotes to enhance the public image of its subject. Boswell gave the public the intimation of getting behind the public view of Samuel Johnson to render a definitive picture of the great man (Sisman, 2000).

Hazlitt and his dinner party would have been alive to this innovation in biography. By acquainting themselves with the private lives of celebrities and linking these details to their public, recorded deeds, they believed that they would gain illumination about those who are truly great. Nonetheless, at the same time, they believed that there is something evasive and mysterious about achieved celebrity. It is one thing for Boswell to reveal illuminating characteristics of Johnson's life, but something Sphinx-like about Johnson remains.

There was a puzzle about the phenomenon of celebrity. It resided in two areas: the secrets of the formation of the star personality from ordinary clay and why some stars implode while others endure. Fame was not just about deeds and personality. It was about the relationship between stars and the use of the biography of fame to shape the time.

This made achieved celebrity into something otherworldly, Sphinx-like and mysterious. Perhaps it reflected the origins of fame in long-forgotten forms of totemism and the primitive notion of the divinity of kings. Achieved celebrities may reveal more about their personalities, they may offer ordinary people lifestyle tips and people skills, but they remain consummate mysteries. So that when one encounters a famous achieved celebrity by chance, even today, one is dazed as if touching a source of energy that is not present in everyday life.

The public celebrity

Our own day may still be dazed by celebrity but it is less willing to see anything of the Sphinx in celebrity culture. Today, it is common for us to feel entitled to know *everything* about the private lives of celebrities. The PR-Media hub satisfies the insatiable public demand for the real person behind the celebrity mask. Cosmetic surgery, food preferences, phobias, political opinions, school memories, relationships with parents and children, exercise habits, favourite brands of toothpaste or shampoo – everything is grist to the mill. Nor is there any sense of balance. Public interest in the private lives of the stars is equivalent, and often disproportionate, to the content of the deeds that made celebrities famous. It is as if it is taken for granted that fame neutralizes any right of celebrities to retain privacy. In putting themselves before the public as figures of note, the celebrity is taken to serve notice that every scintilla of their life is up for grabs. Although the question of the invasion of privacy is at the heart of celebrity culture, the general view appears to be that celebrities are fair game. The notion of building an exclusive, private relationship with the celebrity now seems cranky. It is the stuff of extreme celebrity worship syndrome and pathological narcissistic idealization. From the mean standpoint, celebrities are viewed as the property of the *polis*. Everyone has a right to a piece of the action.

Nor are achieved celebrities today conventionally regarded as universally belonging to a superior (higher) world. A more equivocal relationship between the stargazer and the star prevails. Stars are presented in the media and understood by the public to be prey to the same anxieties, neuroses and perturbations of spirit as ordinary men and women. The personality is no longer separated from culture and society as it was in Hazlitt's day. Personal details humanize stars by making them appear, on one level, to be just like everyone else. This is transparently the case with celetoids, who are perceived as, often grotesque, versions of Everyman. But nowadays the cultural distance between superstars and society is also seen as drastically reduced. The superstar possesses talents and accomplishments that are not distributed in the mass. Nonetheless, the fact that they hail from the ranks of ordinary people and are vulnerable to the same battery of psychological, social and cultural challenges that we all face, is an important part of the appreciation process. *We* learn through *their* struggle.

This has an important consequence for how celebrity is positioned before audiences and fans. We have shifted from a perspective that seeks to discover definitive, final readings of celebrities, to one in which fame is viewed as perpetually changing in form. Nothing is any longer set in stone. For example, Peter Ackroyd's renowned biography of Charles Dickens (1991) was presented by the publishers as an unsurpassable achievement in understanding the great man.

However, it has spawned a lively counter biographical literature that seeks to expose the faults and gaps in Ackroyd's account. Thus, Lillian Nayder's biography (2010) of Dickens's wife, Catherine Hogarth, is entitled *The Other Dickens,* implicitly suggesting that existing accounts of the writer that focus on genius and personality, rather than the relationship of genius and personality to primary relationships and society at large, are distorted and one-sided. The book aims to reclaim Catherine as a seminal, misunderstood and poorly remembered influence on Dickens's life and writing. The accent is now upon challenging the facade of fame. Achieved celebrity is understood to be intrinsically a matter of talent, accomplishment and *representation*. The facade of celebrity is commonly regarded as a PR-Media related mask that needs to be resisted. Celebrities are themselves caught up in the public mania to dispel the public face and flourish insights about the self behind the mask.

Hence, Tom Cruise's (2005) disastrous appearance on *Oprah,* and Tiger Woods's (2010) public TV confession of deceit and adultery, overturned long-standing assumptions and violently changed popular perspectives. Cruise could no longer be accepted as the movie-star master of self-control and buttoned-up discretion; while Woods kissed goodbye to his highly lucrative public image as an incorruptible, clean-cut sports hero. Yet a superstar as well versed and adept in public presentation as Cruise surely knew what he was doing, even if he misjudged the payoff; while Woods must have known that he was playing with fire in denying allegations of infidelity. Perhaps both had grown weary of the hall of mirrors of celebrity culture and a tiny, unfulfilled part of them wanted to break free from the celebrity straitjacket and be acknowledged for who they really are.

Who can say? What is beyond reasonable doubt, is that only the naive in the *polis* believed that the real men behind the celebrity facade were thus revealed. In media-saturated cultures, there is no authoritative core to celebrity, only the constant ebb and flow of the celebrity image. When we ask who was the 'real' figure behind a celebrity supernova, we are unable to supply a satisfying answer. The 'real' John Lennon, Bob Marley, Marlon Brando, Kurt Cobain, Elizabeth Taylor or Michael Jackson remains elusive. Interestingly, the development of the celebrity image of these stars shows no sign of abating. For example, the 'real' circumstances of Jackson's sudden death became an issue almost as soon as his death certificate was signed. The public had been used to viewing Jackson as wacky, out of touch with reality, spoiled and mixed up in sinister ways with children. Now, overnight, he was redefined as a media victim, a lamb slaughtered by the malevolence of the fame industry. There is no 'truth' here, but rather an array of competing representations, none of which is unifying. Similar questions derive from John Lennon's involvement with violent, militant groups and his hounding by the CIA as an 'undesirable' alien. Was Lennon a covert supporter of terrorism to advance the cause of liberation? Did he see this as the price to pay for building a society of 'no possessions'? Or was he a well-meaning political halfwit, gulled into supporting causes that he did not fully understand and activists who pulled the wool over his eyes?

When Elizabeth Taylor died in 2011, tribute programmes and obituaries referred to her as the 'last of the real stars'. By this was meant that her fame was formed in an era of Hollywood when stars had to be remote from the world of ordinary men and women. They were required to obey the law of being more beautiful, more pure, more steadfast, fitter, more health-conscious, kinder, better with their children, more heroic and energetic than ordinary men and women. The law, of course, was an absurdity concocted by the Hollywood dream machine. Taylor's own life, with eight marriages (she married Richard Burton twice), ill health, depression, struggles with weight, battles with alcohol and drugs, was hardly conducted with the gods on Mount Olympus free from the tawdry complaints and miserable temptations that afflicted mere mortals. The obituaries and tribute shows did not stint in recounting disclosures of personality and life history that revealed her to be a victim of consumerism, double-talk, unhealthy obsessions and damaging addictions, just like the rest of us.

In becoming relentlessly more public, is celebrity culture killing the goose that lays the golden egg? If we become aware of how like us they really are, why should we any longer see celebrities as elevated, incandescent beings? Take away the mystery behind celebrity and you remove its power to bewitch.

But the *raison d'être* of celebrity is not the capacity of the PR-Media hub to persuade us that celebrities are special, nor is it our admiration of the skills and accomplishments that we see in individual celebrities. The *raison d'être* lies elsewhere. It rests in the human need for transcendence. The sheer transcendence of fame over ordinary life and the different aspects of the celebrity image, represented in the various pictorial, aural and written texts devoted to celebrity, provides most of us with pleasurable involvement and drives some to the obsessional behaviour characteristic of celebrity worship syndrome and narcissistic idealization. This reflects an important transformation in the relationship between the audience and the celebrity since Hazlitt's day. Popular participation with media representations of celebrity is now continuous. Over the last thirty years it has been 'naturalized'. The media has become our second skin. We do not need to burrow for celebrity news or titbits. Rather, they are *drilled* into us perpetually via multiple commercial media channels. This is noteworthy. It is tantamount to silently recognizing that most people understand, without necessarily consciously acknowledging, that the inevitable corollary of celebrity is the PR-Media hub. We take for granted the vast global information highways that transport truckloads of celebrity data. We find nothing remarkable in our familiarity with the private lives and public careers of stars. Quite simply, today, more people know more about celebrities, living or dead, than at any point in human history. This is the direct result of the gigantic multiplication of supply outputs, namely celebrity TV shows, celebrity TV channels, celebrity podcasts, celebrity biographies, celebrity magazines and celebrity gossip columns. Undeniably, the expansion of supply side factors since the 1980s has contributed to make celebrity ubiquitous.

Celebrity and the need for transcendence

Nonetheless, it really is untenable to explain celebrity culture merely, or even primarily, in terms of supply side factors. Celebrity culture is ubiquitous because it affords access to the deep human need for transcendence and meaning. The PR-Media hub is as caught up in this as much as stars and stargazers. In premodern society, the body, the community, society and the whole world are regarded to follow the plan of Creation. In modern society, science, technology and commerce have led to the fragmentation and decline of cosmological values. Over the whole of society, their force is much diminished. For most people today, the body is without religious significance. God is not respected as an influential presence in human life. To be sure, in some quarters, among relatively large numbers of people, belief in deities, totems, spirits and magic survives. But the majority of men and women are agnostic. They prefer to let their beliefs reside in the testable propositions of science, medicine and technology.

Yet the need for transfigured experience and the memory of transhuman rituals survives and flourishes. John Castles is hardly alone in noting the occurrence of states of 'ecstasy' and 'revelation' in rock and popular music concerts (John Castles, 2008: 63; see also Wilson, 1975). The outstretched hands of the crowd, or the lighting-up of lighters, are the physical representation of the yearning for, and recognition of, a bigger, higher spiritual whole.

Similar states of being are claimed for mass sporting events, some television shows and the cinema. To go into this matter fully would require another book. However, common observation of celebrity culture quickly leads to the hypothesis that spectator sport, music concerts and music festivals and cinema seem to operate with models of transcendence that contain memory traces of abolished religious events and totemic rituals. Celebrity is associated with elevation, just as worship of the totem or the divine rights of kings was associated with higher life. Participation in celebrity culture requires fans to go through initiation rites and rites of passage. At the simplest level, fans escape from time. They live under a different metric governed by transcendent engagement with the celebrity rather than the laws of chronology and Nature. But the labour of following a celebrity provides a discipline and purpose to individuals that echoes religious meaning. This is reflected in dress, cosmetics, the organization of speech patterns, the development of political and spiritual belief systems, identification with various celanthropic causes, the belief in a higher purpose to life and much else besides.

The landscape of celebrity culture is full of echoes of religious memories and impressions of half-forgotten totemic ritual. Film, television, sport and popular music play with the motifs of the struggle between good and evil, the gaining of knowledge through ordeals, the quest for purity, the mysteries of transformation, the difference between the world and paradise and wholeness and the interactions between heroes, demons, princesses, maidens and trusty friends (Payne, 2000; Hedges, 2010). So Jake Gyllenhaal plays the heroic Prince Dastan who, in a quest for the Dagger of Time, falls in love with Princess Tamina in Disney's Prince of Persia (2010). Or Nicholas Cage plays the sorcerer, Balthazar Blake, in The Sorcerer's Apprentice (2010) and recruits Dave Stutler (Jay Baruchel) to save New York from the powers of darkness. The British Heavyweight boxer David Haye, the Filipino boxer and politician Manny Pacquiao; the tennis stars Roger Federer, Rafael Nadal and Serena Williams; and the soccer stars Lionel Messi and Cristiano Ronaldo are portrayed in the media as heroes engaged in quests for success who are willing to endure ordeals against foes. These contemporary film plots and sporting narratives draw on our pagan and religious past, recycling character types, redefining set pieces and rebooting sacred rituals so that their origins become almost unrecognizable. But once the link between religion, totemism and contemporary rituals of celebrity is made, it does not require much perspicacity to detect the ghosts within.

Celebrity culture offers a multicoloured cloak of transcendence to a world habituated to the centuries-long waning of cosmology. Narcissistic idealization and hero worship have their roots in the human need for elevated, transcendent forms of meaning. The desire for larger-than-life versions of ourselves, or superhuman gods, leads to the birth of stars. Because the majority in society are obliged to be self-controlled, to be sexually prudent, to minimize risks and to put aside pennies for a rainy day, the image of a frontier existence, conducted on the edge, elevated from ordinary experience, in which the delight of boldness and carefree living are unapologetically stressed and celebrated, is intoxicating. Transcendence here refers not only to a larger-than-life existence, but also to freedom from the moral codes and economic constraints that regulate ordinary life.

Celanthropy intensifies these developments. It is only natural to want to make a difference. But celebrities seem to live with the supreme confidence that the world would be an inconsolably poorer place without them and that what they do carries global significance. Small wonder that they arouse acclaim, provoke identification and generate indignation and disapproval in comparable measure. Stars who pack stadiums on Saturday, generate millions at the box office every year and, in their free time, use their power to bring relief to the Third World are the big citizens that most of us secretly want to be. Just as surely as their willingness to speak on behalf of mankind is sometimes abhorred as unspeakable arrogance and their personal wealth is rejected for making them cocksure and vain.

The fear of idolatry

Fame is indeed often twinned with contamination. Celetoids and achieved celebrities, who spend a good deal of their pre-fame existence coveting acclaim, frequently seem at a loss to manage it when it comes. Far from producing the elevation of spirit and the consolidation of self-worth that is associated with transcendence, fame is experienced as a burden and sometimes a curse. This is a consequence that is keenly felt in the public mind and actively fanned by some sections of the media.

What evidence can be marshalled in support of this hypothesis? Take the case of Anna Nicole Smith. It is not exactly self-evident that Smith coveted celebrity.

She was certainly aware of her physical charms and used them to become a *Playboy* centrefold. She certainly understood the connection between sexual allure and acquiring a fortune. But the evidence that she sought out a wealthy suitor is not strong. Smith appears to have been hunted, rather than to have taken the path of the hunter. An octogenarian oil baron, J. Howard Marshall II, became smitten with her when she worked as a stripper in a Houston adult club. He eventually proposed. The two were married in 1994.

This should have been Anna Nicole's triumph. In fact, it is now widely held to be the start of her downfall and demise. Marshall, who was sixty-three years older than Smith, died within thirteen months of the marriage. Smith claimed half of his $1.6 billion estate. This precipitated a bloody and protracted series of court proceedings between her and the Marshall Estate that continues to this day. Smith was dragged through the mincer by the media, who portrayed her as a gold-digger. She seemed visibly unable to cope with the strain and tension of the relentless court proceedings and media muckraking. Her public life became more erratic and suggested severe difficulties in her private life. Her fledgling film career constantly misfired. She became a face on the 'Events' circuit and a perpetual item in the gossip columns. The media circulated stories of her as a talentless, but striking wannabe. She rapidly adopted the persona of a long-life celetoid, a model and TV personality addicted to, and produced by, the PR-Media hub and driven to ever more desperate fame-spikes to keep her face and name in the public eye.

In 2002 her reality TV show, *The Anna Nicole Show*, debuted on the *E!* cable channel. It positioned her as a dizzy blonde who was not in control of her life and who seemed emotionally damaged and out of sorts with the trappings of Hollywood lifestyle. Like the more successful reality TV show, *The Osbournes*, the *Anna Nicole Show* positioned the protagonist as a sort of holy fool, apparently oblivious to the absurdity of her life and oddball status.

Media stories of Smith's dependency on drugs and alcohol created the widespread public impression that she was doomed. The public recognizes morbid romance as being destroyed by the same gods who rewarded you with excess and gratified your every whim. Even if Smith gained control of a large chunk of the Marshall Estate, she was portrayed as a profoundly lost character. Her death, from an accidental drug overdose, in 2007 was not unexpected. To be sure, it was not difficult to detect a sense of righteous fatefulness about her drug overdose, as if she had paid the price for the Icarus complex.

The repeated public reaction to a celebrity elevation without trace is to await the inevitable descent and falling. The baying of the media, and the public's appetite for descent and falling in celebrity status, echoes the war against the idols in

Christianity. We look for defects in the facade and for personal character flaws in those who have a brush with fame. The media participates in this by mounting the idolatry funfair. Undercover investigative journalists, muckrakers, phone-tappers and computer hackers regularly engage in illegal activities to outwit celebrity exposure management strategies. Newspaper and TV stories about the cracks in the celebrity facade are paraded before a gluttonous public. The media has developed various entrapment strategies to expose celebrity sexual misdemeanours, drug issues, alcohol dependency and violence. The main justification is that the public interest is being served. However, the most prominent interests are newspaper and magazine circulation figures and the ratings wars.

The compulsion to bring down achieved celebrities and celetoids is hardly new. The ordeal of descent and falling is a seminal primitive myth. In the Judean tradition, Lucifer's temptation of Eve in the Garden of Eden and Cain's slaying of Abel are classic examples. In both instances, forbidden actions bring disgrace and punishment. The corruption of nature, abhorred, but assimilated by a merciful God, paves the way to rites, festivals and rituals of redemption and ascent. The Oriental tradition, which holds that introversion is the road to truth, is rejected as a delusion. Salvation requires public redemption to overcome the original sin. The Judean and Christian instrument of redemption is to act upon the world in order to transform it in one's own image. This is what achieved celebrity superstars do. Through their deeds, they provide intimations of transcendence and models of practice that ordinary men and women can appreciate and follow.

Good and evil derive from the same source, namely God. For, in creating mankind, God equips us with the potential to take the path of righteousness or to stray. The authenticity of transcendence is a pivotal issue in Byzantine, Muslim and Christian traditions. The outbreaks of iconoclasm in these traditions are part of the vehement and intransigent revolt against idols. Just as good and evil are regarded as springing from the same source, the true and virtuous are regarded as being integrally joined with the base and the false.

I have already touched upon the theological doctrines behind this in Chapter 7. I am raising them here again because the modern idolatry funfair carries unmistakable echoes of puritan disapproval of the luxury of fame. It is driven by the urge to expose stars as fakes. Undue media attention is focused upon the vulnerabilities and bad habits of the famous. The use of entrapment strategies treads a narrow line between enticing celebrities to behave badly and merely faithfully representing their flaws and defects.

The counter-world of narcissistic idealization in celebrity culture is to treat celebrities as if they are just like us. However, the idolatry funfair is disproportionately obsessed with bringing celebrities down to earth and making sure that their vulnerabilities receive their just desserts. At its worse, it is a pernicious distortion of fame that is no better than narcissistic idealization and hero worship. Indeed, it is part of the same syndrome that has placed the business of celebrity at the forefront of our culture, taking up the equivalent amount of airtime and column inches to news and opinions about politics, the economy, medical research, science, the arts and the like. The question is, has this really gone too far?

Conclusion: 'When You Wish Upon A Star...'

The old Harline and Washington song 'When You Wish Upon A Star' was first used in the Disney movie *Pinocchio* (1940). The Jiminy Cricket character sings it in the opening credits. Over the years, the song has gone on to become a trademark of the Disney Corporation, widely used in product placement and advertising campaigns.

The fable of Pinocchio is an apposite metaphor for the story of achieved celebrity and celetoid culture. A wooden puppet is miraculously transformed into a living thing and is informed that if he wants to be a real boy he must prove himself by his deeds. This anonymous person from society is identified by the PR-Media hub, elevated into public prominence and prevailed upon to be a heroic role model and unofficial life coach for the people. 'Ours must be a leadership democracy,' wrote Bernays, 'administered by the intelligent minority who knows how to regiment and guide the masses' (Bernays, 1928: 127).

Bernays and his followers were right to maintain that complex societies, organized around democracy, require more than words, laws and a financial surplus to run smoothly. They need glamorous figureheads whose presence persuades, enlivens and entreats the masses to greater things. But it is bad propaganda to argue, as Bernays does, that, at its best, the PR-Media hub does no more than this. For the PR-Media hub is judged not simply by its output in making democracy more perfect, but also by the private interests of the business executives, government officials and corporate stockholders that it serves. The growing importance of celebrity culture for capitalism in reproducing order and maximizing accumulation has allowed the genie to escape from the bottle. The popular desire for fame now precedes, and is often disturbingly indifferent to, questions of talent, accomplishment, dedication and skill. Narcissistic idealization and hero worship have transformed recognition and acclaim into popular entitlements. There is ambivalence about celetoid culture and the idolatry funfair, but there is no serious attempt to curtail or eliminate these features from the face of society. The only meaningful form of regulation advocated is self-regulation. But what does self-regulation mean in a celebrity culture in which optimizing impact is the name of the game?

The culture of fame is now as fundamental to the wellbeing of capitalism as is oil and nuclear energy. But just as pollution and environmental degradation is associated with the latter, so it is with the former. Fame culture produces fame attack in which the desire for celebrity results in obsessional personalities and dangerously skewed types of behaviour. A sizeable proportion of those touched by the hand of fame end up as prima donnas, or corrosive, pampered princes and little princesses who think nothing of dealing with the dilemmas of personality distortion by throwing tantrums, abusing others and resorting to acts of self-harm as a form of penance or a way of coping. We have seen that their mortality rate is higher than the mean, and that they are more prone to mental collapse, emotional disturbance and physical injury.

But the perils of celebrity are not confined to the famous. In as much as we live in an age of achievement famine, in which the urge for fame is general, but the conditions for its attainment are meagre, fame attack affects ordinary people in ways that we do not fully comprehend. We know about celebrity worship syndrome and have studied it in this book. But the costs of living in a culture in which social impact for the majority is out of reach, where commodified magnetism is frequently mistaken for charisma, and a sense of popular fraternization is mediated through commercialized para-social relationships (*Pop Idol, The X Factor, Got Talent, Big Brother*) are tricky to estimate. No one can survive comfortably or prosper in society without effective self-presentation. But in a culture where facade and impact are kings, and a belief in oneself regardless of talent or accomplishment is no longer regarded as impudent, genuine modesty, humility and balance have become handicaps to achievement. Meretricious conduct gets noticed, even if it also elicits criticism and disapproval. Look at the astonishing success of Lady Gaga.

But what if standing out in a crowd disassociates oneself from the concerns, values and interests of the crowd? What if leaders and figureheads really do regard their fellow men as a herd, in Bernays's sense of the term (Bernays, 1928)? What if wanting to be noticed drifts over into demanding acclaim and reverence as non-negotiable entitlements? What if the only sincerity recognized as 'working' is spray-on and cosmetic? Celebrity culture produces shining stars to follow, but it also unleashes many demons.

Mostly, when we wish upon a star, our dreams do not come true. The more we put into worshipping a celebrity, the less space we have for developing as an independent person. Celebrity is necessary to provide us with a sense of transcendence, especially in societies in which organized religion is a weaker force than it used to be. But there is no point in denying that it extends and reinforces the culture of dependency, where people look up to others rather than to themselves, and where PR images, celebrity endorsement and marketing sound bites are allowed to do your thinking for you. Adding to the fame of others saps us of the energy that should be used for self-knowledge and social responsibility. Being born again by latching on to a star in celebrity culture is to voluntarily submit to a kind of modern serfdom. The serfdom in question is the bondage to consumer culture, where branding stands in for personal presence and packaging becomes the primary and salient form of cultural experience. When Angelina Jolie and George Clooney tell you what cause to follow and what charity to give tax-deductible donations to in the morning; when Jay-Z and Kanye West show you what shirts and cologne to wear in the afternoon; and when Natalie Portman is unveiled as the new (desired) face of Dior, and Rihanna fronts a new ad for Reb'l Fleur perfume in the evening, for you to follow and buy, what is left of the person under such conditions?

Despite condescension in the media and alarm in the public, celebrity culture is not going to go away. We need to stop thinking of it as trivial and compartmentalized from the rest of life. There are ways in which it can be used to enhance democracy and personal well-being. But there are also ways in which it is used to gull consumers into mindless emulation and develop a fixation with form over content, which contributes to dehumanization and toxic social life.

Fame has been described as a spur.[1] It is also a slip-on boot, stamping on the face of independence to demand conformity, and substituting real life with vicarious existence that is ultimately empty and unfulfilling. It is wise to take celebrity culture seriously because its effects permeate deep into our subconscious. The PR-Media hub that boosts its profile in society and positions it to sell products and politics to us has become so artfully adept that we have stopped noticing its presence. Celebrity culture is 'normal' in everyday life and the PR-Media hub is the 'natural' means of communicating fame to the public. However, the 'invisible government' of business and political interests and 'people-skills' professionals, who are ultimately behind the culture, are acutely conscious of its seductive power and potential for exerting social control. That is why they devote substantial corporate revenues and government reserves to the task of exploiting and developing celebrity throughout the *polis*. Only outwardly is celebrity culture about selling things. At the heart of the matter is a battle for the mind. Those who see celebrity only in terms of harmless fun or exuberant liberation, without recognizing its immense power for codifying personality and standardizing social control, do not see celebrity at all.

Notes

Preface

1 Middleton's parents went on to become millionaires by founding *Party Pieces* (1987), a mail order company that sells party supplies and decorations.

2 An important exception is the work of Stuart Ewen (1996). Ewen was one of the first critical academics to take the public relations industry seriously.

Chapter 1

1 There is some dispute about the extent of the decline of organized religion. Much depends upon the definition. If 'organized religion' means regular churchgoing, there is no doubt that there has been dramatic post-war decline. However, if it refers to a belief in God and an afterlife, the situation is more equivocal. Either way, the force of organized Christian religion in Western society is less prominent than it was in 1945.

2 Tom Payne (2009) has made a heroic effort to demonstrate consistency between the ancient gods and goddesses and modern celebrities. But I find his treatment is rather laboured. The central issue in celebrity culture is that contemporary celebrities follow in the footsteps of the ancient gods and goddesses. Rather it is that both ancient myths and modern celebrity culture addresses the human need for transcendence.

3 Leadership seems to be a human universal. No societies have persisted based on the principle of egalitarianism. Advanced industrial societies require leaders to counteract the anonymity and specialization of everyday life. Celebrity culture plays an important role today in providing role models and informal life-coaching.

4 The doctrine of divine rule held that the monarch was the appointed delegate of God to bring the grace of God to the people. In traditional society the monarch was the primary achieved celebrity. The fact that monarchs were understood to be God's representatives provided a certain force and confidence in their dealings with society and culture.

5 Jade Goody was a British *Big Brother* contestant who became a national figure and leading celetoid until her death in 2009. William Hung is a Chinese-American singer who initially gained fame for his dubious rendition of Ricky Martin's song 'She Bangs' on *American Idol* (2004).

6 The 7:10 figure comes from comes from Blyton and Jenkins (2007). If service work requires people skills, it clearly places celebrities in an important position in the labour market. Celebrity people skills – the power of celebrities to persuade and attract – is what ultimately accounts for their economic and social rewards. If celebrities are the top in people skills, it follows that they constitute a significant resource in popular pedagogy. In short, the people-skills literacy of celebrities provides psychological and social materials that can be transferred to ordinary people in the job market and in primary relationships. In this sense, celebrities can be described as informal life coaches in contemporary society, providing ordinary people with pedagogy as well as transcendence.

Chapter 2

1 Andy Warhol's prediction has passed into popular culture (along with much else that he invented). The recorded origins of the statement seem to be a catalogue reference to Warhol in an exhibition of his works at the *Moderna Museet* in Stockholm (1968).

2 Rebooting celetoids is by no means an indefinite process. In fact it is subject to the law of diminishing returns. Long-life celetoids usually depend on a human-interest element to prolong their impact with the public. For example, the diagnosis of Jade Goody with terminal cancer both extended her impact and redefined it. From being a vulgar *Big Brother* also-ran, she was redefined as a courageous mother and national heroine.

3 The perspective that casts audiences as puppets is most powerfully expressed in the work of the Frankfurt School. In particular, the interest of Adorno (1991) in Hollywood forms of mass communication led him to hypothesize that the desires and opinions of the audience in mass society is governed by the culture industry. By and large, the notion of the passive audience is rejected in contemporary audience studies. Instead the emphasis is upon the active interpretive capacities of audiences. New digital technologies enable audiences to influence intellectual property, especially in the form of recorded music, on their laptops.

Chapter 3

1 The late Christopher Lasch (1980) deserves credit for being one of the first critical intellectuals to take celebrity seriously. His work makes clear connections between the cult of celebrity and the proliferation of traits of narcissism in society at large. He identifies the media as the key to this process:

> The mass media, with their cult of celebrity, and their attempt to surround it with glamour and excitement, have made Americans a nation of fans, moviegoers. The media give substance to and thus intensify narcissistic dreams of fame and glory, encourage the common man to identify himself with the stars and hate the 'herd'. (Lasch, 1980: 21)

We would now need to add the role of public relations staff to that of the media in making celebrities modern cultural skyscrapers. However, we would not depart from Lasch's conclusion that the preoccupation with 'personality' and 'reward' in celebrity culture produces social malaise:

> Thriving on the adulation of the masses, celebrities set the tone of public life and of private life as well, since the machinery of celebrity recognizes no boundaries between the public and the private realm. The beautiful people – to use this revealing expression to include not merely wealthy globetrotters but all those who bask, however briefly, in the full glare of cameras – live out the fantasy of narcissistic success, which consists of nothing more substantial than a wish to be vastly admired, not for one's accomplishments but simply for oneself, and without reservation. (Lasch, 1980: 321–2)

2 While the term 'the mirror effect' has become recently famous through the work of Pinksy and Young (2009), it originates in the writings of Daniel Boorstin. Boorstin writes:

> One of the deepest and least remarked features of the Age of Contrivance is what I would call the mirror effect. Nearly everything we do to enlarge our world, to make life more interesting, more varied, more exciting, more vivid, more 'fabulous', more promising, in the long run has an opposite effect. In the extravagance of our expectations and in our ever increasing power, we transform elusive dreams into graspable images within which each of us can fit. By doing so we mark the boundaries of our world with a wall of mirrors. (Boorstin 1962: 255)

3 *Frontierism* is a term introduced here to refer to the ideological and spatial zone occupied by celebrities, which is on the edge of society. Characteristics of frontierism include wealth, access to financial, government and media power, licence for sexual experimentation, drug use and temper tantrums. The frontier is the place where the rules of everyday life have thin existence.

4 The timidity of modern men and women to grasp the nettle and get the most out of life is a long-standing theme in Western philosophy. Friederich Nietzsche's discussion of 'the superman' can be read partly as a criticism of the shallowness of everyday culture.

5 In describing the mirror effect, Pinksy and Young (2009) seem unaware of Veblen's (1899) work on leisure and emulation. The parallels are inescapable. Veblen maintains that the leisure class (consisting of the super-wealthy) cultivates various practices of conspicuous consumption to signify their freedom from the need to engage in paid employment. This is a matter of status distinction since wage labour is regarded as bound to a life of necessity and burdensome obligation. However, for Veblen, the practice of conspicuous consumption sets the bar for the behaviour of the majority employed in wage labour. Wasteful consumption trickles down the system as a mark of social distinction. The behavioural pattern of the mirror effect follows the same general course. The narcissistic behaviour of the star is emulated by the stargazer. Waste and dangerous risk-taking, which should be concentrated in the frontier zone, seizes popular dominion.

6 Superstars often complain of extreme isolation. In part, this reflects the security risks that celebrity brings. Superstars may command the adulation of sizeable sections of the public, but they are insulated from contact with others by bodyguards and live in gated communities. Superstars also see themselves as isolated from ordinary people by virtue of their talent. This is another nuance of frontierism. Talent isolates. It provides justification for prima donna-ism and the urge to save mankind rather than show respect and tolerance to ordinary people.

7 Ideation is a medical term for suicidal thoughts.

Chapter 4

1 Max Weber describes charisma as 'a certain quality of an individual personality by virtue of which he is considered extraordinary and treated as endowed with supernatural, superhuman, or at least specifically exceptional powers or qualities' (Weber, 1968: 241). He goes on to note that the powers of charisma are not accessible to an ordinary person and are regarded to be 'divine'. Charisma is an entirely personal relationship based on the devotion of a charismatic community to the calling of a leader. There are no 'officials' or constitution of rules. The genuine charismatic leader demands obligations by virtue of revelation, oracle, and inspiration of the power of his own will.

2 Adolf Hitler was a charismatic leader. To refer to Kershaw:

> Hitler's power was of an extraordinary kind. He did not base his claims to power (except in a most formal sense) on his position as party leader or on any functional position. He derived it from what he saw as his historic mission to save Germany. His power, in other words, was 'charismatic', not institutional. It depended upon the readiness of others to see 'heroic' qualities in him. (Kershaw, 1998: xxvi)

3 The main benefits of celanthropy are fundraising, brand-building, access and insight. Celanthropy works on what Bono calls 'conscious consumerism'. That is an awareness of the power of consumerism to be used responsibly (Bishop and Williams, 2008: 201, 209).

Chapter 5

1 The shallowness of celetoid culture and the onslaught of celebrity gossip contribute to the perception of celebrity culture as trivial.

2 The nude photos in question were taken by Martin Schreiber in February 1979. Four were published in *Playboy* Magazine in 1985.

3 This line of thinking reproduces the culture industry thesis that the audience is passive, and is open to the objections already made (see Chapter 2).

4 A problem in managing intellectual property is that the digital age has not produced an effective method of policing. This complicates the gatekeeper function of exposure managers.

5 As a general principle, frank disclosure is the best policy. If celebrities are exposed as dissemblers they face an uphill struggle in re-engineering trust relationships with the public.

6 Cognitive dissonance refers to the tension between the expectations and experience of someone occupying a specific status or role.

Chapter 6

1 *E! Online* is one of the main Web sources dedicated to celebrity issues and gossip.

2 Achieved celebrity presupposes a degree of intimacy between the star and the stargazer. This follows from the emergence of achieved celebrities from the ranks of the unprivileged. Photo shoots and interviews milked this to enhance trust relations between the audience and stars.

3 Social Darwinism is the doctrine of the survival of the fittest. It is inherently problematic in celebrity studies, since the idea of natural fitness is invalidated by the practices of cultural intermediaries.

4 Stallen *et al.* (2010) claim to have identified a link between neural patterns in women and celebrity endorsement. The Dutch researchers scanned the brains of twenty-four women as they looked at photographs of celebrities and non-celebrities wearing certain brands of shoe. The team documented increased activity in the medial orbitofrontal cortex. They conclude they this activity is produced by 'the persuasiveness' of fame itself.

Chapter 7

1 Emotional deficit is common in societies based upon high levels of social and geographical mobility. Where people are required to move around a lot to find work, celebrity culture may function as a stabilizer. It gives mobile individuals a sense of continuity and stability.

2 Ascribed celebrity is based on fixed status and a prescribed role. This gives little room for manoeuvre. Celebrities have a defined role to play from a clear status position. If they step out of role or change status, it affects their traditional impact.

3 The main charities associated with Princess Diana are: The Diana, Princess of Wales Memorial Fund (now disbanded); The British Red Cross Anti-Personnel Landmines Campaign; Centrepoint Soho; English National Ballet; The Leprosy Mission; National AIDS Trust; Great Ormond Street Hospital for Children NHS Trust; and American Red Cross.

4 These two Revolutions dramatically exposed the obsolescence of systems of status and privilege organized around ascribed celebrity. Thereafter, achieved celebrity gradually expanded and consolidated its influence over society.

5   Thomas Rainsborough was a Colonel in the New Model Army who participated in the Putney Debates. In the course of the debates he famously declared: 'For really I think that the poorest he that in England hath a life to live, as the greatest he.' This was an important statement of English radicalism.

6   The term 'bus class' is used by the nouveau riche in South Africa. It is a useful phrase to adopt in celebrity studies because fame is so closely associated with mobility. The term bus class indicates that large sections of society simply do not have a ticket to acquire the status of fame.

7   Sheen's 'My Violent Torpedo of Truth/Defeat is Not An Option Show' (2011) was widely seen as erratic. The *Hollywood Reporter* review of the Detroit performance captured the issues well:

> What the audience got was egomania gone wild … Sheen's haphazard act was neither standup nor confessional memoir, despite repeated promises that he was going to dig deep and dish secrets. It was closer to a motivational statement, but one in which the speaker was also the key beneficiary … There's a certain trainwreck fascination in watching a meltdown in progress, but this anthropological study of the *homo loco* species wore very thin very fast. (Rooney, 2011)

Chapter 8

1   Modernity is a multi-faceted concept. At its heart is an approach to society and social relations in a state of flux, motion and 'ceaseless movement' (Frisby, 1985: 13).

2   The pattern here confirms McCutcheon *et al.*'s (2004) Absorption-Addiction Model.

3   The terms 'dominant', 'emergent' and 'residual' elites come from Raymond Williams (1958).

4   Johnny Cash's support for prisoner's rights was exemplary in this regard. He regularly played concerts to prisoners. The first was in 1958 at San Quentin State Prison.

Chapter 9

1   Celebrities are vulnerable to the charge of being absentee managers. This is because their key status derives from participation in the entertainment sector. For this reason, other activities are liable to be regarded by the media and the public as subsidiary.

2   This is tantamount to acting as an unappointed ombudsman for the public. Again, Cruise emphasizes the heroic aspect of celebrity advocacy: the lone star against the pharmaceutical companies.

3   Cruise is right to say that psychiatry does not have an unblemished record. The use of electroshock therapy and drugs to pacify behaviour has attracted an enormous *ad hominem* attack that portrays psychiatry as witchcraft. The attack comes across as unbalanced and hot-headed. Hence, the damage done to Cruise's public image, which hitherto had been seen as moderate and humane.

Chapter 11

1   The phrase was used as a title of a wartime novel by Howard Spring (1940).

Bibliography

Anonymous (1993) 'RTC v Robin Scott' *US District Court*, Central District of California No 85-71917.

Ackroyd, P. (1991) *Dickens*. London: HarperCollins.

Adorno, T. (1991) *The Culture Industry*. London: Routledge.

— (2000) *The Psychological Techniques of Martin Luther Thomas' Radio Addresses*. Stanford: Stanford University Press.

Alexander, J. (2007) 'The Celebrity Icon'. *(Mimeo, Not Published.)*

— (2010 (a)) *The Performance of Politics: Obama's Victory and the Democratic Struggle for Power*. Oxford: Oxford University Press.

— (2010 (b)) 'The Celebrity Icon'. *Cultural Sociology*, 4(3): 323–336.

Andrejevic, M. (2004) *Reality TV: The Work of Being Watched*. Lanham: Rowman & Littlefield.

Aristotle (2005) *Poetics*. Cambridge: Harvard University Press.

Barbas, S. (2001) *Movie Crazy: Fans, Stars and the Cult of Celebrity*. Basingstoke: Palgrave-Macmillan.

Barraclough, L. (2009) 'Susan Boyle Breaks UK Record'. *Variety* (30.11.2009).

Baum, M. (2007) 'Soft news and foreign policy: how expanding the audiences changes the policies'. *Japanese Journal of Political Science*, 8(1): 115–145.

Belk, R. (2010) 'Sharing'. *The Journal of Consumer Research*, 36(5): 715–734.

Bellis, M., Hennell, T., Lushey, C., Hughes, K., Toque, K., and Ashton, J. (2007) 'Elvis to Eminem: Quantifying the price of fame through early mortality of European and North American rock and pop stars'. *Journal of Epidemiology and Community Health*, 61: 896–901.

Berlin, J. (1996) *Toxic Fame: Celebrities Speak on Stardom*. Darby, Penn: Diane Pub Co.

Bernays, E. (1928) *Propaganda*. New York: Ig.

— (1935) 'Moulding Public Opinion'. *The Annals of the American Academy of Political and Social Science*, 179: 82–87.

— (1947) 'Engineering Consent'. *Annals of the American Academy of Political and Social Science*, 250: 113–120.

Bhusnurmath, M. (2010) 'Celebrity Endorsements Can Be A Two Edged Sword'. *Times of India*.

Bishop, M., and Green, M. (2008) *Philantrocapitalism*. London: A & C Black.

Blyton, P., and Jenkins, J. (2007) *Key Concepts in Work*. London: Sage.

Boorstin, D. (1962) *The Image*. Harmondsworth: Penguin.

Borkowski, M. (2008) *The Fame Formula*. London: Sidgwick & Jackson.

Boswell, J. (1791) *The Life of Johnson*. London: Thomas Tegg.

Bourdieu, P. (1993) *The Field of Cultural Production*. Cambridge: Polity.

Bourdieu, P. (1984) *Distinction*. London: Routledge.

Brooks, D. (2010) 'The Gospel of Mel Gibson'. *The New York Times*.

Budd, T. and Mattinson, J. (with Myhill, A) (2000) *The Extent and Nature of Stalking*. London: Home Office Research Study 210.

Bunz, M. (2009) 'Susan Boyle On Britain's Got Talent Is 'You Tube's' Top Video of 2009'. *The Guardian*.

Burke, M., and Barrett, W.P. (2010) 'Celebrity Charities: Good for Image, But What About Good Works?'. *Forbes*.

Butler Breese, E. (2010) 'Meaning, Celebrity, and the Underage Pregnancy of Jamie Lynn Spears'. *Cultural Sociology*, 4(3): 337–355.

Cashmore, E. (2006) *Celebrity/Culture*. London: Routledge.

Castells, M. (2009) *Communication Power*. Oxford: Oxford University Press.

Castles, J. (2008) *Big Stars*. Perth: Network Books.

Cheung, T. A., Lee, C., and Chen, T. (2007) 'The influence of media reporting of the suicide of a celebrity on suicide rates'. *International Journal of Epidemiology*, 36(6): 1229–1234.

Cicero (1969) *Selected Political Speeches*. London: Penguin.

— (1993) *On Government*. London: Penguin.

Colley, L. (2009) *Britons: Forging the Nation 1707–1837 (3rd edition)*. New Haven: Yale University Press.

Cooper, A. (2008) *Celebrity Diplomacy*. New York: Paradigm Publishers.

Couldry, N. (2003) *Media Rituals*. London: Routledge.

Cowell, S. (2004) *I Don't Mean To Be Rude But ... The Truth about Fame, Fortune and My Life in Music*. London: Ebury Press.

Dannan, F. (1991) *HitMen: Power Brokers and Fast Money Inside The Music Business*. New York: Vintage.

Dawkins, R. (1976) *The Selfish Gene*. Oxford: Oxford University Press.

Dobuzinskis, A. (2009) 'Susan Boyle Breaks Past 100 Million Online Views'. *Reuters*: 20.04.2009.

Dovey, J. (2000) *Freakshow: First Person Media and Factual Television*. London: Pluto.

Dufrenne, M. (1973) *The Phenomenology of Aesthetic Experience*. Evanston: Northwestern University Press.

Dumont, L. (1980) *Homo Hierarchicus*. Chicago: University of Chicago Press.

Eliade, M. (1957) *The Sacred and the Profane*. New York: Harcourt, Brace, Jovanovich.

Engelbrekston, L. (2010) 'The rock poster boy as idolmaker'. *Variety* (13.04.2010).

Etzersdorfer, E., Voraceck, M., and Sconneck, G. (2001) 'A dose response relationship of imitational suicides with newspaper distribution'. *Australian & New Zealand Journal of Psychiatry*, 35: 251.

Ewen, S. (1996) *PR!: A Social History of Spin*. New York: Basic Books.

Fowles, J. (1992). Washington: Smithsonian.

Franks, S. (2010) 'Why Bob Geldof has got it wrong'. *British Journalism Review*, 21(2): 51–56.

Frazer, J. (1909) *Totemism and Exogamy, 4 Volumes*. London: Macmillan.

Frisby, D. (1985) *Fragments of Modernity*. Cambridge: Polity.

Fu, K. W., and Yip, S. F. (2007) 'Long-term impact of celebrity status on suicide ideation'. *Journal of Epidemiology and Community Health*, 611(6): 540–546.

Fuhrman, C. (1989) *Publicity Stunt*. San Francisco: Chronicle Books.

Gamson, J. (2001) 'Normal Sins: Sex Scandal Narratives as Institutional Morality Tales'. *Social Problems*, 48(2): 185–205.

Gellner, E. (1985) *The Pscyhoanalytic Movement*. London: Paladin.

Gilligan, A. (2010) 'Africans don't rate Bob Geldof, so why should we?'. *The Telegraph*.

Glyn, E. (1927) *It*. New York: Macauly.

Gould, M., Jamieson, P., and Romer, D. (2003) 'Media Contagion and Suicide Among The Young'. *American Behavioral Scientist*, 46(9): 1269–1284.

Gundle, S. (2008) *Glamour*. Oxford: Oxford University Press.

Hartley, J. (2008) *Television Truths*. Malden: Blackwell.

Hattenstone, S. (2011) 'Zeta Jones' disclosure of bipolar treatment will have huge impact, charities predict'. *The Guardian*.

Hazlitt, W. (1930) 'Of Persons One Would Wish To Have Seen', in G. Keynes (ed) *Selected Essays of William Hazlitt*. London: Nonesuch Press. 523–539.

Hedges, C. (2009) *Empire of Illusion: The End of Literacy and the Triumph of the Spectacle*. New York: Perseus Books.

Hill, A. (2008) *Restyling Factual TV*. London: Routledge.

Holt, D. (2004) *How Brands Become Icons*. Boston: Harvard Business School Press.

Horton, D., and Wohl, R. (1956) 'Mass communication and para-social interaction: observations on intimacy at a distance'. *Psychiatry*, 19: 215–229.

Indiana, G. (2006) *Schwarzenegger Syndrome: Politics and Celebrity in the Age of Contempt*. New York: The New Press.

Inglis, F. (2010) *A Short History of Celebrity*. Princeton: Princeton University Press.

Jeffries, S. (2009) 'Jade Goody, Obituary'. *Guardian, 23.03.2009*.

Johnstone, I. (2006) *Tom Cruise: All The World's A Stage*. London: Hodder.

Katz, J. (1988) *Seductions of Crime*. New York: Basic Books.

Kellner, D. (2009) 'Barack Obama and the Celebrity Spectacle'. *International Journal of Communications*, 3: 715–741.

Kershaw, I. (1998) *Hitler: 1889–1936, Hubris*. London: Penguin.

Khaldoun, I. (1989) *The Muqaddimah*. Princeton: Princeton University Press.

Kierkegaard, S. (1962) *The Present Age*. New York: Harper & Row.

Klapp, O. (1949) 'The Fool As A Social Type'. *American Journal of Sociology*, 55(2): 157–162.

Kolakowski, L. (1999) *Freedom, Fame, Lying and Betrayal*. London: Penguin.

Laing, R. D. (1961) *Self and Others*. Harmondsworth: Penguin.

— (1970) *Knots*. New York: Pantheon.

— (1982) *The Voice of Experience*. London: Penguin.

Lamont, D. (2006) 'Even Madonna's adopted baby has privacy rights'. *The Guardian*.

Lasch, C. (1980) *The Culture of Narcissism*. London: Abacus.

Levi-Strauss, C. (1968) *The Savage Mind*. Chicago: Chicago University Press.

Livingstone, S., and Lunt, P. (1994) *Talk On Television*. London: Routledge.

Lum, K., Polansky, J., Jackler, R., and Glantz, S. (2008) 'Signed, sealed and delivered: "big tobacco" in Hollywood, 1927–51'. *Tobacco Control*, 17(5): 313–323.

Magninini, V., Honeycutt, E., and Cross, A. (2008) 'Understanding the Use of Celebrity Endorsers for Hospitality Firms'. *Journal of Vacation Marketing*, 14(1): 57–69.

Maltby, J., Houran, J., Ashe, D., and McCutcheon, L. (2001) 'The Self Reported Well Being of Celebrity Worshippers'. *North American Journal of Psychology*, 3: 441–452.

Marling, K. A. (1994) *As Seen On TV*. Cambridge: Harvard University Press.

Marx, K. (1977) *Capital, Volume 1*. London: Lawrence & Wishart.

McCutcheon, L., Lange, R., and Houran, J. (2002) 'Conceptualization and Measurement of Celebrity Worship'. *British Journal of Psychology*, 93(1): 67–87.

McCutcheon, L., Maltby, J., Houran, J., and Ashe, D. (2004) *Celebrity Worshippers: Inside the Minds of Stargazers*. Baltimore: PublishAmerica.

Meek, R. (1973) *Studies in the Labour Theory of Value*. London: Larence & Wishart.

Mekesmon, C., and Glantz, S.A. (2002) 'How the tobacco industry built its relationship with Hollywood'. *Tobacco Control*, 11(81–91).

Morin, E. (1960) *The Stars*. New York: Groove Press.

Nayder, L. (2010) *The Other Dickens: A Life of Catherine Hogarth*. Ithaca: Cornell University Press.

Newman, G., Diesendruck, G., Bloom, P. (2011) 'Celebrity Contagion and the Value of Objects'. *Journal of Consumer Research Inc*, Electronic version (paper version in press).

Ottinger, R. J. (2008) 'Give with the stars – but make it count'. *Financial Times*.

Parr, M. (2009) 'The power of sepia – an expert's take on the Madonna image'. *The Guardian*.

Payne, T. (2009) *Fame*. New York: Vintage.

Pemble, J. (1987) *The Mediterranean Passion*. Oxford: Clarendon Press.

Penfold-Mounce, R. (2009) *Celebrity Culture and Crime*. Basingstoke: Palgrave-Macmillan.

Pinsky, D., and Young, M. (2009) *The Mirror Effect: How Celebrity Narcissism is Endangering Our Families – And How To Save Them*. New York: HarperCollins.

Pringle, H. (2004) *Celebrity Sells*. Chichester: John Wiley.

Rank, O. (1990) *The Myth of the Birth of the Hero*. Princeton Mythos.

Reid Melloy, J. (2001) *The Psychology of Stalking*. New York: Academic Press.

Rieff, P. (2007) *Charisma*. New York: Pantheon.

Riley, A. (2010) *Impure Play*. Lanham: Lexington Books.

Roach, J. (2007) *It*. Ann Arbor: University of Michigan Press.

Rogers, H. (1980) *Walking The Tightrope: The Private Confessions of a Public Relations Man*. New York: William Murrow.

Rojek, C. (1993) *Ways of Escape: Modern Transformations in Leisure and Travel*. Basingstoke: Palgrave-Macmillan.

— (2001) *Celebrity*. London: Reaktion.

Rooney, D. (2011) 'Charlie Sheen: My Violent Torpedo of Truth (Review)'. *The Hollywood Reporter*.

Rousseau, J. J. (1984) *Discourse on the Origin of Inequality*. London: Penguin.

Schickel, R. (1985) *Intimate Strangers: The Culture of Celebrity*. New York: Doubleday.

Schlesinger, L. B. (2006) 'Celebrity Stalking, Homicide and Suicide'. *International Journal of Offender Therapy and Comparative Criminology*, 50(1): 39–46.

Segrave, K. (1994) *Payola in The Music Industry: A History 1880–1991*. Jefferson: McFarland & Co.

Shuttleworth, J. (1998) *Fools and Jesters at the English Court*. Stroud: Alan Sutton.

Singh, A. (2009) 'Malawi Government Supports Madonna's Adoption Bid'. *Daily Telegraph*.

Sisman, A. (2000) *Boswell's Presumptuous Task*. London: Penguin.

Smith, A. (1759) *The Theory of Moral Sentiments*. London: Penguin.

Smith, D. (2006) 'Images of icy beauty come out of the cold'. *The Observer*, 13.08.2006.

Stallen, M., Smidts, A., Rijpkema, M., Smit., Kulchrev, V.A., and Fernández, G. (2010) 'Celebrities and shoes on the female brain: The neural correlates of product processing in the context of fame'. *Journal of Economic Psychology*, 31(5): 802–811.

Stone, G. (2007) '"Murderabilia" Sales Distress Victims' Families'. *ABC Online – http://abcnews. go.com*.

Story, L. (2006) 'Seeing Stars'. *New York Times*.

Street, J. (2002) 'Bob, Bono and Tony B: the popular artist as politician'. *Media, Culture & Society*, 24: 433–441.

Suddath, C. (2010) 'How the Internet Made Justin Bieber a Star'. *Time*, 17.05.2010.

Sylvan, R. (2002) *Traces of the Spirit*. New York: New York University Press.

Theroux, P. (2006) 'Bono aid is making Africa sick'. *Sunday Times*.

Thrall, A. T., Lollio-Fakhreddine, J. Bernet, J., Donnelly, L., Herrin, W., Paquette, Z., Wenglinski, R., and Wyatt, A. (2008) 'Star Power: Celebrity Advocacy and the Evolution of the Public Sphere'. *The International Journal of Press/Politics*, 13(4): 362–385.

Todorov, T. (2010) *In Defence of Enlightenment*. London: Atlantic.

Turner, G. (2010) *Ordinary People and the Media*. London: Sage.

Veblen, T. (1899) *The Theory of the Leisure Class*. London: Allen & Unwin.

Ward, P. (2011) *Gods behaving Badly*. London: SCM Press.

Weber, M. (1948) *From Max Weber*. London: Routledge.

Welsford, E. (1935) *The Fool: His Social and Literary History*. London: Faber.

Wenner, J. (1981) *Lennon Remembers; The 'Rolling Stones' Interview with John Lennon and Yoko Ono*. London: Penguin.

Williams, R. (1958) *Culture and Society*. Harmondsworth: Penguin.

Wilson, B. (1975) *The Noble Savages: The Primitive Origins of Charisma and its Contemporary Survival*. Berkley: University of California Press.

Winterman, D., and Kelly, J. (2010) 'Five Interpretations of Lady Gaga's meat dress'. *BBC News Magazine*, 14.09.2010.

Wykes, M., and Gunter, B. (2005) *The Media and Body Image*. London: Sage.

Young, S. M., and Pinsky, D. (2006) 'Narcissism and Celebrity'. *Journal of Research in Personality*, 40(5): 463–471.

Author Index

Subject Index